UNEARTHING THE TRUTH

UNEARTHING THE TRUTH

An Unauthorized Commentary
on AMERICA UNEARTHED Season 1

Jason Colavito

ALBANY, NEW YORK
JasonColavito.com Books
2013

Versions of the material included in this book first appeared on JasonColavito.com. Some material included in the historical background to "Episode Twelve" also appeared as "The Zeno Brothers' Voyage of Discovery" in *Faking History: Essays on Aliens, Atlantis, Monsters, and More* (2013) by Jason Colavito.

This book is not produced or endorsed by *America Unearthed*, Committee Films, or A + E Television Networks.

This book has been typeset in Charis SIL

ISBN-13: 978-1489548238
ISBN-10: 1489548238

www.JasonColavito.com

CONTENTS

The Story of America Unearthed

D id European visitors come to North America before Columbus, penetrate deep into the country's interior, and stake an early claim to much of the land that would become the United States? According to *America Unearthed*, the answer is yes, and the people involved were a European order of knighthood dedicated to protecting the direct lineal descendants of the secret marriage of Jesus Christ and Mary Magdalene. The story of *America Unearthed* begins, however, with a chunk of rock uncovered in the backwoods of Minnesota more than a century ago. Known as the Kensington Rune Stone, this alleged evidence for Scandinavian visitors to the pre-Columbian interior of America would lead directly to the H2 channel's first original program, which debuted on December 21, 2012 to record ratings for the recently-rebranded sister channel to cable powerhouse History.

The origins of the Kensington Rune Stone are murky. In 1898, a Swedish immigrant farmer named Olaf Ohman claimed to have discovered a large, flat stone inscribed with runes, the medieval alphabet used to write Old Swedish, on his farmland near Kensington, Minnesota. The text inscribed on the rune stone appeared to tell of a journey by eight Götalanders and twenty-two Northmen in 1362 from Vinland, the Viking colony now known to have been located at L'anse-aux-Meadows, on the Canadian coast. They were traveling on a journey of "exploration." The stone told how ten of the men were killed while some members of the group were fishing. The stone asserted that the inscribers had additional men waiting with their ships a fortnight's journey from Kensington, which they described as an island or peninsula—despite the area being no such thing:

> 8 Göter ok 22 Norrmen po opdagelsefærd fro Vinland of vest. Vi hade læger ved 2 skjær en dags rise norr fro deno sten. Vi var po fiske en dagh; æptir vi kom hem fan 10 man röde af blod og ded. A. V. M. fraelse af illu.
>
> Har 10 mans ve havet at se æptir vore skip 14 dagh rise from deno öh ahr 1362.

> *8 Götalanders and 22 Northmen on an exploring (or acquisition) expedition from Vinland west. We camped by 2 skerries one day's journey north from this stone. We were a-fishing one day; after we came home we found 10 men red with blood and dead. A. V. M. (= Ave Maria) Save from evil.*
>
> *(There) are 10 men by the sea (or lake) to look after our ships 14 days' journey from this island (or peninsula). Year 1362.*[1]

The story seemed possibly to relate to a letter sent from the famous mapmaker Mercator to the English occultist and polymath John Dee in 1577, in which Mercator wrote of what he had read in the now-lost work of Jacobus Cnoyen of the people of King Arthur who had traveled across the North Atlantic and lived eight generations before returning to Norway. (In the Middle Ages, some believed King Arthur had colonized Greenland and Iceland.[2]) These people were "...part of the army of King Arthur which conquered the Northern Islands and made them subject to them. And we read that 4000 persons entered into the indrawing seas who never returned. But in A.D. 1364 eight of these people came to the King's Court in Norway. Among them were two priests, one of whom had an astrolabe, who was descended from the 5th generation from Bruxellensis: One, I say: The eight (were sprung from?) those who had penetrated the Northern regions in the first ships."[3] But Cnoyen's men were British, not Götalanders or Northmen, and they had been in their homeland five generations, not a few months.

Suspicions ran high about the provenance of the rune stone. It did not help matters that no one other than those close to Ohman had witnessed its discovery, and none of them could get their stories straight, claiming different seasons for its discovery (sometimes April, sometimes November) and different times of day as well (sometimes afternoon, sometimes evening). They also couldn't quite remember exactly *who* made the discovery: Olaf Ohman, his son Edward, two workmen, a neighbor named Nils Flaten, or any combination of the above. Skeptics early on noted the coincidence that a Swedish immigrant living in an area filled with Swedish immigrants happened upon a rune stone written in Old Swedish that served to tie the new immigrant community to a long and storied history on land that had, in living memory, been won from the Native American tribes displaced from the region around the time of the 1862 Dakota War. Skeptics also wondered whether there was a connection between the discovery of the stone and current events: At the World's Columbian Exposition in nearby Chicago just five years earlier, the Swedish government had sent a fantastic recreation of a Viking ship, the *Viking*, from Norway—then a restless province of Sweden—across the Atlantic to the Exposition. Surely it was beyond coincidence that the rune stone told of a joint expedition of Norwegians and Swedes along nearly the same water route.

Opinions differed about the authenticity of the stone, and by 1910, the Minnesota Historical Society, following the lead of Newton Horace Winchell, a geologist, was prepared to declare the stone genuine based on his geological evaluation that the weathering of the stone meant that it must be five centuries old. By contrast, George T. Flom, a linguist, determined that the language was modern, not ancient, and was certainly a modern hoax. He also determined that the geology favored a recent date of carving. Interestingly, even at this early date Flom called attention to a strange rune, unattested in any other runic inscription in the world known to that point, that took the form of an **X** with a small crossbar emerging perpendicularly from the upper right stave (X), a character Scott Wolter would come to call the "hooked X." Flom simply considered this one of several "unusual" characters he believed to be the result of poor copying on the part of the hoaxer.

This was where the debate stood for the next ninety years, with supporters of the stone's authenticity, led by the stone's new owner Hjalmar Holand, appealing to geology and detractors appealing to philology, and both delivering increasingly complex arguments about the faults with the other's position. Arguments came forth about whether the language of the stone could have been used in Sweden in 1362, while others questioned the science behind the weathering of the stone. In 2004, the discovery of a set of runic notes from 1883 and 1885 by a Swedish journeyman named Edward Larsson, featuring the hooked X (X, X̊, and X̊) and other variants found only on the Kensington Rune Stone, suggested a source for the stone's inscription. Larsson's runes may have been used as a private code by a guild or other organization, and in this way they could have been transmitted to America by Swedish immigrants.

Scott Wolter entered the debate in 2000. Wolter was then (and now) president of American Petrographic Services, a geology firm that did most of its work testing concrete for structural faults and other, similar mundane tasks. He was asked to testify about evidence obtained from concrete at a murder trial and forever after claimed the title of "forensic geologist," by which he continues to identify himself today. Since the 1980s the University of Minnesota graduate, who holds a bachelor's degree in geology and is licensed by the state of Minnesota as a geologist, also claimed an "honorary" master's degree in geology, but the university had no record of this degree. For twenty-five years it sat on his résumé until the state licensing board and I questioned it. Wolter told me the story behind his non-existent degree, which he said was never anything more than whipped cream. After giving a lecture to his former undergraduate instructors

> ...six of my former professors asked me technical questions which I answered to their satisfaction. Afterward, they had an informal reception in the Professors' lounge where they gave me an honorary degree with a whipped cream-topped coffee as my "certificate." They gave it to me as I have always presented it to be, a sympathy degree. At the time I was quite proud and when I told my then supervisors at my new job at Twin City Testing, they published the story in the company newsletter and added it to my résumé. Not long ago, the question was asked by the State

licensing board if it was an official degree and I said no. Because I didn't want my professors who [are] now in their eighties to have to answer questions about this, I removed it from my résumé.[4]

Wolter attributed his acceptance of Twin City Testing's action to his grief at the recent death of his father. He did not explain why he had allowed the mistake to remain on his résumé and to be used in professional and media reports about him for more than two decades.

On the advice of chemist Barry Hanson, the Kensington Runestone Foundation asked Scott Wolter to examine the Kensington Rune Stone and determine its true age scientifically, a tall order since modern science recognizes no methods to provide absolute dates for rocks within timeframes narrower than millennia. Wolter admitted that needed help figuring out what to do, so he invited some of his former professors to recommend ways to test the stone's age.[5] The group examined the stone under an electron microscope, and in the process Wolter invented what he calls a "new science," archaeo-petrography, or the study of archaeologically significant stone. According to Wolter, his study revealed that the mica degradation of the stone's surface and the carved letters was identical, indicating that both were of the same age. He could not, however, determine whether that age was "decades" or "centuries," only that he was certain it would take a "long time" for the mica to weather so much.

In 2001, Wolter was cautious about asserting that his new science could only suggest the stone was "at least" two hundred years old; however, by the time of *America Unearthed*, that same research had now "convinced" him that the stone was from the fourteenth century. However, reevaluations of Wolter's work by other experts—including Runo Löfvendahl, whom Wolter cited as a supporter—determined that if Wolter were correct about the geology of the stone, the weathered surfaces were between two thousand and twelve thousand years old, not consistent with the claim that the stone was shaped by the Swedes in 1362. Worse, accusations started flying that Wolter had been dishonest in his handling of the Kensington Rune Stone, a small piece of which he held on to while claiming ignorance of its location until documentary evidence proved other-wise. His former writing partner, Richard Nielsen—who remains a believer in the stone's authenticity—broke with Wolter over what he had come to see as Wolter's tendency to speculate beyond the evidence. The two had written a 2005 book on the Kensington Rune Stone in which Wolter at-tempted to connect the hooked X on the rune stone to unrelated but super-ficially similar symbols around the world as part of a broad conspiracy featuring the Knights Templar. Nielsen objected to Wolter's handling of the book, which was published over Nielsen's objections about specific passages. Wolter came to believe that the hooked X represented symboli-cally the womb of Mary (**V**) and the penetrating penis of Jesus (Λ), with the crossbar on the stave the embryonic child in Mary's womb.

But even if it were genuine, the Kensington Rune Stone would do much less to rewrite history than Scott Wolter claimed. The Norse were known to have landed on the North American continent around 1000 CE, in an area they called Vinland but which we know today as Newfoundland in Canada. Indeed, the identity of Vinland and North America had been deduced from medieval sagas as early as 1835 by the Danish antiquarian Carl Christian Rafn and was championed by several Victorian archaeolo-gists, including an influential paper by Sir Daniel Wilson published in 1892, just a few years before the Kensington Rune Stone's discovery. Ac-cepting the Kensington Rune Stone at face value merely asserts that the known Viking colonization of Greenland and Vinland included an expedi-tion a bit further into the American interior—hardly a dramatic revision of history.

Scott Wolter, however, saw something more in the Kensington Rune Stone. He saw in it a "land claim," an assertion of ownership by the (large-ly French) Knights Templar of the entire Mississippi watershed—despite the fact that the rune stone says no such thing. The only evidence for this was an ambiguous secret code of Wolter's own device, whereby certain disputed marks on the Kensington Rune Stone could be made to spell out the German word *gral*, as in Holy Grail—the true prize the Knights Tem-plar meant to hide in America—if one picked selected marks and ignored others. Wolter had become convinced that the Holy Grail was in America, that the Knights Templar from France had encoded this fact in Old Swedish, and that he was on the trail of the final descendants of Jesus Christ, right there in Minnesota. Wolter began evangelizing his claim wherever he could find an audience. He attended the 2008 Atlantic Conference, a diffusionist gathering sponsored by Steven St. Clair and Niven Sinclair, both of whom were investigating whether their ancestor Henry Sinclair (St. Clair) had sailed to America in the 1380s or 1390s. Wolter accepted the claim and decided that Henry Sinclair had led the Templar charge into the United States and had built the Newport Tower to "align" to the Kensington Rune Stone as part of a grand plan to lay claim to North America in the name of the Grail Kings.

It was against this backdrop that Scott Wolter met Maria and Andrew Awes, a pair of television producers with Committee Films, a rather minor documentary film company based in Minnesota. According to production documents I obtained from Minnesota Film and Television, Maria Awes stated that she became interested in the Templar-America connection after meeting Wolter, and in 2008 Awes decided to feature Wolter as the "key expert" in a documentary called *The Holy Grail in America*, which she would sell to the History Channel in 2009. The pitch for the film would win Maria and Andrew Awes the 2009 non-fiction Emerging Producer of the Year award from Cable U, a cable TV research firm, presented at the National Association of Television Program Executives conference. The Awes asserted in press materials for *Holy Grail* that they intended it as a pilot for a future series, and they explicitly claimed that their film could tie in with the then-current Dan Brown *Da Vinci Code* prequel movie, *Angels and Demons*. The similarity between the *Da Vinci Code* and Wolter's bloodline of Christ theory was uncanny—and indeed derived from the same source, the 1982 book *The Holy Blood and the Holy Grail*.

The Holy Grail in America had a budget of more than $360,000 and received $19,468.57 in funding from Minnesota Film and Television, of which fifty percent came from tax dollars and the rest from privately-donated matching funds. The thesis of the documentary was that the Kensington Rune Stone was carved by the Knights Templar in order to claim the entirety of what later became the Louisiana Purchase as well as much of the Midwest and Deep South. "If you could prove you navigated to the headwaters of a major waterway and buried this land claim," Wolter stated in the film, "you could claim that entire waterway and the land adjacent to it. By placing a land claim, these people claimed the Mississippi watershed and the Red River watershed to the north all the way to Hudson's Bay, which is essentially over half of the North American continent." Remember that the Kensington Rune Stone says nothing about land claims and instead offers only a warning about hostile Natives.

In the documentary, the Templars, who started a new society in America, became the Freemasons, who in turn secretly infiltrated the fledgling United States government in order to perpetuate their dissenting view of the "sacred feminine" in Christianity. According to the film, the "separation of church and state" was of "Masonic design" to protect Templar interests. Niven Sinclair appeared in the documentary to present the Sinclair apologists' version of events, based, as we shall see later in this book, on extremely faulty evidence. The concepts laid out in the film exactly match those developed at length in the first season of *America Unearthed*.

But this would not be the Awes' only excursion into "alternative" history. At the end of 2009, the production team started work on a follow-up documentary for the History Channel, tentatively titled *America B.C.*, named after Barry Fell's 1976 book in which the marine biologist attempted to demonstrate that ambiguous markings on rocks around the world were proof of the global transoceanic voyages of various European groups in Antiquity and the Middle Ages. With a budget of $575,000, the two-hour film examined claims for Japanese, Chinese, Polynesian, Hebrew, Roman, Norse, Welsh, and Irish contact with prehistoric North America. Unlike the previous film, this one mixed scholarly theories with out-and-out speculation, giving it more than a patina of seriousness. Its Welsh and Irish claims would return, in modified form, in *America Unearthed*. Minnesota Film and Television reimbursed the Awes $53,254.41, of which half came from public tax money. The program aired on the History Channel in 2010, under the name *Who Really Discovered America?*

Both of the Committee Films documentaries were ratings successes for the History Channel, which had also seen great success with another pseudo-historical documentary, *Ancient Aliens*, which also aired in 2009. That program explored the work of Swiss writer and convicted embezzler Erich von Däniken, who had claimed that space aliens were responsible for ancient earth monuments. History ordered *Ancient Aliens* to series, premiering in 2010 to great success, attracting two million weekly viewers at the height of its popularity. It seemed that there would be nothing to stop the Awes from following through with their stated plan to turn *Holy Grail in America* into a weekly series. But the History Channel—now rebranded as "History"—was undergoing a change in focus. Historical documentaries, even those as absurd yet successful as *Ancient Aliens*, no longer fit the brand, which would instead focus on "character-driven" non-fiction programming such as *Ice Road Truckers*, *Axe Men*, *American Pickers*, and *Pawn Stars*.

At the end of 2011, History announced it would move *Ancient Aliens* from its main channel to its little-watched sister station, History International, which was undergoing a rebranding as H2. At the time, the channel averaged just 196,000 prime time viewers, according to *Broadcasting & Cable* magazine. At the start of 2012, H2 offered only History reruns and new episodes of three former History series: *Ancient Aliens*, *Modern Marvels*, and *The Universe*. When *Ancient Aliens* successfully improved the network's Friday night audience to the better part of a million weekly viewers, History decided to order a companion series to focus on *Ancient Aliens'* key demographic: young, upscale, undereducated males. The president of ad sales at H2's parent company, A + E Networks, Mel Berning, told *Ad Age*, "It's such a good cut of audience, the upscale male. Male viewers watch a lot of sports, a lot of news, but news skews really old."[6] He told the magazine that H2 was therefore aimed at men who don't watch news, don't watch sports, and don't watch broadcast television.

Thus, it seemed that H2's ideal viewer would be young, wealthy, and a low-information consumer. Not coincidentally, this was also the ideal market for advertisers, who are interested in wealthy consumers who are willing to accept televised claims without solid evidence. But the advertising department's needs contrasted with the programming department's stated aims. Dirk Hoogstra, the senior vice president of development and programming at History and H2, told *Ad Age* that while most History viewers were not interested in traditional, fact-based programming (preferring character-driven reality shows), "There's a portion of our viewers that still want the deeper dive. So we said 'If they are out there looking for that information, let's give them a home.'"[7] Splitting the difference between the "deeper dive" into facts needed to attract a different audience from History (to avoid competing against another A + E brand) and advertiser demands for programs that would attract an audience willing to accept claims without proof, H2 turned to the producers of History's successful alternative history documentaries, the Awes.

In late 2011 or early 2012, Maria Awes made the case that "audiences are eager to entertain alternative theories to accepted history."[8] Based on the success of *Holy Grail* and *Who Really,* she received an order for a new project to pair with *Ancient Aliens* on the nascent H2 channel, set to air at the end of the year. According to production documents, Awes had told H2 that the program would cover a range of "alternative" history claims, including Thomas Jefferson's "secret" knowledge of treasure buried in the Louisiana Purchase, a medieval Welsh princess buried in upstate New York, Minoan copper mining on Lake Superior, and an Egyptian royal tomb in the heart of the Grand Canyon. Only one of these would make it to air in the first season of the new series. At the very same time Awes was telling H2 about how hungry America was for "alternatives" to history, Committee Films was also busy producing a National Geographic special for PBS's *Nova* on the mystery of Easter Island. Based on the controversial but scholarly work of Terry Hunt and Carl Lipo, the film offered a straightforward investigation into one possible way the Easter Islanders had moved their giant statues. This sober hour aired in November 2012, just weeks before the debut of *America Unearthed* and testified to the different editorial standards at PBS and H2, as well as Committee's willingness to work with both.

Maria Awes's first decision for her new diffusionist show was to turn to her old friend Scott Wolter to host the series. She described him in glowing terms as "the guru of all pre-Columbian mysteries" and the "chief investigator" of such mysteries as crystal skulls and odd artifacts, despite the fact that he was largely unknown outside the narrow world of Kensington Rune Stone and Templar-Freemason investigators. She promised that he would "blend his science with the research of scholars, authors, and other scientists worldwide to explore alternatives to accepted American history."[9] As the "key expert" on *Holy Grail*, Wolter was intimately involved with the story of the Holy Grail in America, and, better yet, he was local to Minnesota, reducing the production costs for the Minnesota-based Committee Films and also qualifying the series for further rebates from Minnesota Film and Television. Prior to the start of filming on the pilot episode, Committee Films filed paperwork requesting more than $100,000 in reimbursements against a budget of $617,000 for the series' pilot and a payroll of nearly $200,000. Minnesota Film and Television approved the request. Principal photography began June 26, 2012, according to production documents submitted to Minnesota Film and Television, although scenes in the broadcast episodes were represented to viewers as having been filmed on the summer solstice of 2012, which took place the week before.

In the course of production, something occurred to change the series' original plan of focusing on European incursions into the Americas in relation to the Holy Grail. The change seemed to be due to the chance to tie the new series to a major alternative history event. Friday, December 21, 2012 was viewed in alternative history circles as the so-called "Maya Apocalypse," the alleged date at which the Maya calendar turned over to its thirteenth cycle, or *baktun*, a date when pundits on H2's own *Ancient Aliens* predicted the return of the aliens and others predicted everything from the destruction of the earth to the inauguration of a new age of wisdom and light. To tie in with the hype, H2 had commissioned a series called *Countdown to Apocalypse*, and it planned to air a day-long marathon of Maya Apocalypse-themed programming on December 21. *Ancient Aliens* would rerun its Maya Apocalypse episode at 8 pm ET and launch its fifth season at 9 pm with a program on world pyramids. *America Unearthed* would join the fun with its first episode, which would send its host to the Maya site of Chichen Itza in search of evidence that the Maya had penetrated as far north as Georgia. The episode aired at 10 pm.

It would be the only episode of the series' first season to feature an investigation into a non-European culture. Nevertheless, H2 used this episode as the launching pad for the series, and their promotional artwork for *America Unearthed*, seen in broadcast, online, and print advertisements, featured a moody and atmospheric shot of the upper reaches of a stepped Mayan pyramid—one never seen on the show itself—emerging from a swirl of brown fog and sand dunes. This clever misdirection obscured for several weeks the series' real purpose, the one Maria Awes had outlined four years earlier—to make a series about the hunt for the Holy Grail in the United States. Many viewers, like me, who didn't know much about Scott Wolter or the show's connection to the earlier History documentaries, were deceived into thinking the new show would examine a broad range of topics drawn from all over the United States to illuminate American history. Only gradually was the truth revealed: This program would occupy the fringe of the fringe, single-mindedly pursuing the fantasy of European penetration of the pre-Columbian Americas as part of a globe-spanning goddess cult devoted to protecting the secret descendants of Jesus Christ. It would also seek to question the very foundations of the American government, weirdly arguing that America truly belongs to a cult of Christ's children and their hidden goddess.

As an investigator into the claims of alternative historians, I've seen and heard a lot. I wrote an entire book about the people who believe that aliens and Atlantis were responsible for ancient civilizations, a book called *The Cult of Alien Gods* (2005); and I've covered the alternative history movement since 2001 on my website, in books, and in the pages of *Skeptic* magazine and other publications. I have never seen anything like *America Unearthed*. The sheer the breadth of its audacity, both in terms of the conspiracy it fabricates and in the low quality of the "evidence" used to support, it astonished me; but more amazing was the response the program garnered. Not only did my reviews of the program, collected in the pages that follow, become the most popular feature on my website by leaps and bounds, the show attracted one of the largest audiences alternative history had seen in almost twenty years, since the mid-1990s, when the broadcast networks offered *The Mystery of the Sphinx*, *The Mysterious Origins of Man*, and *Chariots of the Gods*, sparking the alternative history craze of those years. *America Unearthed* was the highest-rated program H2 had ever broadcast, averaging 824,000 viewers in its first four weeks, and breaking one million by January 25, not counting reruns and online viewing.[10]

Something in the show struck a nerve, and in reviewing the show episode by episode I came to learn exactly what. Read on and unearth the truth about H2's hit show.

American Mayan Secrets

Airdate: December 21, 2012

Episode Summary

Scott Wolter uses geological testing to link pigment found at the Maya city of Chichen Itza to clay deposits near the Track Rock Archaeological Site at Ocmulgee, Georgia, and he concludes that the Maya built Track Rock, operating it as a mining camp to supply the Yucatán with blue pigment.

Historical Background

Around 4500 BCE, Native Americans in the region now known as Louisiana began piling dirt up in enormous heaps to form great earthworks that came to be known as mounds. By 1500 BCE, the people of Poverty Point had constructed the earliest and most impressive mound city of its age, filled with semicircular mounds row on row, and in 1450 BCE they built the Bird Mound, a mound so massive that for more than 2,500 years it stood as the largest structure in the entirety of what would become the continental United States. The influence of Poverty Point and its vast trade network spread mound building throughout the Mississippi basin and beyond, yielding far-flung mound building cultures that used such structures variously for cemeteries, as temples, and as platforms for elite housing. So numerous were the mounds that more than ten thousand stood in the Ohio valley alone.

The fabulous Adena mounds were aligned to the stars, and the mounds of the Mississippian culture from 800 to 1500 CE were the most famous of all, including Monk's Mound at Cahokia, the largest earthen mound in all of the United States. One hundred feet tall, the mound's base was larger than the Great Pyramid of Egypt. It stood at the center of a complex, six-square-kilometer city so large that no American city would equal its forty thousand inhabitants until Philadelphia in 1800. The city stood at the heart of a vast trade network that reached from the edges of Mesoamerica to upstate New York, circulating goods, foodstuffs, and religious symbolism and ideology. But by 1300 CE, Monk's Mound (named for a European monastery built atop it much later), had begun to fall into disrepair. By 1400, Cahokia had collapsed, and by 1500 Native peoples were building only one or two very small mounds in tiny villages, a far cry from the days when a city like Cahokia might sport more than one hundred.

When the first European explorers encountered the remnants of the mound building cultures of the southeastern United States, they wondered exactly what these structures might be, and who built them. The answer was quite obvious, however, for many Native groups were still constructing their small mounds at the time of the Spanish explorations of the sixteenth century, and several explorers observed mounds under construction. Nevertheless, the larger cousins of these small structures retained an air of mystery. The Spanish thought they might be full of gold, but several exploratory digs turned up nothing but bones, dirt, and more dirt.

Many explanations were given for the mounds, some fanciful and others serious. They were variously attributed to Hindus, wandering Jews, the Irish, Toltecs from Mexico, a "lost race" of white men, or even the giants from the book of Genesis. In this cloud of speculation, their true origin was lost. Thomas Jefferson excavated a mound in America's first scientific archaeological dig[1]—and wouldn't that have made a great episode of *America Unearthed?*—and discovered the truth: They were Native American. But his findings weren't accepted for a century, until an archaeologist working for the Bureau of American Ethnology named Cyrus Thomas put to rest the myth of white mound builders and demonstrated through careful excavation that the mounds were indisputably the work of Native Americans.

However, an interesting question remained: The mounds of America seemed very similar to the stone-built platform temples of the Toltecs, Aztecs, and Maya. Could there be a connection? It was, of course, indisputable that corn (maize) had originated in deepest Mexico and spread northwards into the continental U.S., but had people moved with it? In the desert southwest, the Native peoples had built ceremonial ball courts just like those of the Mesoamericans, and Native tribes of the southwest like the Hopi and the Zuni shared motifs in their myths with the Mexicans, including a belief in the cyclical end of the world. Further, the religious art of the Mississippians, called the Southeastern Ceremonial Complex, bore suspicious similarities to that of Mexico, including such items as serpents with feathers, like the god Quetzalcoatl.

In the southwest, there was clear and demonstrable evidence of sustained contact with Mesoamerica. The problem, however, was that no solid evidence connected Mexico and the Mississippians to the east. The first piece of such evidence, in fact, only emerged in 2002, when Alex W. Barker et al. reported that tests on an obsidian scraper found at Spiro Mounds in Oklahoma, a Mississippian site, demonstrated that the object had originated in Hidalgo, Mexico.[2] Scholars have been working for more than a century and a half to prove a connection between the Mississippians and Mesoamerica, but aside from this one scraper, they haven't been able to pin anything down—though not for want of trying. The scholarly consensus is that direct contact between Mesoamerica and the Mississippians was either non-existent or very rare, and that the only limited contact would have been the diffusion of ideas and the movement of raw materials along trade networks, without direct movement of peoples. However, more than a few archaeologists seriously speculated that a band of traveling merchants, most likely the Aztec *pochteca*, could have evangelized Aztec religion while questing for raw materials. If these merchants did in America as they did in Mexico, they would have taken control of weaker societies, imposed their ideology, and ruled among them.[3] But there is no evidence of contact, let alone control. According to Stuart J. Fiedel, the lack of Mesoamerican linguistic incursions in the Southeastern languages and the direct evidence of a gradual evolution of Mississippian culture rules out any major migration of Mesoamericans.[4]

That was the state of knowledge about the contact between Mesoamerica and the southeastern United States when forensic geologist Scott Wolter and *America Unearthed* went in search of the Maya in the middle of Georgia.

The Episode

I wasn't sure what to expect going into *America Unearthed* because the program's advertisements made it seem like a serious show about the actual archaeology of ancient America, but at the same time I remembered Scott Wolter for an article he had written for the diffusionist popular magazine *Ancient American* about the Bat Creek Stone, a supposedly ancient rock containing a Paleo-Hebrew inscription. Originally published in 2010, his article claimed that the stone, discovered in the nineteenth century in a mound, was not as widely believed a hoax but rather a real ancient Hebrew artifact discovered in the United States. The article was fresh in my mind because an ex-neo-Nazi and convicted pederast named Frank Joseph, the former editor of *Ancient American*, had collected it in an anthology of the magazine's back catalog, and the book's publisher, New Page Books, had sent me a copy to review on my website.[5] I wasn't impressed by Wolter's confusing, non-linear writing style, which freely mixed unclear discussions of scientific investigations with repeated jeremiads about unethical academics working to suppress the truth and impugn the reputations of those who challenged orthodoxy. In retrospect, I should have realized that this style would carry over to his television show.

The production values on the show impressed me immediately; they were several steps above those of *Ancient Aliens*, with almost movie-quality cinematography and high-end graphics closely resembling those of Fox News, though in a greener shade of blue alongside the requisite red; but the program also relied heavily on obviously reenacted or scripted conversations in which Wolter "investigated" ancient mysteries. At various points, long tracking shots showed Wolter walking, and we saw him standing, posing, and reciting dialogue that had very clearly been practiced ahead of time. The first episode did not provide much by way of description or context as it barreled through its mystery, making it very difficult to pinpoint at times exactly what the program was talking about and thus forcing the viewer to simply go along with Wolter, facts be damned. As would become a recurring fault in the series, Wolter neglected to provide enough of a historical context to understand the ancient site in question, what experts on the subject truly think about the site, or how the conventional view was assembled from various strands of evidence; instead, any academic idea is merely presented as dogma.

This episode discusses what it calls the "Track Rock site" in Georgia, a mound site which Wolter claims is evidence that the Maya came to Georgia. It contains several terraces lined with rough, dry-stacked stones atop an earthen mound. Wolter travels to Georgia, where he meets with Richard Thornton, an alternative history author, who tells him that the Creek in the area are ethnically Maya, which they are not. Thornton is the originator of the hypothesis that the Maya came to Georgia, and Wolter bases his arguments on Thornton's original claim, which was briefly made national headlines in late 2011 before archaeologists explained that not a single Maya artifact or cultural marker was found anywhere in the Track Rock site.[6] Sadly, this led to still more charges that academia was "suppressing" the truth, foreshadowing Wolter's later claims. Archaeologist Mark Williams, in debunking Thornton's ideas, said that "There's a feeling that people are hiding the truth. Someone needed to stand up and say: 'This is silly'."[7]

Thornton's evidence is the same as that offered by the Atlantis theorizers of the past: coincidences of architecture and language. He believes that the Track Rock site is shaped like a Central American pentagonal mound, and he feels that the Native village name of Itsate (as recorded by early mapmakers, not known for their phonetic fidelity) is "identical" to the Itza Maya's word for themselves. He claims that a similar nearby place name, "Itsaye," means the "Place of the Itza" in Itza Maya, but standard works on the Itza Mayan language give "Location of the Maya" as "Tah Itza" and its derivative Tayasal. "Itza" as a modifier *follows* the noun; it does not precede it—hence Chichen Itza (Well of the Itza) and Petén Itzá (Island of the Itza). After this episode aired, Thornton accused Wikipedia, the U.S. Forest Service, and the Cherokee of conspiring to discredit both him and Wolter as part of an ongoing suppression of the "truth."[8]

In the episode, Wolter asserts that the U.S. federal government prohibits access to the Track Rock site, and he asks Thornton whether the "academic community" might be working to "shut down" his investigation. Both agree it's a possibility, a comment put in new context in reviewing Thornton's 2011 experiences. At first the producers of the show imply subtly through lighting and mood music that this prohibition is for conspiratorial reasons, but later Wolter just explicitly says so. He has a clear problem with authority figures, and his contempt showed through, breaking the superficially friendly and soft-spoken façade he presents as show host. These glimpses of the passionate, angry Wolter beneath the mask would gradually become more prominent as the first season wore on. Despite what *America Unearthed* claimed, the Track Rock Gap Archaeological Site was and remains open to the public (for free, no less), and on the site's web page the government offers directions to help visitors get there and brochures to help them find their way around the site. The only thing prohibited is archaeological excavation without following the formal application process. The U.S. Forest Service has a web page debunking the claim that the Maya built the mounds and stone walls found at what is properly called the "Track Rock Gap Archaeological Site." The mounds were constructed by the Creek and Cherokee around 1000 CE, after the Classic Maya had collapsed.

Wolter and his crew were denied access not by conspiratorial government bureaucrats but rather because the Creek and Cherokee governments of the region objected to television filming on the site, which archaeologists have suggested was once a necropolis, I was told by Gary C. Daniels, who also appears in this episode to show Wolter some spirals carved on a boulder that both assert is a star map—possible, but no proof of a Maya connection since most Native tribes had astronomical knowledge. Wolter's anger occurs because the U.S. Forest Service originally issued permits for filming until the Native Americans objected. I am not sure why they did so, but I can't imagine that the Cherokee were much pleased to have Wolter promoting his research on the Bat Creek Stone in early 2012, with the attendant claim that the Cherokee played host to Hebrew overlords. At any rate, Wolter asserts from afar that the Track Rock site must be the work of the Maya, essentially because it is large and complex. He gleans this not from looking at archaeological site reports or maps but rather by dramatically taking to the air to use high-tech surveillance equipment to make his own map of the site from the sky, which he compares to the layout of Mesoamerican cities, but not to other American mound sites, which contain similar elements, including mounds, courts, etc.

The Creek built mounds like most southeastern tribes during the Mississippian period, so there is no need to postulate Maya influence unless you want all the mounds of the Americas to be Mayan—in all their tens of thousands. Note, too, that the Post-Classic Maya built with their major monuments of stone, not dirt, in the period under discussion. As discussed above, there has been limited evidence of trade with an *influence* from Mesoamerica on Mississippian culture, but not the direct movement of large numbers of peoples from Mexico to Georgia, as Wolter implies. This would neatly account for similar iconography and the movement of materials between the two cultures, but in Wolter's view, the Maya came in multitudes to run a full-scale mining operation in Georgia as their civilization was collapsing in Mexico. Worse, Wolter asserts that any suggestion of Maya involvement is simply "taboo" for academics; however, as seen above, such claims have been widely discussed in archaeological literature, often with regret that the strong suggestion of influence has found no archaeological correlate. I mean, for crying out loud, the idea was in the archaeology textbooks I read in college at the turn of the century!

The reason we know that the Maya didn't relocate en masse to Georgia at the end of their civilization is (a) they continued (and continue) to live in Mexico, and (b) no indisputably Maya artifact has ever been found in Georgia. Ocmulgee (Track Rock) was very much part of the Southeastern Ceremonial Complex, which is clearly part of a continuum of native cultures that stretched from Mexico to New York. Wolter makes a big deal out of a plate image of a "Feathered Dancer" found in Georgia and claims it is uniquely related to a Maya image from Chichen Itza. The plate depicts a dancer shaking a rattle and holding a severed human head; he is superimposed over a stylized set of bird wings and a bird's tail. Wolter does not tell you that the feathered dancer is a widespread image found as far afield as the Siouan and Winnebago peoples; it is the common heritage of the Mississippian culture. The specific image shown in the program was found at Etowah, not Ocmulgee, and is thus not direct evidence of the Maya at Ocmulgee, even if we agree that it represents a copy of a somewhat similar Maya relief image found on a wall at Chichen Itza in the Yucatan. This spawns a trip in which Wolter travels to Chichen Itza to speak with Alfonso Morales, a Mexican archaeologist, and the only non-white expert consulted in the entire first series of the show. Morales shows Wolter a Mayan figure who also holds a severed head and a rattle, but the position of both, as well as the position of the wings and that of the dancer are very different. Severed heads, rattles, and feathers are common motifs in both Mississippian and Maya art, and it is far from unlikely that the three elements would show up in combination in both places. Several Mississippian pieces show men with rattles (or clubs) and severed heads, as well as many birdmen, though only one combining both traits. None of these elements is unique to these two cultures, of course. Peoples from the Aztec to the Winnebago used the same elements.

The Etowah plate uses the common stock of artistic conventions found from Mexico to Minnesota that were diffused across the Americas from at least the time of Poverty Point, the oldest mound-building culture. There is simply no need to postulate the movement of thousands of people when the movement of goods and ideas explains the similarities Wolter found between Mexico and the mound builders of America. In a heavily-edited clip, Morales says he can see a "relationship" between the sites, by which he appears to mean a diffusion of iconography sometime in the past, but which Wolter steps in to say means direct movement of peoples that "rewrites" history. Morales is only shown smiling and beginning to speak, at which point we cut to commercial and never hear his reaction. Wolter speculates that the Maya sent a large delegation to Georgia, built the mound site as a colony, and ruled as overlords—a scenario we've seen scholars propose in slightly different form. As supporting evidence earlier in the hour Daniels had offered the fact that three Native peoples in Florida had the "Maya" as syllables in their names, the Mayaimi, Mayayuaca, and Mayaca, although these names were only recorded five hundred years after the construction of the Ocmulgee citadel. However, the name of the Mayaca is a Spanish name, recorded only after 1575, and the Mayaimi (Miami) said their name referred to the Muskogee term *miaha*, or "wide," not the Maya. This is because they called themselves the peoples of the wide water, their name for Lake Okeechobee, known as to them as Lake Mayaimi, as Hernando d'Escalante Fontenada reported in 1575: "They are masters of a large district of country, as far as a town they call Guacata, on the Lake of Mayaimi, which is called Mayaimi because it is very large."[9] Additionally, the "Maya" spelling is merely conventional; Spanish reports also used "Maia," "Mia," and other variants.

Wolter tries to prove a connection between the Maya and Georgia by creating "Maya Blue," an artistic pigment used in Maya art, with clay from Georgia. The pigment is also found in other Mesoamerican cultures, like the Aztec, indicating much broader trade than Wolter allows. (Remember the traveling Aztec *pochteca* from the archaeological literature? Wolter doesn't know them despite appropriating the entire scenario wholesale and changing Aztec to Maya.) The Maya, in fact, specifically considered the clay from which the pigment was made a valuable item of trade, a fact known for at least fifty years. The sample (from a deposit first reported many decades ago) chemically matched that from Chichen Itza under the analysis Wolter had done at a lab, though again details weren't provided to let us judge whether the match excluded all other sources, such as Yucatan deposits. Again, though, trade networks do not require the movement of peoples, only the movement of goods. Amber moved across Europe without people accompanying it, and this clay could very well have followed the same route. Mesoamericans are known to have visited the

American southwest for turquoise, and Mississippian artifacts have been found at a Classic Maya site in the Yucatan. Robert Hall, for example, also found clear ritual and myth diffusion from central Mexico to Mississippian cultures as far away as the Winnebago (though, of course, not everyone agrees). That such connections happened is not a taboo subject, though the question of the direction and degree of influence is still debated.

"There are a whole host of academics who refuse to believe that there were cultures that came to America prior to Columbus," Wolter states. "And this is bullshit!"

Scott Wolter therefore "proved" a connection that archaeologists have been working on for ages and did it while complaining loudly about how the "establishment" was "suppressing" the very information they are actively investigating *and which he used in his own show!* At least, however, his alternative theory was only a few steps beyond the facts, somewhat plausible, and conditioned upon a scientific test others could repeat to confirm or refute. Future episodes would increasingly depart from the fact-based grounding of the first episode.

After this episode, I thought that, as entertainment, *America Unearthed* was no *Ancient Aliens*. *America Unearthed* relied heavily on the wooden delivery of an unpracticed Scott Wolter—which would improve in time— instead of a wide range of pundits. Because it focused on just a single topic per hour, the show came across as very, very slow and very repetitive. Long, lingering shots of Wolter looking plaintively at trees and rocks abutted interminable pauses between sound bytes and repeated shots of nature. The cinematic photography failed to mask the paucity of facts and information, or the barely-coherent conspiracy mindset both Wolter and the show's producers irresponsibly promoted—a problem that would only grow as the show moved from the Maya to its true focus, Europeans.

Medieval Desert Mystery

Airdate: December 28, 2012

Episode Summary

Scott Wolter investigates a stone in the Arizona desert that is inscribed with runes. Wolter concludes that these runes date to 1200 CE and record the death of an Englishman, who Wolter believes taught the art of building cliff dwellings to the Native Americans.

Historical Background

In southwestern New Mexico stands the Gila National Forest, comprised largely of evergreens perched on a rugged landscape of canyons, highlands, and shallow rivers. Amidst the splendor of the forest there is a large cliff formed from by the activity of an ancient volcano. This massive cliff has five alcoves that created a natural shelter high above the trees. It is within these caves that the Mogollon culture built an impressive series of interlocking rock, earth, and timber structures, the Gila Cliff Dwellings, now a national monument. The wooden beams used in the construction have been dated using dendrochronology, a method of counting tree rings, to 1276-1287 CE, the time when the cliff houses were in use.

The Mogollon occupied the southwest from possibly as early as 250 BCE to 1450 CE; however, "Mogollon" is not what they called themselves. Instead, the name comes from mountains named for an eighteenth century Spanish governor of New Mexico where the first Mogollon artifacts were found. The Mogollon were the neighbors of the Hohokam and the Anasazi, and they lived in an area stretching from Arizona and New Mexico south into what is now Chihuahua in Mexico. It is not certain whether the Mogollon emerged from local Desert Archaic peoples or whether they migrated from Mexican farming regions to the south. Whatever the case, they produced distinctive pottery that helped set them apart from their neighbors. The most famous branch of the Mogollon was the Mimbes people of the Gila River, known for their spectacular black and white geometric pottery.

The Mimbes seemed to prefer high-altitude locations, and over time, the size and complexity of their settlements grew. Early hamlets of small pit houses interspersed with semi-subterranean ceremonial rooms (often compared to Anasazi kivas) gave rise to rock, earth, and timber pueblos in the eleventh century. These pueblos contained up to 150 rooms organized around large plazas with rectangular or square semi-subterranean ceremonial rooms. The Mimbes people, however, suffered a serious population decline in the twelfth century, and they stopped making their distinctive pottery. In the thirteenth and fourteenth centuries, they built cliff dwellings, possibly due to an increase in intergroup conflict and warfare in those centuries. The Gila Cliff Dwellings are the most famous of these, and they probably housed between ten and fifteen families. By 1400-1450, the Mogollon had disappeared, possibly merging with later Pueblo and Zuni peoples. All that remained was their ruins.

The Hopi record legends that changes in climate and changes in religion led the migration of people away from the Cliff Dwellings, and the exact cause of their abandonment has not been established. It does, however, parallel similar abandonments of other similar sites among the Anasazi and the Hohokam, attributed to climate change and warfare by many archaeologists. The Gila Cliff Dwellings sat forgotten until 1878 when a man named Henry B. Ailman found them while trying to avoid jury duty. He and some friends organized a prospecting trip as an excuse, and in the process came across the ruins. The site became a national monument in 1907.

The Episode

"Medieval Desert Mystery" begins with a dramatic reenactment of a couple of white guys dressed in medieval style dying in the sandy wastes of the Arizona desert in view of some Native Americans. We then cut to Scott Wolter in his glowing blue-black laboratory reading a letter from a concerned viewer who claims to know of a stone in Arizona covered in medieval European runes. Obviously such as a stone threatens to rewrite history since dogma says that no European capable of writing in runes traveled to the continental United States before the Age of Discovery. Wolter reenacts for the camera the excitement he felt in learning of this stone and makes plans to travel to Arizona to see for himself the mystery of the desert rune rock.

So we travel to the Mustang Mountains in Sierra Vista in southern Arizona to view the rune stone in an over-produced montage of a convoy of SUVs traveling while bombastic music provides a manly cover of serious purpose. This leads to a lengthy montage of rock climbing in which very little occurs until we finally are taken to the cave. Beneath the entrance, stony and dry in the bright desert sun, the camera shows us a stone covered in what look like runes. At first glance, the letters look more like stylized Latin letters than the Northern European runic alphabets of Scandinavia (derived from Old Italic), but we are informed that this is because they are meant to be "Anglo-Saxon" runes, which look much more like Latin letters. Unfortunately, the show never explains which of the various runic systems in use in medieval England this was meant to be, and for good reason. Although I cannot read runes, those who can and who have examined the images shown on *America Unearthed* have told me that the runes are primarily Elder Furthark, not Anglo-Saxon, though some Anglo-Saxon characters—a completely different alphabet—are inexplicably mixed in. In any case, those who can read Elder Furthark explained that the symbols are in no coherent order and are nonsensical gibberish. Worse, Elder Furthark vanished from European cognizance after 800 CE, all knowledge of its very meaning lost until the nineteenth century. Anglo-Saxon runes are derived from the Germanic Elder Furthark, expanded to

26-33 characters from the Elder Furthark's 24, but this script, too, died out no later than 1000 CE, with all knowledge of it whatsoever vanishing with the coming of the Normans.

More interesting is what the show leaves out. Wolter notes how fresh the carvings on the rune stone look, and he tries to explain why they seem carved only years—not centuries—ago. On the wall of the cave, photographs and eyewitness testimony prove nearly identical "fresh" runic inscriptions can be seen. One could argue that these are simply later graffiti, but they call into question the authenticity of the similar runes on the stone just feet away. The key, of course, is that when the cave site was discovered in 1984 and recorded by the Arizona State Museum, the runes weren't there. They do not appear in any documentation done at the cave, so they are almost certainly a modern forgery, as the Arizona State Archaeologist, Steve Ross, tells Wolter.

Wolter makes a valiant case that the floor of the cave had been dug out after 1984 (it was vandalized sometime in the past thirty years), thus making the runic rock seem younger than it is because it had been hidden in the floor and did not experience weathering. So, one might ask, why did the runes on the walls not weather either? The show doesn't want us to know of these runes, so they are passed over in silence. Nor is the state archaeologist convinced. A silly staged bit of cell phone discussion with an unseen correspondent—in an area where tourists routinely report a lack of cell coverage—leads Wolter to believe that the rock was a grave marker, though the text message he read aloud from the his hidden source was quite clearly planned before filming began, giving a patina of fabrication to Wolter's investigation of a stone that is itself covered thickly in the patina of fabrication.

A great deal of cave exploration follows, leading to little more than speculation that some spiral petroglyphs found within the caves were star maps or Fibonacci spirals of sacred geometry—even though, quite obviously, the spirals are not in the Fibonacci proportions. (A Fibonacci spiral is instantly recognizable because the curve's width doubles with each pass around the point of origin, and these cave spirals do not do this.) Whether the spirals are a star map is open to interpretation, but even the most generous interpretation fails to lead to the direct conclusion that they must be of European origin; Native Americans were capable of understanding the stars. Wolter then tells us how big a deal a European presence at the cave *would* be *if* it really existed. Arizona's state archaeologist, Steve Ross, explains that a permit is needed to excavate, but Wolter refuses to go through the permit process because no one involved in this production cares much for facts so much as they do making a documentary as quickly and cheaply as possible. Hence, we see long scenes of Wolter staring at a computer and writing notes, when a better program might have commissioned some actual archaeology.

According to Wolter's staged phone call with a guy identified as "Mike" (Mike Carr) the runes carved on the stone reveal that the rock marked the grave of a twelfth-century Englishman. That would be a neat trick since most runes had been replaced by the Latin alphabet for all but specialized ritual use in Europe by the twelfth century, and as we have seen above, in England, Anglo-Saxon runes (never mind the Elder Furthark these really are) ceased to be used for inscriptions after the ninth century and fell completely out of even scholarly and antiquarian understanding after the Norman Conquest, according to standard texts on runes. In fact, fewer than two hundred runic inscriptions survive from medieval England, none after 1066. Thus, twelfth century runes are several centuries late for even an educated explorer to have used in carving a gravestone. An educated Englishman of the time would have used Latin, or possibly Norman French if he were particularly progressive; and an uneducated man wouldn't have written anything at all. English vernacular wouldn't have been used for significant religious or monumental inscriptions until around Chaucer's time.

Steve Ross, the state archaeologist, throws cold water on Wolter's enthusiastic embrace of the runes as genuine medieval writing by pointing to the logical and physical problems with doing so—not least of which are (a) the lack of notice given the rock in 1984 and (b) the complete lack of any other European artifacts of influence in the area—but none of the people on the program is an expert in European archaeology or writing and thus they speak largely from preconceived ideas rather than evidence. Ground-penetrating radar is used to reveal a change of density in the cave floor near the rune stone. Wolter interprets this as a grave spreading out before the rune stone, which he infers from this must therefore be a headstone. That said, Wolter had just finished arguing that the stone had been *moved* when the cave was vandalized, and now he claims it is resting *in situ* as a gravestone! (For both things to be true, the rock would have needed to have been dug out from the floor, and the floor then leveled around the stone, an unlikely scenario for vandals.) Once again, the "investigation" is stymied not by government conspiracy but by Wolter and his crew refusing to apply for permits to conduct real research that could settle the speculative claims.

Another staged cell phone intrusion by "Mike" provides his translation of the runes. He tells us that the runes identify the deceased as Peter "Rough" Hurech, a name associated with Staffordshire in England. As we shall see momentarily, this man likely never existed. According to Mike, the rune stone reads: "The body in contrast with the soul fits/lays / Rough Hurech here / He enjoyed entertainment, joy, merriment, the secret stolen / Rough Hurech's body—fame and glory / Dust beyond Eden / Eden's temple." Remember that others with knowledge of runes have analyzed the rock and concluded it was gibberish and does not contain any name whatsoever. We do not hear how Mike translated the runes, but I was able to find parts of the translation appearing verbatim in the *Bosworth-Toller Anglo-Saxon Dictionary*, where the entry for the word *líc* (body) gives the specific definition "*the body* in contrast with the soul or vital principle..." The translator of the rune stone appears to have misunderstood the explanatory definition and included the entire explanation in his translation. Similarly, the three synonyms "entertainment, joy, merriment" smack of a dictionary definition, not unlike Bosworth's "joy, music, musical accompaniment of a song, mirth, jesting" given for *gleow*. The amateur effort on display in taking *all* possible synonyms as part of a single meaning strongly smacks of fakery, or at least a translator out of his depth, seeing connections where none exist in ambiguous, random lettering. In fact, his whole "translation" seems to be a collection of unrelated, unconnected dictionary definitions. I also wonder if the otherwise unattested nickname "Rough" came from finding "rough" as the definition for *hrio, hrúh,* and *hreó,* words very similar to Hurech.

The odd phrase "Eden's temple" appears to be a reference, probably of Mike Carr's own devising, to Beth-eden, the "house (i.e. temple) of Eden," on the plain of Damascus, in Amos 1:5, which speaks to God's promise to destroy the pagans of Eden and the surrounding region, but also implies that Mike means to relate Hurech to the Crusaders, who around 1200 had just lost control of Damascus and the Holy Land to Saladin. It is impossible for me to say at a distance, but the translation appears to be geared toward providing a putative justification for Hurech's travels—that he had left England for the Crusades.

Mike also tells Wolter to travel to the Gila Cliff Dwellings in New Mexico but won't say why. The program presents this as a mystery, but this bit of deceptive stagecraft helps undercut the claims to truth on the show since the filming permits at Gila Cliff Dwellings National Monument were arranged and an interview with a ranger there was also planned. (The site is run by the U.S. Forest Service under an agreement with the Department of the Interior—the same Forest Service that "conspired" against Wolter in Episode One.) Nothing of interest seems to happen as we visit the Gila ruins other than wasting time looking at sites with no connection to England whatsoever ... that is, until Wolter goes to England and tries to connect the Mogollon buildings to European builders. After a long montage of Wolter traveling by car across England to Staffordshire, he meets up with Alan Butler, an alternative history author whose research has focused on ancient goddess religions and his belief that the Knights Templar and Freemasons perpetuate goddess ideology. He also tried to sue me back in 2005 for reviewing in *Skeptic* magazine without permission a book he and Christopher Knight wrote about megalithic architecture in which they claimed that an Atlantis-like civilization encoded cosmic information into the measurements of Neolithic stone circles. I didn't think much of the book, and I thought less of him and Knight after their threatened lawsuit.

Butler claims that county records in Staffordshire associated a certain Peter Hurech with the Whittington Inn, a manor house built in 1310, converted into an inn in 1783, and now serving as a pub. The building stands atop land that paranormal researchers looking into the inn's alleged ghosts say was purchased by Hurech for twenty shillings for a farm back in the 1100s. However, according to the *History of the County of Stafford*, the land actually belonged from the 1160s to Philip de Kinver, also called Philip Helgot, who was in debt and had to forfeit the land to Thomas fitz Bernard from 1181 until Geoffrey fitz Peter took over in 1183, before returning six months later to Philip de Kinver, who held it past the point when Hurech would have left.[1] Philip was compelled to pay £20 to build a hunting lodge for King Henry II to settle the back rent he owed on the farm; it is this lodge that eventually grew into Whittington Inn when a nobleman of that name expanded the lodge into a manor. Peter Hurech, should such a man have existed, would therefore have been a tenant of Philip, though only the elite could own significant property such as a manor; but Butler claims he actually *built* the Whittington Inn, the present form of which is not older than 1310, and mostly rebuilt after the 1600s. Since we know who actually owned the property, this Peter Hurech could not be an actual nobleman of any note, raising the question of where a tenant farmer got the money to fund an expedition. Hurech, Butler asserts, can be traced in English records down to around 1200, but he left no offspring and his surname died out in Staffordshire after 1200. We never see a single actual record, only Butler reading a text message he asserts came from the county records office. This is highly suspicious.

Obviously, I was not willing to take Butler at his word given our history. I contacted the Staffordshire Record Office in March 2013 and inquired about the claims made on the program. The duty archivist at the records office was unfailingly polite but quite obviously concerned about the claims made for information provided by her office. Not only did the county records office not provide any information about the Hurech family to *America Unearthed* or to Alan Butler, but there is no existing record for *anyone* of the name Hurech in Staffordshire or Stoke on Trent in any extant index for *any* century, not in the electronic index nor the manual index. No record of "Hurech" or any similar name appears in any of the indexes to twelfth century records in the four volumes of the Collections for the History of Staffordshire series published by the Staffordshire Records Society (formerly the William Salt Archaeological Society) that cover the relevant century. The archivist cautioned that such indexes are compiled based on archivists' judgment and therefore are partial, so an obscure name may exist within the body of the records without being indexed; but the county has no record of any family by the name of Hurech.[2] On the program, the research discovering the "Hurech" records is presented as having taken but an afternoon, an impossibility given that the name is not indexed.

This is only to be expected, of course, since surnames only began to be adopted among the Norman nobility in the twelfth century and only filtered down to the common people in the thirteenth and fourteenth. It is only after 1300 that we see surnames passed from father to son, thus creating family names. So where did *America Unearthed* get its name from? That I do not know for sure. It is possible that the name was created backward from Mike Carr's fanciful reading of the fake Arizona runes. It is also possible that the "Hurech" Butler was referring to was an attempt to retroactively Anglo-Saxonize the Norman name of the known Staffordshire nobleman Hugh fitz Peter (died c. 1210), the son of Peter de Birmingham, who was active around this time and held lands in Staffordshire. Although no such name appears in Anglo-Saxon records, *Hu-* ("mind") is a Saxon first element cognate with Hugh (Old French *Hue*, meaning "mind," "heart," or "soul"), and *–ric* ("ruler") a second element, so the name *Huric* is a possible construction that someone might mistake for a Saxon form of Hugh, especially in back-constructing a moniker for a ruler named Hugh. It might also be a mistake for other Peters operating in the area, like Peter de Broc (de Brok), if the "B" was misread as an "H." This family shares many of the traits ascribed to Hurech, for Peter de Broc, who died in 1219, was the last of his line, after which his family vanishes from Staffordshire—his lands reverting to Hugh de Loges. The last occurrence of the de Broc name occurs in the *Book of Fees* in the 1300s, but not in Staffordshire but rather in Hampshire. That Alan Butler pronounces Hurech as "Hr-OAK" suggests that this reading ("Hroc" for "Broc") is plausible.

The most likely scenario, however, involves a British ghost hunting group, Elite Paranormal, who investigated the manor for ghosts in 2011. Their website is the only other place where the name Peter de Hurech appears, and they claim he held the land (as a "manor," or estate) prior to 1187 as a tenant of Philip of Kinver, although they give no source for the claim. When I contacted them they said that they obtained the text for their website from an unremembered third party. They correctly note that the current manor house itself was not built until the 1300s. I would imagine that the *America Unearthed* team read this webpage, misunderstood it, and derived their claims about Peter from that.

Butler takes Wolter to the Kinver Rock Houses, the inspiration for Tolkien's hobbit houses, which Wolter claims are "reminiscent" of the Gila Cliff Dwellings, if by "reminiscent" you mean that they are buildings with rooms in some sort of relationship to large rocks. These impressive houses look like the façades of homes but they are carved from the living rock. The Kinver Rock Houses were not built on cliffs as at Gila but rather were built into sandstone rock walls, mostly at ground level (though some abut a "street" that rises far above ground level), by carving rooms into the living rock, much like the city of Petra in Jordan. The Kinver Rock Houses date back to perhaps 1500 CE (though some think they may be older) and were used down to the 1960s. Some are carved as proper English houses, with straight walls, even floors, and well-proportioned rooms in the style of an English country house, with some having three stories and brick chimneys. Others are more like caves, but all were carved completely out of the relatively soft living rock. Here is how they were described in 1904:

> Kinver is situated at the south-western edge of the county of Stafford, just where it joins Worcester and Salop. It is a small town on the banks of the river Stour, some four miles from Stourbridge, and about four and a-half

miles from Kidderminster. The only access to the place, unless one prefers to walk, is by the electric tram from Dudley or Stourbridge. Passing through the main street, an enjoyable walk brings us to what is known as Kinver Edge. This is a great ridge, or edge, of new red sandstone, which terminates abruptly above the river Stour, the extreme headland of which is 542ft. above the sea-level. Between this headland and the valley below lies a remarkable mass of isolated crag which goes by the name of the Holy Austin Rock. This is literally honeycombed with habitations in three storeys, or stages, with families occupying each level, although at present all the dwellings are not tenanted. It was here that we made our first stay and the photographs of the old lady at the well and the old gentleman at his door were taken. The old lady, Mrs. Chance, informed us that she had lived in the rock-house eleven years, and paid £8 1s. 8d. a year rent for it. The old gentleman, who had occupied his house thirty-five years, however, lived rent free, the parish also contributing 3s. 6d. a week towards his maintenance. His house consisted of three rooms, or caves, in one of which he lived, one he used as a storeroom, and at the end of a long tunnel running from the living-room was a large cave hollowed out of the solid rock, in which, he stated, "many years ago, as many as fifty people had danced." It may be interesting to mention that these rock-houses and the adjoining lands belong to Mr. P. H. Foley, the well-known Worcestershire cricketer, who lives at Prestwood, close to Kinver, and who is Lord of the Manors of Kinver and Compton, his agent, who collects the rents of these houses, being Mr. H. K. Foster, another famous cricketer, and one of the well-known Worcestershire family of that name.[3]

Contrary to Wolter's assertion that the Gila dwellings were completely artificial and thus just like the Kinver houses, archaeologists believe that the Mogollon people built the Gila houses within five naturally-occurring caves created by ancient volcanic activity, with large brick, irregular brick rooms and structures constructed within the caves. Again unlike the British site, the Gila dwellings have uneven floors, open fire pits, storage pits, and heavy plastering. They clearly represent a very different cultural tradition both in their construction and in the use implied by their layout and design. The Gila dwellings were built after 1275 CE (which we know from tree-ring dating of wood at the site) and occupied for only a few decades. Thus they are a century too late to have anything to do with Wolter's imaginary "twelfth century" explorer, or with sixteenth century English rock houses. These cliff houses were also clearly meant for defensive purposes since they are high and inaccessible, again in contrast to the British examples atop which were the pens for livestock and which had ground-level doors and large windows.

Therefore, Wolter's entire evidence for an English presence in twelfth-century Arizona is nothing more than a rock with an anachronistic carving that was almost certainly fabricated in the past thirty years. The rest is nothing but illogical speculation.

Great Lakes Copper Heist

Airdate: January 4, 2013

Episode Summary

Scott Wolter tests copper found around Lake Superior for purity and uses that test to determine that the copper supply for Bronze Age Europe came from Lake Superior. He concludes that the Minoans colonized the Lake Superior basin and ran it as a mining operation.

Historical Background

The area around Lake Superior has long been known as one of the only places in the world where large amounts of pure copper could be extracted and used without the need for smelting. For thousands of years, the Native Americans of the Lake Superior basin did just that, at first taking copper straight from where it lay on the surface, and later digging it out of the ground, first with simple sticks and later in larger mining operations. This may have begun as early as the Paleo-Indian period. Artifacts from this operation have been found from Wisconsin to the Eastern Seaboard, and they number in the tens of thousands of known objects—a mere fraction, of course, of the actual number produced, traded, and reused down to the contact period. Much of the copper was eventually buried with the dead, where it would eventually turn up in nineteenth century excavations of burial mounds, to the shock of the Victorians. The copper was used in place of stone for everything from projectile points to fish hooks.

The people who did this mining are known as the Old Copper culture,

a local variant of the Lake Forest Late Archaic societies, and they flourished between 3000 and 2500 BCE. After them, copper mining continued,
and the metal traveled across trade networks as far afield as the southeastern United States, where it became prized as a sign of social prestige,
as evidenced by its use in ritual ornamentation and grave goods. Although
systematic mining ended around 1000 BCE, copper artifacts from that period were preserved and handed down right up to the period of European
contact, confounding the Jesuits, who wondered why these items were
held sacred.

The Chippewa had a story about copper and the long-vanished Old
Copper culture, or at least what they had inferred from its remains. Their
legend tells of Missibizzi, a terrible god who lived on a floating island of
copper and presided over fabulously rich copper mines in and around Lake
Superior, each haunted by fearsome spirits. Four young warriors who
paddled out to Michipicoten Island, the third largest in Lake Superior,
near Sault Ste. Marie sometime in the distant past. There, they stole from
the deity Missibizzi four glowing red stones—copper ingots—and immediately launched their canoe back to the mainland. The god stood on the
shore and thundered after the warriors, causing one to die of fright immediately and a second to die upon reaching shore. The third young man
died returning home, and only one survived to bring the copper to the
tribe before expiring himself. Thereafter, Michipicoten was considered
taboo, though copper items were held to be irreplaceably sacred and objects of worship, to the annoyance of Jesuit missionaries, who noted that
the Chippewa knew nothing of mining.[1]

When questioned about Missibizzi and his mines, the Chippewa would
refer only to a lost race of copper miners who had worked the mines in
the fabulous past. They themselves had nothing to do with the mines,
fearsome places where dread spirits lived. The Lake Superior copper mines
remained in the memory of Native peoples down to the time of European
contact. The Algonquin presented Samuel de Champlain with a gift of a
large copper ingot, which he dutifully sent back to the king in France, and
he told the king that the Algonquin had taken the ingot from the "bank of

a great river flowing into a great Lake," almost certainly the Ontonagon River and Lake Superior. But since copper was neither valuable nor rare, later French explorers did not follow up on the copper, questing in vain for gold and gems instead, and working tirelessly to try to coax the Chippewa to tell them myths of any other metal besides their many stories of copper. But in the 1660s, the French sent expeditions to determine the source of the copper, and they discovered ancient and abandoned pit mines rich with copper. There was so much copper that whole boulders of it sat in river beds and on islands, sometimes weighing several tons. In 1672, the French sent Marquette and Joliet to search out all the lake's copper, but, taking a different direction, they found the Mississippi instead. Eventually, the stories of the copper wealth of Superior led to Isle Royale being granted specifically to the United States in the Treaty of Paris in 1783, thanks to American businessmen appealing to Benjamin Franklin to secure its inclusion.[2] We have them to thank for this episode of *America Unearthed.*

Following this, the old copper mines sat vacant until 1822, when some New Yorkers proposed to start mining them anew, specifically citing their ancient pedigree. This led to a copper boom in the area, and mining continued down to the twentieth century before all the copper it was profitable to extract had finally been exhausted.

In the meantime, speculators began to wonder just how anyone had been mining copper prehistorically. Since the Chippewa were considered ignorant of mining, it was quickly suggested that a lost race of white people were responsible for the mining operation, for Victorian intellectuals felt that Native Americans were savages, of a lesser level of physical and mental development, and therefore not capable of developing metallurgy unaided by a superior culture. A man named Bertholet speculated that carved symbols at Lake Superior and on the Canary Islands proved that the two shared a common, ancient culture.[3] In 1882, Ignatius Donnelly, the U.S. congressman who singlehandedly resurrected Atlantis as a genre of alternative history, wrote that it was shocking that so little copper had been found among the Native peoples, and he implied that copper mining originated around Lake Superior, that it gave rise to the Bronze Age, and that it was the work of the lost race of Atlantis.

...among the Chippeways of the shores of Lake Superior, *and among them alone*, we find any traditions of the origin of the manufacture of copper implements; and on the shores of that lake we find pure copper, out of which the first metal tools were probably hammered before man had learned to reduce the ore or run the metal into moulds. And on the shores of this same American lake we find the ancient mines from which some people, thousands of years ago, derived their supplies of copper. [...]

[I]f we are to seek for the source of the vast amount of copper brought into Europe somewhere else than in Atlantis, may it not be that these supplies were drawn in large part from the shores of Lake Superior in America? The mining operations of some ancient people were there carried on upon a gigantic scale, not only along the shores of the lake but even far out upon its islands. At Isle Royale vast works were found, reaching to a depth of sixty feet; great intelligence was shown in following up the richest veins even when interrupted; the excavations were drained by underground drains. On three sections of land on this island the amount of mining exceeded that mined in twenty years in one of our largest mines, with a numerous force constantly employed. In one place the excavations extended in a nearly continuous line for two miles. No remains of the dead and no mounds are found near these mines: it would seem, therefore, that the miners came from a distance, and carried their dead back with them. [...] Such vast works in so remote a land must have been inspired by the commercial necessities of some great civilization; and why not by that ancient and mighty people who covered Europe, Asia, and Africa with their manufactures of bronze-and who possessed, as Plato tells us, enormous fleets trading to all parts of the inhabited world-whose cities roared with the continual tumult of traffic, whose dominion extended to Italy and Egypt, and who held parts of "the great opposite continent" of America under their control? A continuous water-way led, from the island of Atlantis to the Gulf of Mexico, and thence up the Mississippi River and its tributaries almost to these very mines of Lake Superior.[4]

Donnelly concluded by arguing that the mines were worked by the builders of America's ancient mounds, whose "race identity" pointed to an "eastern, over-sea origin."[5] Such claims set the stage for arguing that the Old World's copper and bronze had a New World origin. But not everyone was happy with the idea of a lost continent. Adolph Froehlke argued instead that the true copper miners were instead slaves of the Phoenicians, and that they had mined thirty to fifty million tons of copper over five centuries.[6] Others blamed the Aztecs. In 1961, Roy W. Drier and Octave J. Du Temple proposed, based on faulty estimates, that too much copper— 1.5 billion pounds—was missing from the mines to be accounted for by the use of mere Native Americans. By 1967, patent lawyer Henrietta Mertz, picking up on the Atlantis theme from Donnelly, suggested in *Atlantis: Dwelling Place of the Gods* that it went to the Old World—and that archaeologists were covering up this fact. In 2011, Gavin Menzies adopted this claim wholesale as the centerpiece of his book, *The Lost Empire of Atlantis,* which proposed that the Minoans had conducted mining operations in the Lake Superior basin and shipped all the copper back to Crete.

Scott Wolter would adopt these claims wholesale without crediting any of the earlier authors.

The Episode

We begin "Great Lakes Copper Heist" with a recreation of some woodsmen felling a tree in Michigan in 1896, filmed in dramatic "old-timey" sepia tone. (Actually, it was tinted in post-production from full-color digital video.) The men look at a rock covered in symbols, and we smash-cut to the opening credits. We start at Isle Royale, Michigan, where Scott Wolter plans to investigate the Old Copper Culture, about which he appears to care nothing beyond imagining that these benighted Natives were simply the playthings of their European masters. The area was copper-rich, and Wolter asserts that the copper "disappeared." As we shall see, this is simply a lie.

We hear that 1.5 *billion* pounds of copper were removed from the area around Lake Superior (a number drawn from Drier and Du Temple without credit), but this number is a fraudulent exercise in extrapolation. No source is given on the show, nor could they give one because the numbers come only from alternative speculation dating back to the 1960s. As Dr. Susan R. Martin explained years ago, "The mythic calculations involve the numbers and depths of copper extraction pits, the numbers and weights of stone hammers, the percentage volume of copper per mining pit, the numbers of miners, and the years of mining duration."[7] It is only by combining and recombining all these assumptions (essentially by picking one's own numbers) that alternative writers, most notably Drier and Du Temple, generated the 1.5 billion pound claim. Scholarly estimates of the Copper Culture's mining are much, much less, thus eliminating the "lost" copper.

According to Martin, the variables used to calculate the amount of copper extracted from the Lake Superior mines—which are better described as dug-out pits—are all estimated, so each estimate compounds the error as they are multiplied with one another. For example, she cites the case of the "percentage of copper in the trap rock" as one case where the estimate throws figures off wildly. In nature, the amount of copper in a rock varies from zero percent (no copper) to one hundred percent, as in the Ontonagon Boulder, two solid tons of pure copper. The amount of copper even within a known course of trap rock can vary significantly. Drier and Du Temple picked an arbitrary number to represent all the copper-containing rock, regardless of its actual copper content, and then compounded that error by multiplying this erroneous number by an estimated number of copper pits (the real number being unknown), an assumed constant size for the pits (which in reality vary greatly), and by projecting the number of pits to areas not surveyed (and thus unknown). Therefore, after multiplying out this many levels of error, the total 1.5 billion pound estimate is off by entire orders of magnitude. Once the archaeologically verified figures are inputted into their calculations, the "missing" copper vanishes.[8]

That said, the Old Copper Culture *did* mine copper for several thousand years, and they removed quite a bit of rock, which in turn yielded much less actual copper. Without any "missing" copper, the rest of the episode becomes irrelevant. Nevertheless, Wolter talks next about an artifact found near the copper pits that allegedly has Old World symbols. The artifact, known as the Newberry Tablet, is at first presented as destroyed (obviously following Barry Fell and Wayne May, who claimed in their separate works that it had vanished), but all the better to create fake drama later on, as we shall see.

Wolter claims he will test Michigan's copper for purity and see if Old World copper artifacts are of the same purity to "prove" they are identical. The scholarly literature has several articles that have attempted to propose ways to distinguish between native (i.e. unrefined) copper and smelted copper, but the academic consensus among experts is that no test can determine this with certainty because the smelting process can produce copper pure enough to be indistinguishable from native copper.[9] The chemical formulae are tiresome to review in detail, but the books I consulted all agree: smelted copper's purity cannot be distinguished from naturally pure copper, so Wolter's purity test is useless. Only a trace element test would have any bearing on the situation, which Wolter, as a geologist, must know since he used that same type of test in Episode One in looking for the clay used in Maya Blue pigment. In fact, the archaeological consensus is that trace element analysis is the only way to distinguish between smelted and native worked copper artifacts, though unworked copper can also be distinguished by a distinctive metallographic structure, one that is lost once worked.[10]

We watch Wolter tramp around some old mine shafts on Isle Royale, mostly to waste time; and at the halfway point of the show, I became bored with the lack of facts or action. Preposterously, the show claims that the native wolf population of Isle Royale has collapsed due to wolves falling into open mine shafts; in truth, a virus devastated the wolf population in the 1980s—not 4,000-year-old pit mines—and skewed sex ratios contributed to reproductive problems. There were perhaps fewer than ten wolves on the island when this episode was shot in 2012, down from 24 in 2009. Although researchers who have studied the island's wolves for the past 25 years were unable to determine the cause of death for most of the wolves whose bodies they recovered, the dead wolves were not found at the bottom of the mines—nor have they ever witnessed wolves falling into the mines. Clearly, mine-shaft falls are not the leading cause of death, or even a significant one, though of course we cannot rule them out. Several wolves died without being found.[11]

"Why wouldn't" Old World people come to Michigan for copper, Wolter asks. Well, that's because they didn't know it existed; also, the island of Cyprus was a well-known source for Minoan copper, negating the need to go to America. But we look at a petroglyph that depicts a canoe or ship with a square sail, which Wolter admits is probably less than one thousand years old but then tells us might well be a depiction of a Minoan vessel—despite resembling Minoan ships in no discernible way. The size and shape of the keel are different, for example. Probably the petroglyph was carved after European contact, at a time when sails had become known to Native peoples. This is supposed to be an indication that the Minoans, a Cretan people who flourished between 2700 to 1500 BCE, sailed to America to mine the Lake Superior copper.

In a staged conversation, Wolter learns from a grizzled old man that the artifact with "Minoan" writing that he calls the Newberry Tablet still exists, and he goes to visit it. This rock is roughly rectangular and contains a regular orthogonal grid in which individual characters are inscribed, one per square. Wolter claims the tablet must be legitimate because it contains "Minoan" writing and was found *before* the Minoan culture was "discovered" by Sir Arthur Evans in 1900. There is no such thing as "Minoan" script, of course, and Wolter never says what he means by it. The Minoans wrote in Linear A script, which has not been deciphered, and a comparison of the characters on the Newberry Tablet and actual Linear A writing shows that the symbols are very different. The Newberry symbols appear to be a jumble of stylized characters from the Greek alphabet, the Phoenician alphabet, northern European Runes, and other ancient symbols placed willy-nilly on the stone.

Ah, but Wolter is fudging here. Some alternative writers have claimed the tablet reflects "Cypriot-Minoan," a term for the Cypriot syllabary, a type of writing used on Cyprus from 1000-400 BCE (predominantly, though, in the 500s BCE), when it was replaced by Greek, just as it had replaced Linear C. Other alternative writers, like David Childress and Barry Fell, claim the stone is written in Hittite or Hittite-Minoan,[12] though this cannot be the case since the Hittites wrote in cuneiform characters or in Anatolian hieroglyphs. The confusion stems from the theory that Cypriot script was a simplified variant of Hittite cuneiform, proposed in the 1880s. The Cypriot syllabary was deciphered in the nineteenth century by Assyriologist George Smith (who also discovered the Babylonian flood myth)—*before* the Newberry Tablet was "discovered," making it likely that this was one source used to hoax the tablet. The Cypriot syllabary's characters are quite similar to the Newberry symbols (as are the even better-known Phoenician letters) as carved by someone who doesn't understand them very well. Not coincidentally, the Newberry Tablet's case was taken up by Henrietta Mertz, the same woman who also was involved in declaring the copper around Lake Superior "missing."

We then travel to a lake where some believe the Minoans left clues below the water level. Wolter takes us to look at some underwater rock piles supposedly made in the shape of "Minoan" characters, though everyone involved with the show admits they've been altered in modern times. Even Wolter notices that the designs appear to be very recent. Therefore, this segment is simply another bit of wasted time, offering no proof of anything.

The hour concludes with a proton-induced x-ray emission (PIXE) analysis of the Michigan copper to try to match it to Old World copper artifacts. PIXE analysis uses the x-rays an object emits when struck by a proton beam to distinguish trace elements in the object since each element produces a unique x-ray signature. The results in the Michigan sample show the presence of germanium, arsenic, and other trace elements, with 99.9% copper purity. But Wolter does not compare the trace elements in the "Minoan" copper he refers to, which is actually a non-Minoan source, the Uluburun shipwreck, a Bronze Age boat found in 1982 that had sunk after leaving copper-rich Cyprus sometime in the years right before 1300 BCE, after the Minoans had already been conquered and absorbed by the

Mycenaeans. Interestingly, this is the exact same evidence Gavin Menzies used in his book on the Minoan voyage to Lake Superior in 2011. Wolter never credits Menzies, whose book Wolter followed nearly point for point in this episode.

Several presumed Mycenaeans were aboard the Uluburun ship, which carried goods from at least ten different cultures, none of which was North American. The ten tons of copper found on this wreck are allegedly the only other copper samples in the world that are 99.9% pure. But as scholars know, the purity of the copper is irrelevant to the match; smelted copper can be taken to 99.9% purity, too, and Wolter purposely fails to mention any trace elements found in the "Minoan" copper. Why? Because they don't, won't, and can't match—the copper is almost certainly from Cyprus. This key omission lets him falsely claim a connection that simply does not exist.

Giants in Minnesota

Airdate: January 11, 2013

Episode Summary

Scott Wolter investigates a claim that a giant is buried on a Minnesota farm as well as a claim that a Norse sword was found at Ullen. Although Wolter finds no evidence of either, he concludes that Minnesota was colonized by the Norse during the Middle Ages.

Historical Background

Tales of giants go back as far as human storytelling can take us. Among the very first recorded stories is that of the Mesopotamian hero Gilgamesh, who battled the giant Humbaba. Giants also grace the pages of Greek mythology, and the Italian humanist Giovanni Boccaccio even recorded the excavation of the skeleton of one Greek giant, the Cyclops Polyphemus, in 1342. The excavators, he said, entered a cave near Tripani (ancient Drepana) in Sicily and "saw opposite the entrance a seated man of immense magnitude, of whom they were much frightened. ... The body of the man also fell apart upon being touched, and it turned almost completely to dust."[1] In 1806 Georges Cuvier put forward the ingenious hypothesis that ancient and medieval reports of giants were actually referencing the misunderstood bones of extinct elephants, mammoths, or mastodons.[2] Being mammals, their teeth and long bones, the most likely parts to survive, closely resemble gigantic versions of those of their human counterparts. In 1706, a German physician recognized the bones of a giant that had been displayed in Switzerland since 1577 were those of an elephant (though he was not aware that the fossil forms were from extinct species), and in 1832, an anatomist revealed that the famous skeleton of the giant Teutobocchus, displayed in France since 1613, was that of an extinct elephant. Today it is recognized that many claims of giant bones refer in reality to the misunderstood bones of the large mammals that died out with the Ice Age, not just elephants and their kin.

Until recently, giants were most familiar to Americans from the King James Version of the Bible, where they appear in Genesis 6:4: "There were giants in the earth in those days; and also after that, when the sons of God came in unto the daughters of men, and they bare children to them, the same became mighty men which were of old, men of renown." These giants, Genesis said, had occupied the earth before the flood of Noah but were now gone with the waters. Such a passage made it essentially an article of faith that good Christians must believe that pre-Flood ruins would contain the bodies of giants. This is why when mammoth or mastodon teeth and bones were carried to Albany, New York in 1705, Cotton Mather, the witch-hunting preacher, immediately used them as proof of the veracity of Genesis, and Gov. Joseph Dudley of Massachusetts, upon seeing one of the teeth in 1706, wrote that he was "perfectly of opinion that the tooth will agree only to a human body, for whom the flood only could prepare a funeral; and, without doubt, he waded as long as he could keep his head above the clouds, but must, at length, be confounded with all other creatures."[3] He could not, however, decide which "rank or classis"—which earthly generation—of giants he belonged to, but gigantic descendant of the fallen angels he must have been.

As the mastodon and mammoth became better understood, it became more difficult to pass off their bones as those of giants. Nevertheless, in the backwoods of America such events continued right down to modern times, and one unfortunate mammoth skeleton continued to be displayed as the remains of a Biblical giant throughout the nineteenth century, despite scientific identification of its real species. But the most famous of the giants was never living at all: The infamous Cardiff Giant was sculpted by a man named George Hull to resemble an oversized petrified body and placed in the ground as a hoax, and biblical literalists, on cue, declared it the remains of a biblical giant once it was unearthed in William Newell's backyard in 1869. One clergyman asserted that it was one of the very sons of God mentioned in Genesis 6:4. Hull wanted to prove that Americans were so willing to believe the Bible that they'd accept anything, and he also hoped to make a fortune off the hoax. He did both, but even though Hull eventually confessed the hoax, the giant has remained on display continuously to the present day.

Further to the west, skeletons of giants began to appear in newspaper reports with alarming frequency, though always vanishing before anyone in an official capacity could document them. In the 1860s through the 1880s, Minnesota settlers despoiling Native American burial mounds claimed to have found skeletons measuring as much as ten feet nine inches in height. Some of these skeletons were Native American, appearing larger because the bones had become disarticulated and fell out of joint. Others were extinct animals' bones. If the Midwest was particularly prone to finding giants it was partly because of the local fame of men like the "Minnesota Giant," a man named James MicIndoo suffering from a glandular disorder leading to giantism. When he died at the age of nineteen he stood seven feet and two inches tall and weighed more than 300 pounds—which by Victorian standards was astonishing. In nearby Iowa, another "giant" worked as a station agent and was forced to endure tourists stopping by train several times a day to gawk at him, which was partially of his own doing, as he had displayed himself as a seven-foot-four human giant at the 1893 Chicago World's Fair. Such men became fodder for local gossip, news reports, and eventually national magazine articles.

More frequently, though, reports of deceased ancient giants were simply hoaxes designed to cause a sensation in a time when scientists were busy debating whether the burial mounds of America were the work of Native Americans, Hebrews, people from Atlantis, or something else. Stories of giants, often called a lost race of white men, played into the debate and helped to foster the myth that the mounds were not Native American. This therefore justified removing Native peoples from their lands to "restore" the lands to their historic white owners, as Andrew Jackson had made explicit in his 1830 State of the Union address and as the U.S. government had undertaken through the nineteenth century. It was surely no coincidence that the reports of "giant" discoveries grew more outrageous over time, with skeletons increasing in both size and number until by century's end there were claims of a *hundred* skeletons at a time being found with heights exceeding ten feet. Needless to say, not a single skeleton was ever recorded by science, and none exists today. They were the figments of fevered imaginations.

The Episode

Of course *America Unearthed* does not acknowledge the long and undistinguished history of giant skeletons in Minnesota. Before I review "Giants in Minnesota," let me stipulate that in the course of the hour Scott Wolter uncovers *no* evidence whatsoever of giants in Minnesota, or the Norse visitors he ties them to. He admits this, so it is not just me saying it. This, sadly, means that there is little factual material to examine, leaving me to critique this show as a television performance. In that light, we can look at the episode as a triumph of editing in trying to make three pointless investigations add up to more than the sum of their parts through carefully cross-cutting among them and avoiding dwelling too long on the inevitable disappointments. The way the show subtly switches from the proposed topic to others designed to garner support for its star is masterfully executed but deeply manipulative.

We begin with a dramatic reenactment of a flannel-clad man using dowsing rods to find hidden treasure. Although this is presented in shadowy tint as a flashback to several years ago, it was actually filmed alongside footage from Wolter's own investigation later in the episode from the dowser's point of view. I've read some fascinating material from Indo-European mythology about the origins of dowsing rods in a misunderstanding of the mythic importance of specific tree branches thought to be related to the thunder-god's lightning:

In England and in France the divining rod is known chiefly for its alleged power of discovering mines, buried treasure, and hidden springs of water, and it is named accordingly; but this is a modern and too limited view of its wondrous efficacy, the boundless range of which is duly signified by the German name *wish-rod* (wünschelruthe). That name implies a rod which endows its possessor with all earthly blessings, health, wealth, fortune, favour—with everything, in short, that heart can *wish.* In the Niebelungen Lied it is called, like the bounteous god Odin, simply "wish." "The wish lay thereunder, a rod of gold." In this larger sense the divining or wish-rod corresponds very closely with the Hindu chark, and also with the mandrake.[4]

In short, the divining rod is merely a bit of superstitious magic; suffice it to say no scientific evidence supports its efficacy. The gruff man mumbles about "giant bones," and then we're off to the opening credits.

After the credits, the dateline tells us we're at Saker Farm in Twin Valley, Minnesota to investigate the bones of an alleged giant. A farmer named Roger Saker tells Scott Wolter that the Minnesota state archaeologist came out to view some Native American bones Saker had found on his land, one set of which was unusually large. He did not provide a date for this, but it is implied that this was a recent event, though the hard-packed ground and tall weeds growing atop the grave suggest otherwise. "They wanted to get this thing buried as fast as possible," he says, implying a conspiracy to suppress the truth. Reburial is no conspiracy; in fact it is merely Minnesota state law, which mandates respectful treatment for Native remains and reburial, except in extraordinary circumstances. State residents don't get to play with old bones like they were toys, nor are human remains there for amusement. The farmer talks about how he ripped apart the bones and played with them, which made me sad.

Wolter displays for Saker a newspaper article from the 1880s about "giants," one of hundreds published in those decades. Wolter, though, thinks the bones Saker found belong to a race of seven to eight foot tall Norse colonists from medieval times. He never explains why he thinks that the Norse were giants, and it is hard to fathom. I think it derives from two threads. The first is recorded by Snorri Sturluson, that Harald Sigurdsson, known as Hardrada, Viking explorer and King of Norway (as Harald III), stood five ells (7.5 feet) tall.[5] He was rumored to have been among the first to travel to Vinland, now thought to have been the area around L'anse-aux-Meadows in New Brunswick, according to one reading of passages in the work of his contemporary, Adam of Bremen. Immediately after describing Vinland as a land of "the best" wine, Adam recorded in 1076 that Harald had recently "searched the breadth of the northern ocean in ships."[6] Some other individual Scandinavian men, like Eric the Red's son Thorvall, were credited with "gigantic" size in sagas and legend. The second thread is a myth recorded by the Inuit that they battled giants. They said of their enemies "that they were a gigantic race, of great strength—were very fierce, and delighted to kill people—that they themselves could not be killed by either dart or arrow, which rebounded from their breasts as from a rock."[7] Some later scholars concluded that the invulnerability was a memory of Viking armor, and Inuit myths called the Norse "giants" because they were several inches taller on average than the diminutive Inuit, whom evolution had selected to be shorter and more compact to retain heat. Others disagreed and attributed such myths to poetic fancy.

Wolter measures the surface of the alleged grave of an eight and a half foot tall giant under a burial mound on Saker's property, which we must take on faith; without a skeleton, we aren't able to confirm this. Humans, however, could occasionally grow to seven feet, especially with hormonal problems, as was the case with the "Minnesota Giant" a century earlier. Such individuals may well have been considered sacred or holy and given special burial. But all we have to go on here is Saker's claim that the head and feet reached to stone landmarks placed atop the burial mound. Saker explains to Wolter that the state's archaeologists "covered up" the burials, and he accuses them of a conspiracy. Again, federal and state laws require respectful treatment of graves, and thus after their Native identity was confirmed, they were reburied. Not content with this, the farmer called in a dowser to probe the burial mound magically. Wolter claims dowsing really works, based on the authority of Einstein, but as with all the show's other "research," this is another lie. There is no published confirmation Einstein said any such thing, and the Einstein Archive lists only two mentions of dowsing, where Einstein expressed curiosity.

Supposedly the dowser found a ten foot giant, but let's not kid ourselves. This is primitive folk magic, the kind that has been practiced in America since colonial days and was the same type of magic that Joseph Smith was an expert in and used to create Mormonism. (He was an expert in the use of crystal-gazing to find buried treasure, for which he was once sued when a dig went wrong.) Wolter tries to "prove" dowsing is real by hiding a metal knife and asking a seventy-year-old dowser to find it. Noting the obviously disturbed grass, the dowser easily finds it, attributing the discovery to his magic rods. Funny, isn't it, that so many trust in the power of dowsing with any old rod, when in Europe dowsing was traditionally believed to only work when using the wood of the rowan (mountain-ash), and only on certain saints' days, taken over from when they were formerly sacred to Odin or Thor, for the rod was a piece of lightning made wood, the begetter of great boons. All we need to know, though, is that there is no scientific evidence dowsing works.

Farmer Roger Saker, in turn, explains that investigation of the mound is limited because he doesn't want to disturb the corn, not because it is illegal to rob Native American graves, even on private land, under Minnesota law. (On federal land, the Native American Graves Protection and Repatriation Act is the controlling legal authority.) The Private Cemeteries Act, last amended in 2007, gives the state archaeologist the exclusive power to authentic human burials greater than fifty years of age and to arrange for their removal or reburial.[8] The show is careful to avoid breaking the law, but they won't tell viewers what that law is, either. The obvious course would be to dig up *the giant's body*, but since they know that is illegal, they dig instead far from the burial mound where they can plausibly claim no bodies were likely to be found. (The trouble with digging up human remains is briefly noted later on, rendering moot the entire premise of the episode, the search for *giants!*)

Wolter brings in Michael Arbuthnot, a Florida archaeologist specializing in underwater sites, to investigate the farm, and Wolter shares the legends and myths of ancient Norse in Minnesota, all of which are of nineteenth century provenance or later. Wolter even notes that the area is filled with Scandinavian immigrants, but he fails to make the obvious connection that the nineteenth century immigrants who settled Minnesota brought with them a sense of their own cultural history and sought to create an imaginary historic landscape of ancient Norse settlers to help make the land truly "theirs" rather than, say, the Native Americans' or even the Anglo-Americans'. This process has occurred across time and space, with old ruins appropriated by new settlers and incorporated into their history. As a brief example, the nineteenth century English attributed Neolithic remains in Britain to the Druids, whom they saw as their true ancestors, in contradistinction to the decadent Romans, identified with the Continent, the home of Britain's rival and enemy, France.

So, anyway, all these characters start digging and found a chunk of cut bone, which I suppose must be animal since they didn't stop digging and call the authorities, as required by law. After the commercial, we head into the second half of the show and two other plot lines. Wolter first travels to George and Becky's Café in Detroit Lakes, Minnesota to view an alleged Viking sword supposedly pulled from the earth. Wolter frames this in terms of the Kensington Rune Stone, the century-old hoax that I explained in the introduction Wolter has attempted to rehabilitate using dubious geological testing. The program does nothing to discuss the stone beyond letting Wolter assert that his geologic tests "proved" its age. As my introduction noted, this is far from settled, but *America Unearthed* treats this as established, scientific fact.

All of this is prelude to our look at the "medieval" Ullen sword, dug up in 1911 at the height of early twentieth century Viking fakes, when such objects were excavated with surprising frequency thanks to a combination of hoaxing and wishful thinking on the part of Scandinavian immigrants. The sword, at first glance, simply looks new, due to a polishing given it in 1911 and not disclosed in the program. It has none of the patina of age around it, but the camera doesn't linger long enough to really get a good look at it. There's a good reason for that. The Ullen sword looks nothing like medieval Viking swords and exactly like nineteenth century German military swords, which even this program is forced to admit anon.

But since this "investigation" is clearly going nowhere, the producers introduce another, lest we get bored trying to follow one from start to finish. Wolter wastes some time traveling to look at a tumbledown house whose foundation was apparently built with boulders allegedly carved with runes. But, as Wolter himself mentioned, the nineteenth century settlers of Minnesota came from Scandinavia, so there is no need to assume that a "runic carving" was necessarily ancient. A revival of interest in runes had taken place in the nineteenth century, and inscriptions could easily be copied from any of a number of books on the subject. The boulders in question can't be seen when Wolter and crew arrive on this particular day, Wolter promises to come back when the house is torn down the next day.

Back at the farm, the Arbuthnot and Saker discover that the modern farm had previously served as a farm (shock!), and had once been a Native American settlement. No Vikings, no giants. More digging follows as we go into commercial.

After the commercial, the show seems to concede that none of the three plotlines is going well. The show keeps intercutting between them, and we are treated to some extraneous scenes of picturesque destruction as we watch the old farmhouse with its rune-boulders get destroyed. Wolter goes looking for the runic boulder in the ruins, and he finds some scratches on one stone that he identifies as "manmade characters." They look like tool marks to me, since they have no relationship to any alphabetic or runic characters and are (at best) three in number. Even Wolter seems to recognize this, though he tries to obscure the fact by, essentially, hoping viewers look away. He quickly expresses shock that some random guy who shows up has runes for a tattoo, and Wolter is delighted to find they spell the man's name as he slowly translates them, pretending that the tattooed man is ignorant of his own tattoo's mysterious meaning! Oh, my... that had no purpose whatsoever beyond wasting another forty seconds of airtime and distracting viewers from the inconclusive tool mark discovery. The program seems to want us to remember "boulder" and "runes" and forget that they aren't connected in any way.

After the commercial we get a recap of the non-findings so far, and we return to Saker Farm to look at still more bone artifacts, evidence of Native American settlement. But they have found nothing European, nor anything from a giant race—whatever the reason is for assuming the Norse were giants. This strand of the investigation closes, but no one bothers to use any sort of non-invasive testing to measure the alleged giant skeleton in the mound, nor does anyone bother to consult the state archaeologist's report about the site—at least not on camera. And we will soon see why.

Back at the Ullen sword investigation, a medieval sword expert shows us the exact page in a German sword catalog where the Ullen sword had been ordered from Germany in the 1800s, and this entire plotline wheezes to a sclerotic close, much to Wolter's disappointment. Wolter says that the facts have "convinced" him that the sword is modern (good to know), but in a non sequitur he then insists that the Kensington Rune Stone is truly medieval. This is infuriating because this show is *not about* the Kensington Rune Stone, which means that viewers have only Wolter's word to go by since no evidence or discussion of the stone occurred outside Wolter's assertion about its age. This whole program is gradually becoming a bait-and-switch designed to convince viewers that the Rune Stone is real while avoiding the need for evidence.

We finish with a visit to the current Minnesota state archaeologist, Scott Anfinson, whom Wolter questions about the alleged cover-up of the "giant" skeleton. Anfinson states that he did not actually view the bones and therefore cannot answer the question. So who reburied the bones? The show doesn't say. Anfinson has been the state archaeologist since 2006, so presumably the dig occurred sometime before then under a different archaeologist. Wolter informs us that the bones of the "giant" were typical of a 5'3" individual, and Wolter presents Roger Saker with this fact. Since we did not hear Anfinson give this information (and indeed he said he wasn't aware of it), it must have come from Wolter reading the state archaeologist's site report, in turn suggesting that both Wolter and the production team knew there was nothing to this story before they showed up to "investigate" it. Saker responds that there is a conspiracy afoot: "These people, they're up to something," he says, insisting that he saw a giant no matter what the facts say. The farmer seems to have become confused by the disarticulation of the bones, which, falling out of their joints, thus appear larger than the body would have actually stood in life.

The show concludes with another assertion—without evidence—that the Kensington Rune Stone is genuinely medieval, thus "proving" that the Norse colonized Minnesota. Since none of the three stories investigated in this episode provided any evidence of Norse colonizers, the entirety of this "investigation" seems custom-designed to create a circumstantial scenario to provide spurious support to Wolter's assertion about the Rune Stone, which he declines to expose to the scrutiny of a mass television audience. This was a subtle, manipulative hour that asked us to believe in an imaginary conspiracy, to believe that emotional responses count for as much as scientific inquiry, and to believe that Wolter's word is good enough to accept without proof.

A Deadly Sacrifice

Airdate: January 18, 2013

Episode Summary

Scott Wolter investigates a carving of a bull found in Oklahoma that he links to a Celtic religious cult worshiping the Roman deity Mithras in the early centuries CE. Wolter concludes that the Celts came to America, crossed into the Oklahoma panhandle, and worshiped Mithras in a cave.

Historical Background

The cult of Mithras was distinctly Roman creation, born from the Roman adoption of the Persian god Mithra, the divinity of contracts, justice, truth, and cattle. The Persian god originates in the Proto-Indo-European concept of *mitra* ("to cause to bind"), a reference to oaths. The Romans would suggest that the name originated in a related word for mediation. Among the Indo-Aryans, he held the name *Mitra, and many of the gods created from him were later associated with aspects of the sun. However, careful scholarly work on the most ancient forms of Mitra has concluded that he was not originally a sun god but only became associated with solar aspects much later, and separately, in India and Iran.[1] Mithra was granted exalted status in cult, behind only the supreme power of Zoroastrianism, Ahura Mazda (Hellenized as Oromazes), and he served as one of the guardians of the bridge separating the living and the dead. The Manicheans adopted the name as that of a savior guarding the power of light.

The Persian Mithra was known to the Greeks since at least the fourth century BCE, and Plutarch records an early Greco-Roman reference to the god, under the Hellenized name Mithras:

> And this is the opinion of most men, and those the wisest, for they be-
> lieve, some that there are Two Gods, as it were of opposite trades—one
> the creator of good, the other of bad things; others call the better one
> "God," the other "Dæmon," as did Zoroaster the Magian, who, they rec-
> ord, lived 5,000 years before the Trojan War. He therefore calls the for-
> mer "Oromazes," the latter "Arimanios;" and furthermore explains that of
> all the objects of sense, the one most resembles *Light*, the other *Darkness*,
> and *Ignorance;* and that Mithras is between the two, for which reason the
> Persians call Mithras the "Mediator," and he [Zoroaster] taught them to
> offer sacrifice of vows and thanksgiving to the one, of deprecation and
> mourning to the other. For they bruise a certain herb called "omoine" in a
> mortar and invoke Hades and Darkness, and mixing it with the blood of a
> wolf they have sacrificed, they carry away and throw it into a place
> where the Sun never comes, for of plants they believe some to belong to
> the good God, others to the evil Dæmon; and similarly of animals, dogs,
> birds, and land hedgehogs belong to the Good, but to the Bad One water
> rats, for which reason they hold happy men that have killed the greatest
> number of such things.[2]

In the first century BCE, the Romans took over the name and some of the iconography of the god, particularly his cattle, but otherwise created a largely new deity from borrowed Persian parts. All of the available evidence indicates that their cult of Mithras bore little resemblance to its Persian counterpart, though the exact degree of any borrowing from the older religious tradition is not known.[3] What is known from iconography and scant textual references is that the worshipers of Mithras believed that the god was born from a rock,[4] slew the cosmic bull (possibly the constellation Taurus) within a cave, and dined atop its hide alongside the sun god. Among the Greeks and Romans, a single text, the so-called Mithras Liturgy, identifies Mithras as the sun, but most scholars believe that this Greek magical papyrus is associated with Greco-Egyptian magic rather than the Mithras cult. In standard cult iconography, Mithras is separate from the sun and dines beside him at a great feast.

Another deity of the Mithraic pantheon is a lion-headed figure whose name is Arimanios, a name derived from the Zoroastrian Ahriman, the evil deity we saw described by Plutarch, though the absence of an association with evil at Mithraic cult sites suggests that the figure was seen as cosmological god. Cult rites were performed in semi-subterranean temples or natural caves, today known as *mitrhaea*, which featured a singular entrance and rear apse with an altar. These caves were places of initiation and symbolized the universe, which Mithras ruled through the zodiac.[5] Initiates were baptized with water and progressed through seven or eight levels of initiation.[6] The cult was most popular among soldiers and flourished between 100 and 400 CE across the Roman Empire but almost never beyond its borders.

In the late nineteenth century, the Mithras cult attracted new attention because of a new movement to explore the origins of Christianity. Extreme skeptics had begun to question the Gospel accounts of Christ, and the "Christ-myth" school held that Christ was an entirely fictional creation. In support of this, Christ-myth scholars sought evidence that the myth of Christ had been concocted from pagan origins. To this end the Mithras cult was drafted into service beginning with Ernst Renan, who in 1882 claimed Mithraism was a rival of Christianity. Sir James Frazer, in *The Golden Bough*, claimed that Mithras was so similar to Christ that the Church Fathers thought it the work of the devil.[7] This derives from Tertullian, who wrote of Satan that he

> baptizes some—that is, his own believers and faithful followers; he promises the putting away of sins by a laver (of his own); and if my memory still serves me, Mithra there, (in the kingdom of Satan,) sets his marks on the foreheads of his soldiers; celebrates also the oblation of bread, and introduces an image of a resurrection, and before a sword wreathes a crown.[8]

Similarly, Justin Martyr wrote of the rite of communion that the "the wicked devils have imitated in the mysteries of Mithras, commanding the same thing to be done. For, that bread and a cup of water are placed with certain incantations in the mystic rites of one who is being initiated, you either know or can learn."[9] In both cases, though, the rites in question were those of bread and water, not of blood, and Justin actually thought that the cult of Mithras had borrowed and distorted the prophecies of Daniel and Isaiah, accounting for the similarity.[10]

The Episode

We open "A Deadly Sacrifice" with yet another dramatic recreation. This time we see a man in a pit bathed in blood from what sounds like a bull sacrifice above the pit. After this gory interlude, we move forward to the opening credits. A sweeping green vista emerges, and the on-screen graphics inform us that "For more than a century, relics with mysterious symbols have been discovered in Oklahoma." Among these was a five hundred pound rock carving unearthed in 2010. The graphics tell us that the carving was of a bull, "a cult symbol... but one from a different era." Different than what? Oh. "Ancient Egypt." Yeah, um, no. Bulls were cult symbols everywhere bulls could be found, which included almost all the Old World. But this is misdirection; the Egyptians won't last the hour.

The "bull carving" actually arrived in Scott Wolter's lab in 2011, but we are treated to a dramatic reenactment of the event. The carving is shown at first only in shaky, quick shots, making it hard to get a look at it. It appears to depict a bovine of some sort, with a hump on the back, long and curved horns, and four parallel wavy lines separating the head and forequarters from the back and hindquarters. The art style does not immediately suggest any ancient culture but looks very much to me like an archaizing modern forgery. The wavy lines, which puzzle both Wolter and someone with Egyptian expertise he called in to view the carving, recall the jewelry found around the neck of the Apis bull in romantic nineteenth century illustrations.

Wolter asks us to trust that the bull carving is ancient, but he provides no evidence in the opening segment to prove this. Instead, Wolter talks to an Egyptologist about the cult of the Apis bull, which was pretty much what it sounds like—the worship of a bull. At one point Wolter confesses that the bull carving could either be really old or recent and aggressively weathered. The show skips over that quickly, though, lest we think too hard about it. Instead, after the Egyptologist explains many reasons why this carving is completely atypical for Egyptians, Wolter plans to go in search of proof of the artifact's ancient origins. The "Egyptian" theory therefore is unceremoniously abandoned.

So we go off to the river near Tulsa, Oklahoma where the rock was found to pull up some more sandstone rocks. Wolter wants to prove that the carving was or was not carved on native Oklahoma rock. (It was.) This leads to a staged scene where the men who claimed to have first discovered the bull carving announce that five miles away still more inscriptions and carvings can be found. The young men lead Wolter to an unfamiliar location they say they have not visited in a long time, even though the camera was already positioned at the site when they get there in a bit of TV fudging necessary to set up the shot. They show off some modern graffiti and an alleged ancient carving of a face that I frankly am unable to see, even with computer enhancement. It looks like paradolia, the principle whereby the brain interprets ambiguous shapes into familiar images.

Wolter dismisses the whole lot of it as modern, but then, sadly, sees a bunch of lines and claims it is Ogham writing, an early medieval linear alphabet from Ireland—following Barry Fell, who allegedly "translated" the material decades ago. (This, of course, explains why the show came here: They're cribbing from Fell.) Since Ogham writing is almost nothing but vertical lines, it's very easy to imagine Ogham in everything from tool marks to natural crevices. "This looks good!" Wolter says, but I need something more than scratches on rocks to establish that this is (a) Ogham writing, (b) ancient, and (c) produced by traveling Irish. Sadly, none of these three points is addressed with anything more than Wolter's visual assessment.

So we learn the truth: This is another bait-and-switch episode! The putative topic was *Egyptians* in America, and now we're on to medieval Celts again. This should not have surprised me, though; over the past decade Wolter has worked closely with Mormon extremists and Templar theorists who see European influence in America as primarily occurring after the Common Era began (as per the Book of Mormon), so his desire to find medieval artifacts is understandable. Ancient Egyptians mess up the Mormon timeline. Wolter's own research in his own right has focused almost exclusively on the medieval period and Northern European incursions into America, so he is predisposed to seeking out these kinds of incursions.

To learn more about Ogham, Wolter jets off to Ireland (well, in the in-show timeline anyway; in reality, these scenes were almost certainly shot out of sequence to accommodate the show's travel budget and limit the amount of time spent in the British Isles, with the shots of "discovery" and "surprise" recreated later on). Wolter talks to an expert in Ogham writing, Damien McManus of Trinity College Dublin, who explains a bit about Ogham writing, early medieval Irish peoples, and the way the position of the lines, not just their shape, is needed to confirm their authenticity. McManus tells Wolter the inscriptions are superficially similar to Ogham, but not likely to actually be authentic ancient Ogham. Wolter then asks a leading question, hypothetically wondering, in essence, if proof of Irish people in America would be proof of Irish people in America by asking about the consequences of confirming that Celts really did carve Ogham writing in America. McManus, of course, can only answer the question that was asked, but the real question is this: Is this writing Ogham?

At this point I realized that Wolter, if he's clever, could compare the Oklahoma bull carving to the famous seventh century Pictish Burghead Bull at the British Museum. The wavy lines on the Oklahoma bull could thus represent the intricate Celtic scrollwork of the original. Of course this unique carving is from the Picts of Scotland, while Ogham was used by the Irish; however, I'm sure Wolter could have found a way around that. Some Ogham inscriptions have been found in Scotland, which did have extensive cross-colonization with Celtic Ireland. As we headed into the second half of the show, I waited to see if I would be proved right. Sadly, I was not, and it meant that I am apparently a better "alternative" historian than

Scott Wolter without even trying! Oh, and the Pictish carving also serves to show that Wolter's later claims that the Celts relied on Egyptian models for their bull art are false, as this is obviously a completely Celtic bull and one carved long after the Egyptians had faded away.

Wolter "returns" to Oklahoma in stagey scene filmed at a low angle to visit the Anubis Caves in Oklahoma to see more "Ogham" carvings from what the cave explorer he meets calls "Celtic" inscriptions, pronouncing the word like the Boston basketball team rather than with a hard "C," the traditional pronunciation. This cave, incongruously, supposedly has a carving of Anubis and Irish Ogham writing, which conveniently turned up on in the 1970s, at the height of that decade's "alternative history" craze. The carvings are extremely crude, and the "Ogham" writing bears nearly no resemblance at all to the genuine Ogham inscriptions we just saw. Indeed, Dr. James Keyser reviewed the published evidence for the cave's Ogham writing in careful detail and concluded that the alleged Ogham writing was anything but and that true believers' attempts to explain away the problems as a secret code were "laughable."[11] The Anubis figure shown in the cave might as easily (and logically) be a native coyote.

The cave researcher claims this is a "monument to their [the Celts'] god Mithras." This immediately gets my antennae twitching since, as we have seen, Mithras (the Hellenized name for the Persian god Mithra) was an oriental god, not a Celtic one. His cult came from the East and was popular among Roman soldiers before the Christian era. But his cult died out around the fourth century CE. The Celts did not worship Mithras as a rule, though in Britain there were Celts initiated into the Mithraic Mysteries, and a separate Celtic group—who did not use Ogham writing—lived in Asia Minor in the Roman period. As a god of oracles, Mithras shared traits with the Celtic god Ogma, and Sir James George Frazer saw a parallel between them; however, modern scholarship makes plain that Mithraism was a very minor cult in Britain, primarily among soldiers, and did not extend to Ireland.[12] Therefore, Ogham and Mithraism should not be found together in any significant way.

From here we get another whopper that ties us back to the opening scene of the hour. We hear from "comparative religions expert" Joe Rose, who is a bookbinder by trade, that the Mithraic mysteries involved throwing the initiate into a pit to cover him in the blood of a bull slain above him, a taurobolium (bull-sacrifice in Latin). This is false and confuses the Roman bull sacrifice (taurobolium) with the Mithraic myth of the god slaying the cosmic bull (called Tauroctony) from whose blood life emerges. The taurobolium was part of the Magna Mater (Cybele) cult after the second century CE, not the Mithras cult. There is no literary or archaeological evidence for a Mithraic baptism in bull's blood. For most of its history, Mithraism was a secret cult, practiced at night in tight quarters without state sanction. There was no place to fit a giant bull, let alone one per initiate. In fact, the early Christian writer Tertullian, who had every reason to play up the salacious aspects of pagan cults, tells us that the Mithras cult used water for their baptisms: "For washing [with water] is the channel through which they are initiated into some sacred rites—of some notorious Isis or Mithras."[13] Nevertheless, this "fact" is used to explain the bull carving from the episode's start: the wavy lines are "blood" from a bull sacrifice!

The actual origin of Rose's claim comes from the identification of the Mithras cult with that of Attis and Cybele—a specious claim, but one once believed by serious scholars. Attis was a young man who died of madness in the presence of the Great Mother of Anatolia, Cybele. He cut off his own genitals and died from the blood loss. He rose again at the spring equinox,[14] and Cybele's priests self-castrated in his honor. This lets advocates adopt blood rites attributed to the cult of Attis for the god Mithras. I think you'll find this passage from Sir James Frazer's monumental but flawed masterwork, *The Golden Bough*, summarizing the Christian writer Prudentius, suspiciously similar to what Joe Rose said:

> In the baptism the devotee, crowned with gold and wreathed with fillets, descended into a pit, the mouth of which was covered with a wooden grating. A bull, adorned with garlands of flowers, its forehead glittering with gold leaf, was then driven on to the grating and there stabbed to

death with a consecrated spear. Its hot reeking blood poured in torrents through the apertures, and was received with devout eagerness by the worshiper on every part of his person and garments, till he emerged from the pit, drenched, dripping, and scarlet from head to foot, to receive the homage, nay the adoration, of his fellows—as one who had been born again to eternal life and had washed away his sins in the blood of the bull.[15]

But Prudentius wasn't describing a real event. He was actually describing the martyrdom of the Christian saint Romanus in a fictional poem, and he has Romanus speak of the pagan blood rite *after* his tongue has been cut from his head. Recent scholarship has demonstrated that Prudentius was not well-informed about pagan practice and was, in essence, making it up to suit his poem's theme.[16] Archaeological and inscription evidence suggests that the rite was little more than a bull sacrifice (derived from an ancient bull hunting ritual), perhaps with the sprinkling of bull's blood as part of a rite of purification. In imperial times, the term taurobolium became synonymous with the entire festival of Attis and Cybele, which included initiation rites. Nevertheless, on virtually this sole authority, scholars from the eighteenth century until the 1980s assumed that a real rite of baptism by blood bath was performed for the worshipers of Attis, despite no archaeological evidence for it. Rose is unaware of modern interpretations, but at any rate, even accepted at face value, this is a rite of Attis, not of Mithras.

Frazer's *Golden Bough* is also responsible for popularizing the incorrect claim that the Mithras cult was similar to that of Cybele and to early Christianity, as we saw above; this meant that Frazer could imagine blood baptisms for Mithras. This claim goes back to the nineteenth century and derives from the scholarly assumption that the slaying of the cosmic bull by Mithras had the same origin as the bull-slaying rites of Cybele, and also from some sculptures from Asia Minor that seem to identify Attis with Mithras (both gods are young men who wear Phrygian caps, for example). The same claim allows Rose to associate the blood rites with Mithras. It was actually a man named Arthur Darby Nock who made Frazer's implication of Mithraic blood baptisms explicit, arguing that the Mithras cult was Phrygian rather than either Roman or Persian and therefore conducted Attis blood rites; he was refuted systematically several times.[17] As we have seen, the Mithras cult baptized with water, and no archaeological evidence of any pits for showering in bull's blood exists.

Equally wrong is Rose's idea that the Mithras cult had anything to do with the Apis bull of Egypt. Mithraism was a Roman imperial cult modeled on (with alterations) *Persian* or *Zoroastrian* rites (Mithras, recall, originates in the Persian god Mithra), not Egyptian ones. The Romans had plenty of mythological bulls of their own; they did not need to borrow Egypt's to plug into a completely unrelated, borrowed, and reformed Persian cult. If they wanted an *Egyptian* bull, they would have turned to the Isis cult or that of Serapis (the Hellenized version of Osiris). Rose is also wrong that Mithras was a sun god; in Roman iconography, he *shared* a banquet with the sun (Sol); he was not himself the sun, except in the singular Mithras Liturgy, which many scholars doubt is genuinely Mithraic.

Rose reiterates his mistaken beliefs about Mithraism while visiting the Anubis Cave with Wolter, and I realize that everything Rose says about Mithraism is derived from late nineteenth and early twentieth century Christ-myth writers who tried to turn Mithraism into a point-for-point duplicate of Christianity to help deny the claims of the Christian mythos. (They claimed, largely, that Christ copied Mithras, though in truth there is no evidence of Mithraism before Christianity.) Rose appears to be repeating information gleaned from works like Edward Carpenter's classic, but wildly inaccurate, *Christian and Pagan Creeds: Their Origin and Meaning* (1920), which includes all of Rose's claims about Mithraic cult rites, including his largely imaginary connection with astronomy and the zodiac.[18] Rose looks at the crude carvings in the Anubis Cave and declares a one that looks like a stick figure wearing a crown to be a "clear" representation of a Mithraic sun god although it most clearly resembles Native American art and modern graffiti. A tiny little carving of what looks very much like a coyote is declared an Egyptian Anubis, despite the obvious problem that Mithraism has no jackal-god and no relationship to Egyptian death cults.

So Wolter and Rose watch the sun shine on the little carvings and they see it as evidence of a precise alignment signifying the sun god and Anubis in conjunction with a mystical event. They have a shadow fall on them at sunset on the autumn equinox (and, by definition the spring one), but there is nothing in this "alignment" that indicates anything more than a shadow passing over these figures. But even if we assume this alignment is intentional, it provides no evidence of any Celtic or European influence as anyone could have marked the walls with chalk, paint, or coal on the equinox by observing where the shadow fell and then carved the figures from the outline. No advanced astronomy needed.

And Wolter didn't even compare the "bull" from the episode's beginning to any real Celtic bull figure! Wolter carefully omits that not a single one of these "Celtic" artifacts was actually dated by any secure means to 500 CE, nor could he find a single genuine Celtic artifact anywhere in the area to support his claims. All we have are some ambiguous carvings, almost certainly modern, some fake comparative religion from an apparently ignorant "expert," and a whole lot of wishful thinking backed up with emotionally manipulative music designed to dull reason and allow emotion to overwhelm critical thought.

I say "apparently" ignorant because Joe Rose was not happy about his depiction on the program. He took to Facebook after the show aired and wrote that "I was in *America Unearthed* Episode 5 and will be in Episode 12 and was shocked by the power [o]f the edit button. Literally, EVERY sentence I said was out of sequence, context, and was not what I had originally said."[19] There are two ways to go about planning and writing a nonfiction program. The first way, and the one given in the textbooks on journalism, is to collect research, do interviews, shoot footage, and then construct the narrative based on what was learned. This involves writing the narration around the interviews, and refraining from drawing firm conclusions until all the information has been gathered. For obvious reasons, this style of writing is difficult because it means that most of the construction of the final narrative has to wait for shooting to be complete, though of course preliminary research gives producers a good idea of how the final product should turn out. It's time-consuming, and on a tight schedule, it can be challenging to pull off.

The second way of producing a show is to write the narration first based on the producers' own research and ideas. Then, the producer prompts the interviewees to say what they need said to fill holes in the narration and conform to the pre-written narrative. The reason this style is frowned on in the textbooks is that it introduces bias into the system, replacing genuine inquiry for a ratification of the producers' views. Obviously, it also skews what the "experts" are saying. As Joe Rose found out the hard way, *America Unearthed* follows the second style.

Stonehenge in America

Airdate: January 25, 2013

Episode Summary

Scott Wolter visits America's Stonehenge, a mysterious stone site in New Hampshire. After examining the rocks and several maps, Wolter finds that the site is "aligned" to Stonehenge in Britain and to Phoenicia. He concludes that the site was likely built by Phoenicians.

Historical Background

Located off Route 111 near Salem, New Hampshire stands the weird site of "America's Stonehenge," the current name of a place known for most of the past century as "Mystery Hill Caves." There, the visitor will find twenty-two stone-built, semi-subterranean structures that have been the subject of fascination for the better part of a century. Mystery Hill is in all likelihood a collection of nineteenth century farming structures, cold cellars, etc. They first enter the historical record with the arrival of Jonathan Pattee, a North Salem resident who fled to the hills after getting in trouble with the law in 1826. From then until 1848, Pattee lived near the site, and his grandson later testified that Pattee heavily re-built whatever it was he found at Mystery Hill, using the resulting structures for the storage of food and supplies. Most archaeologists believe he built the site, though a few think that he may have reused earlier, colonial storage houses. Sometime after his death, a construction firm began quarrying stone at the site and transported it to Lawrence. Drill marks from the 1830s onward indicate the continuous rearrangement of the stones.

In this ruined state, it attracted little attention. In fact, the first known literary reference to it, published in 1907, reads in its entirety: "Jonathan Pattee's Cave. He had a house in these woods 70 yrs. ago; took town paupers before the town farm was bought. This is a wild but beautiful spot, among rough boulders and soft pines, about which the most weird and fantastic tale might be woven. There are several caves still intact, which the owner used for storage purposes."[1] In the 1930s, newspaper writers speculated that the caves might have been colonial structures used to guard against attacks from Native Americans, or else a stop on the Underground Railroad for slaves fleeing to Canada.

Everything changed in the mid-1930s, when William Goodwin, a Connecticut insurance executive with an enthusiasm for archaeology, read the newspaper reports, visited the site, and purchased it. Goodwin had a penchant for arguing vehemently with historians and archaeologists in favor of unconventional views, which did not endear him to professionals. He convinced himself that Celtic migrants from Ireland had built the site's stone structures in the Middle Ages. After 1937, he began to "restore" the structures to what he felt was their "original" configuration, thus creating the pseudo-Celtic, pseudo-Neolithic look of the place as it is seen today. Any claims about astronomical alignments at the site, of course, are therefore largely false because the stones' positions have been heavily and repeatedly altered. If the site as it currently stands is a modern fake, there *is* evidence of "megaliths" at Mystery Hill. Native Americans came there thousands of years ago and used the large boulders in the area to chip away stone tools. This left behind large stone cores from the quarrying that could be mistaken for fallen megalithic architecture. (And who knows, maybe some ancient Native group thought it would be cute to arrange them artistically.) These Native occupations likely contributed to the radiocarbon dating of charcoal near the site to thousands of years ago.

Although Goodwin always favored Irish monks as the builders, the explanations offered for Mystery Hill changed in time with the zeitgeist, particularly after the site was sold to Bob Stone in 1955. It has remained in the Stone family ever since. The Irish monk idea continued in the alternative literature down to the 1970s, when, in keeping with New Age mysticism, for a time the new owners of Mystery Hill seriously promoted the claim that the whole site was a giant pictogram of an Asian face wearing a peaked hat—a depiction of a ten-thousand-year-old shaman. When traditional views about Native Americans began to change in the 1980s, the site promoted the idea that every stone was a prehistoric food preparation device, like the Mexican *metates*.[2] In the 1990s, the site, now called America's Stonehenge, proclaimed itself four thousand years old and evidence of ancient seafaring voyages from Phoenicia on down to the Irish, in keeping with that decade's penchant for finding Atlantis-like civilizations. Alternative writers who abandoned the Celtic hypothesis and suggested the site was built by Phoenicians, cited as evidence ambiguous scratch marks on some of the rocks (almost certainly tool marks from quarrying) that fringe writers like Barry Fell found to be evidence of not one but three ancient languages: Phoenician, Ogham, and Iberian-Punic. These alphabets are particularly easy to "find" in random scratch marks because they are composed largely of straight lines and angles. Needless to say, archaeologists identified this "writing" as the result of nineteenth-century quarrying efforts, which only enflamed true believers into asserting a conspiracy. Some eventually accused archaeologists of actively destroying evidence for pre-colonial occupation.

I've visited the site (I have relatives in the area), and I was not impressed; the first time I saw the place, when I was sixteen, it was one of the biggest disappointments of my life.[3] Before this episode aired, promotional materials stated that Scott Wolter would "uncover" a mysterious "sacrificial table" at Mystery Hill, supposedly carved with a channel to collect the blood of human victims. I found that hilarious because I have a photograph of me lying spread-eagle across the "sacrificial table," taken surreptitiously on my teenage visit, in contravention of the site's rules. Publicity puffery aside, there is no way to "uncover" the main attraction on full display at the center of the site! The alleged "sacrificial table" is actually a colonial-era stone used in farm work. One such stone is a lye-leaching stone used in soap-making. Similar stones were also used for apple pressing and other tasks. These stones, just like the "sacrificial table," featured an incised groove to allow liquids to drain off. Needless to say, no sacrificed remains were ever found around Mystery Hill.

It is often said that the famed horror writer H. P. Lovecraft, a key figure in the creation of the myth of ancient aliens, based the stone circle atop Sentinel Hill in *The Dunwich Horror* (1928) on Mystery Hill, and nearly every guidebook to the site or to weird things in New England repeats the claim. However, many authors say Lovecraft visited in 1937—impossible, since he lay dying in a Providence hospital—or other years long after *Dunwich* was written. As Lovecraft scholar S. T. Joshi has pointed out, there is no evidence Lovecraft visited the site prior to writing the story, and the only evidence he ever saw it was the much later recollection of H. Warner Munn that he was fairly certain he must have taken Lovecraft to see the site sometime in the 1930s. If that were the case, there might be an echo of Mystery Hill in the stone circle and sacrificial slab featured in "The Diary of Alonzo Typer" (1935)—"a dismal-looking hill on whose summit is a circle of great stones with another stone at the centre"—but Lovecraft's familiarity with the general concept of stone circles from his reading of ancient history does not require such direct influence. Indeed, Lovecraft refers to the "Typer" circle as a *cromlech*, a Brythonic word for the megalithic stone works of the British Isles.

The Episode

"Stonehenge in America" opens with a sepia-toned recreation of a Depression-era barbershop with a faux news report playing on the radio describing the New Hampshire stone site then known as Mystery Hill Caves. An actor, presumably portraying former site owner William Goodwin, then drives past a recreated 1930s sign for the site to view its stony ruins in great awe. This is presented as a major discovery, but the presence of the sign is the first clue that this is not what it seems. Then we smash-cut to the opening titles, and we're off to a discussion of the site now known as America's Stonehenge.

We start by looking at England's Stonehenge, which is composed of around 150 upright stone monoliths, which Scott Wolter claims to be the work of an "advanced" civilization. The New Hampshire site is *absolutely nothing* like Britain's Stonehenge. To begin with, the New Hampshire structures are built of piled stones into small, cave-like structures, while the British site is made of monoliths—large, standing stones. They are as different as two stone sites can be.

"America's Stonehenge is a prehistoric site in Salem, New Hampshire," Wolter intones, but it is not "prehistoric"; that is an alternative history assumption. As noted above, while there is a layer of pre-colonial Native occupation, the stone buildings are colonial constructions historically used as cold cellars; its sacrificial table is a farm implement, and the "aligned" ring of standing stones was rearranged in the 1930s and 1940s by the site's diffusionist owner, William Goodwin, to "restore" them to the positions he assumed were "original." There is simply no way to verify that these stones were in positions claimed for them prior to 1937. The earliest reports make no mention of a stone ring but rather to the heaps of stone formed into rough caves. Rather than acknowledge this, Wolter reviews past episodes and lauds "the ancient practice of archaeoastronomy," apparently blissfully unaware that the "archaeo-" comes from "archaeology" and refers to *studying* ancient peoples' astronomical knowledge, not a discipline ancient people practiced!

Wolter and Kelsey Stone, the son of the current site owner, speculate on the gradual movement of the earth's axis over time and how that proves that the "alignment" of the stones of the site has changed due to earth changes. They completely ignore the fact that these rocks were repositioned in the 1830s due to rock quarrying in the area and again in the 1930s by William Goodwin. Any alignments are therefore speculative until and unless one can prove that the rock has been in its current position for more than a century. We then see a bizarre sequence in which Kelsey Stone uses Google Earth to show that a "straight" line drawn from the "summer solstice" alignment of one particular rock at Mystery Hill will pass along a northeast line through the center trilithon at Stonehenge in England and the Phoenician homeland in Lebanon. (Incidentally, the solstices were not always among the claims made for the alignments at Mystery Hill; some earlier maps of the site claim only equinox and mid-season alignments.) I could not believe what I was seeing.

The "straightness" of the alignment is due entirely to the projection Google Earth is using for the earth and it does not correct for the curvature of the earth. The line *looks* straight because the globe has been flattened into two dimensional space, but as shown on *America Unearthed* the globe used in this "alignment" has been titled far outside its actual north-south orientation. But if you look at the globe in a standard projection with north at top, you'll see that the "straight" line only appears straight because you are looking at a very broad curve from "above" such that the curve is masked by the curvature of the earth. That said, yes, a curved line does pass between the two sites of Mystery Hill and Stonehenge, just as a curved line can be drawn between *any* two points on the globe. The "Phoenician" part of the alignment crosses no major Phoenician site and can be discarded, unless we'd like to include Germany and Ethiopia in the alignment as well, as both places are also along the same curved line. This curved line, however, is not a "northeasterly" line, which would take you to Iceland, as navigation charts show. Instead, the line twists wildly off of true northeast. (Try looking at the sites' latitudes to confirm that they have no directional alignment.)

This is due entirely to the fact that *any* two points on the earth's surface can be connected by a circle equal to the earth's circumference, called a Great Circle, and this line is always the shortest distance between any two points on the earth's surface. A Great Circle passing between Salem, N.H. and Salisbury in Britain would have an inflection point in the mid-Atlantic, meaning that you'd stop going northeast and start heading southeast. Further, because any two points can be connected by a Great Circle, that circle is bound to hit a third location that has some point of interest. For example, a Great Circle drawn through my house in Albany, N.Y. and the Inca temples of Peru passes directly through Guantanamo Bay, Cuba, and a Great Circle drawn from my house to the Coliseum in Rome passes through the Neolithic stone monuments of Western France. But does it mean anything? No. According to Google's "Great Circle Mapper," the shortest distance on the earth's surface from Salem, N.H. to Beirut, Lebanon passes through the area around Stonehenge, though I caution that this is not the same as traveling in a continuous northeasterly direction from Salem, as the program claimed. It is, however, a Great Circle, meaning it is on a line equal in distance to the circumference of the earth. But so much other territory is included as well, including parts of Cyprus, Austria, Germany, etc.—all lands with equal or better claim to ancient cultures capable of the same feats ascribed the Phoenicians.

However, the accuracy of the alignment lives and dies by the accuracy of selecting the intended place of observation: the arbitrary selection of a center point for Mystery Hill (the observation point needed to "see" any alignment) to generate the "alignment" to the "solstice" marker stone, which of course was only moved into its current position in the 1930s! The line Kelsey Stone drew isn't a projection from Mystery Hill toward the sun but an extension of the line drawn from an arbitrary observation point at the center of Mystery Hill (as it currently stands, after "reconstruction") to the pointy tip of the rock supposedly marking the solstice. This "observation line" goes north and east even though the sun itself is not, but the entire alignment is dependent on (a) the observer standing at the point Kelsey Stone selected as the correct observation point, and (b) selecting one specific point on the solstice stone to align with the sun. A shift of even a few inches will produce a line that will miss Stonehenge entirely.

"This rewrites a huge chapter of American history. This isn't kidding around!" Wolter enthuses. I know he's not a stupid man, but, man, this one makes no sense, even by his standards. After all, so many "alignments" have been proposed for America's Stonehenge that a Great Circle drawn through *any* of them is bound to hit *something* ancient elsewhere in the world.

Wolter next expresses his belief that the site could not be colonial because it "reeks" of being old and no one would bother to build in stone when they had wood to use. Apparently he is ignorant of the British animal pens that colonial people took as their models; they were made of stone using dry stone construction, and people coming to America, especially Scots-Irish immigrants, used dry-stone enclosures and fences here in the United States and continued building them into the middle 1800s under the supervision of Scots-Irish craftsmen. Additionally, cold cellars and spring houses were built using the exact type of stone building techniques on display at Mystery Hill, and they bear a close resemblance to the Mystery Hill site because, as we have seen, that is what Jonathan Pattee used them for in the 1820s and 1830s. You can visit many colonial dry stone constructions today.

After this we see some squiggles on a rock that are claimed as a Canaanite inscription to Baal (the Phoenicians of the Bronze Age called themselves *Kenaani*), but it looks like no Phoenician writing I've seen. What bothers me is that all of the adventurers who supposedly came to America were terrible at their own cultures and were unable to carve recognizable letters, write coherently, or draw pictures in the style of their own cultures. Nor were the Mediterranean peoples shy about proclaiming their accomplishments; the famed Periplus of Hanno the Carthaginian (the Carthaginians being an offshoot of the Phoenicians) tells much about his trip around Africa in the sixth century BCE and was put on display for all to see, but somehow every traveler to America was some kind of ignoramus who couldn't scratch his own name in his own alphabet without turning it into a giant mess.

Finally we come to the sacrificial table! It's still very obviously a colonial-era apple-pressing table or lye-leeching table, of which hundreds of examples exist in the United States. Nevertheless, the site owner tells us that this was used for human sacrifices—none of which, conveniently, have ever been found. Wolter notes the exfoliating weathering, but he neglects to consider the damage done to the stone as a result of the agricultural or industrial use to which it was likely put, thereby allowing him to make the table seem thousands of years old. We also look at some of the dry stone caves and the echoes they make (including one called the Oracle Chamber), which the owner attributes to "shamans" or "priests" making noises around non-existent human sacrifices. The problem is that Phoenicians did not use the faux-Neolithic architectural style of Mystery Hill, nor did they squat in tiny caves. They built very nice buildings that look like buildings. Even adapting to local materials, ancient people did not abandon every marker of their culture when colonizing a new area. As is almost certainly the case, the effects Wolter examines are the result of later reconstruction efforts.

Wolter next travels to Mount Holyoke College in Massachusetts to talk to an actual scholar, Mark McMenamin, who explains what we know about the Phoenicians and their Mediterranean trade network, which was based on their ability to navigate by the North Star at night. Wolter again confuses "archaeoastronomy" (the science of studying ancient peoples' astronomical knowledge) with plain old astronomy (twice proves it's no mere *lapsus linguae*) and claims that the Phoenicians, because they knew the North Star was in the north, must therefore have understood celestial mechanics in all their complexity, a logical leap the program asks us to accept on faith. Sadly, though, McMenamin is not a scholar of the Phoenicians; he is a geologist, like Wolter. His alternative history claim is an idea he proposed in 1996 that a Carthaginian coin depicts a map of the world, including what he says is North (but not South) America, with both Florida and Mexico visible. Given that the Americas are shown as smaller than what he identifies as Spain, it is much more likely that if this really is a map, the blob represents Britain or the Azores or other known lands. He also claims that another coin, not shown on the program, depicts similar markings with both "Britain" and an unexplained blob, but these markings are so small (fractions of a millimeter) that I can't see anything in them other than the chance design of an ancient die-maker. Ancient dies simply weren't that good to have such tiny pictures (they had to be inscribed by hand after all), and McMenamin relied on computer enhancement to "restore" the map and make it visible, a telltale sign of problems. It gets worse: He supported his view with a coin showing an uprooted palm tree. This, he said, demonstrated that the Phoenicians planned to "transplant" their culture to America, a culture whose existence is proved by a few Phoenician coins found in America, coins he conceded were in fact forgeries. He believes they are ancient fakes, but more likely they were Victorian souvenirs. How likely is it that only counterfeit coins came to Phoenicia's American colony?

McMenamin cites Diodorus Siculus in support, when Diodorus describes a fantastical island outside the Pillars of Heracles, a veritable paradise: "The Phoenicians, then, while exploring the coast outside the Pillars for the reasons we have stated and while sailing along the shore of Libya, were driven by strong winds a great distance out into the ocean. And after being storm-tossed for many days they were carried ashore on the island we mentioned above, and when they had observed its felicity and nature they caused it to be known to all men."[4] Yet somehow despite this global fame, we are also asked to believe that the island was kept a big secret, as per McMenamin's suggestion. There are several theories about Diodorus's island, which include: (a) it was fiction, (b) it is the Azores or the Canaries, and (c) it represents the Americas. There is no archaeological evidence to support the latter two theories, though occasional reports, unconfirmed, of Phoenician or Carthaginian artifacts in the Canaries or Azores suggest these are the most logical choice.

Following this, we travel to the actual British Stonehenge at the summer solstice to discuss irrelevant material about the ancient site, which is so wildly different in construction, style, and function that even unobservant viewers must have noticed it is nothing like "America's Stonehenge." Wolter tries to make a connection to astronomical alignments at both sites, but as I explained, we can't know where the New Hampshire rocks were once placed, so any connection is pure speculation. Wolter shows the Google Earth "alignment" to archaeologist Dr. Henry Chapman, who, essentially, laughs at him; and Chapman seems confused about why a weird curve is being taken as an "alignment" when it has no relationship to actual directions on the spherical earth, though he is too polite to say so. Wolter suggests that Stonehenge was built by the Phoenicians, an idea first formally proposed by Aylett Sammes (from widespread earlier speculation) in his *Britannia Antiqua Illustrata* in 1676. He believed that all of ancient British culture, including the very name Britain, was of Phoenician origin on little more than wishful thinking and fabricated etymologies. (He believed that the Phoenicians spoke Biblical Hebrew.) Influential in inverse proportion to accuracy, Sammes' book appealed to British pride, finding a nobler origin for Britain than backwoods Druids, who, being Celtic, were unfit as ancestors of Anglo-Saxons—the then-current overlords of the Celts. (English attitudes about Celts changed with the political needs of Britain—in the 1500s the Celtic exploits of Prince Madoc of Wales served the Tudor cause, as we shall see, but in the 1600s this had changed.) The idea was picked up and promoted by people who believed that the British were the descendants of the Lost Tribes of Israel, and the most famous proponent of the Phoenician origins of Britain theory was L. Austine Waddell, who believed the Phoenicians originated in Sumeria. Others argued that Stonehenge was the work of Picts, Druids, Romans, European warrior tribes, African giants, Merlin the magician, and more before archaeology was invented and was able to excavate the graves of those buried near the site to learn about its origins thousands of years earlier than any early modern writer suspected.

After Wolter's idea that the Phoenicians were involved in building Stonehenge gets shot down, he instead claims it "could have been a sacred sanctuary for them," which I suppose is possible, though there is no evidence of a Phoenician occupation at Stonehenge. Wolter concludes by asserting that "the elite" who ran Stonehenge "came over here" to build Mystery Hill because "there's no doubt" the two sites are "connected." The connection is nothing more than a Google Earth artifact and the fact that both sites feature astronomical alignments (dubious ones in the case of Mystery Hill). But, by the standards of *America Unearthed*, this was some of the most solid evidence yet uncovered, which is to damn it with faint praise.

Mystery of Roanoke

Airdate: February 1, 2013

Episode Summary

Scott Wolter investigates whether inscribed stones found in the Carolinas and Georgia are evidence that the sixteenth-century English colonists at Roanoke trekked into Georgia and died there. He eventually concludes that the colony split in two, with some traveling to Georgia and others staying in North Carolina, on the site of what would eventually be a golf course.

Historical Background

In 1583, Sir Humphrey Gilbert attempted to colonize St. John's in Newfoundland, one of the first English attempts to found a permanent colony in North America. Gilbert had a royal charter from Elizabeth I, and he had ambitious plans to colonize what he thought was Norumbega, a fictional advanced civilization we shall encounter again in Episode Thirteen. He had claimed all of Newfoundland for England and issued his first orders as colonial governor: levying taxes on fishermen. Then, lacking supplies, he and his crew attempted to return to England. His ship, the frigate *Squirrel*, sank with all aboard, including Gilbert, who reportedly died reading a copy of Sir Thomas More's *Utopia*.

The next year, on March 25, the Queen granted Gilbert's charter to his half-brother, Sir Walter Raleigh, on condition that Raleigh immediately establish a permanent colony somewhere in North America to return American treasure to England and to form a base to send privateers to menace the Spanish treasure ships. In 1585, an expedition reached Roanoke Island off the coast of what is today North Carolina. The men built a small fort and ran afoul of the local Native Americans, against whom they fought. In 1586, they accepted return passage to England with Sir Francis Drake when promised reinforcements from England failed to materialize. The reinforcements came too late, and a token force was left behind to maintain claim to the land.

In 1587, a new expedition was launched to reestablish a colony at Roanoke, and they found that all the men left behind in 1586 had vanished, presumably killed. The new colony attempted to forge positive relations with the Native peoples of the area, but several tribes remained hostile. Governor John White returned to England to seek help for his colony, leaving behind about 118 colonists, including his new granddaughter, Virginia Dare, the first English baby born in North America. When he returned in 1590, almost three years later, nothing remained of the colony except for the word "Croatoan" carved on a tree, by which White inferred the colonists had decamped for Croatoan Island, now called Hatteras Island, the home of the only tribe on friendly terms with the Roanoke colonists. Due to a storm, he did not venture to Croatoan and instead returned to England. Subsequent expeditions in 1590 and 1602 found no new evidence, and neither made it to Croatoan. A little more than a century later, the Croatoans reported that they had intermarried with the Roanoke colonists:

> These tell us, that several of their Ancestors were white People, and could talk in a Book, as we do; the Truth of which is confirm'd by gray Eyes being found frequently amongst these Indians, and no others. They value themselves extremely for their Affinity to the English, and are ready to do them all friendly Offices. It is probable, that this Settlement miscarry'd for want of timely Supplies from England; or thro' the Treachery of the Natives, for we may reasonably suppose that the English were forced to cohabit with them, for Relief and Conversation; and that in process of Time, they conform'd themselves to the Manners of their Indian Relations.[1]

In 1988, an archaeological excavation found sixteenth-century artifacts likely belonging to the Roanoke colonists, including a signet ring, on Hatteras Island, the former Croatoan.

Today several tribes claim partial descent from Roanoke colonists, though it is not firmly established which (if any) actually are; such claims may be the result of fictive genealogies meant to ingratiate the tribes with the new dominant power in the region. It is, however, suggestive and clearly indicates that the assumption—down to the twentieth century— was that the colony had merged with the Croatoan tribe. In 1907, Alexander Hume Ford went so far as to claim he had solved the "mystery of mysteries" and located the descendants of the lost colonists among the Native peoples of South Carolina, the last descendants of the Croatoans, supposedly still speaking a language filled with obsolete fossils of Elizabethan English. He wrote that these pale-complexioned Native Americans were the "distant offspring" and the fruit of the colonists "who joined with the native Americans at Roanoke when both bade farewell together to the 'mother' vine, to carry white blood into the regions of the west, there to mingle with the red."[2] According to Hume, the colonists intermarried and were forced down into South Carolina as a result of population displacements in the late colonial era, particularly Tuscarora incursions.

That assumption of intermarriage changed in the twentieth century. In 1937, Roanoke Island played host to an outdoor play funded in part by the Works Progress Administration called *The Lost Colony*, which helped introduced the idea that the disappearance of the Roanoke colonists was a "mystery" as part of the celebration of 350th anniversary of the colony's disappearance. The play still runs to this day, and it helped spark a wave of revisionist histories that sought a more dramatic—and less multicultural—ending for the colonists, attributing their disappearance to all manner of nefarious possibilities. But first, as part of a publicity stunt to promote the play, a man tried to interest local collectors in some newly-carved stones with antique inscriptions related to the failed English colony. He planted several on the island to generate interest in the play. Later, the people of Roanoke would testify that this man met the description of the man who by sheer coincidence claimed to have found the first Eleanor

Dare stone several years later.

These Dare Stones, inscribed with writing supposedly carved by Eleanor Dare herself and found between 1937 and 1940 in three locations along a single route between Roanoke and Atlanta, told of the dramatic trek the Roanoke colonists made from their island home deep into Georgia—compressing Ford's generational displacement into mere months. The first stone, well-weathered, was apparently the gravestone of Ananias and Virginia Dare. If there is any truth to the stones, this one, found near the lost colony, is possibly the only authentic stone. Geologists of the time determined it was four hundred years old, and some scholars continue to believe it is an authentic sixteenth century artifact. In 1937, historian Dr. Haywood Pearce deciphered its inscription and declared it genuine. He offered a reward for more stones, paying out up to $1,200 (almost $20,000 in today's dollars) per stone. Suddenly, stones flooded in from South Carolina and Georgia, all found by just four people. I wonder why. Pearce submitted an article about the stones to the *Saturday Evening Post*, and the magazine assigned Boyden Sparkes to investigate.

According Sparkes's April 26, 1941 *Saturday Evening Post* analysis of the stones, which is never mentioned on *America Unearthed* despite being the most important piece ever written about them, a single person found two of the stones in two separate states, and one was even buried near the man's own house! Sparkes discovered that all four individuals who "independently" found the Dare Stones were known criminals who all knew one another, and at least one had approached famed director Cecil B. DeMille about turning the stones' story into a movie. Experts discovered that some of the carvings appeared quite recent, and some of the words used on the stones did not match forms known from the 1590s. (Elizabethan English could be faked easily if crudely since the works of Shakespeare were available in any public library.)

Pearce, for his part, lashed out like modern alternative theorists, threatening to sue the *Post* for revealing the hoax. After the *Post* story, one of the original "discoverers" of the stones, William Eberhart, called the professor he had fooled into accepting the Dare Stones, the same Haywood

Pearce, in 1937 to report a new find, a large carved stone head. Even the credulous professor recognized the stone as a fake, made with hammers and colored with purple vegetable dye. Eberhart later confessed to participating in a hoax and to accepting payment for the hoaxing, as well as admitting to blackmailing Pearce by threatening to reveal the Dare Stone hoax unless Pearce paid him off. He later denied making these sworn and witnessed statements.[3]

These stones (with the slightly possible exception of the first stone) are now considered a hoax by almost all archaeologists, but *America Unearthed* decided they must be real—and evidence of a Roanoke conspiracy.

The Episode

If this episode sounds familiar, it is. Back in 2006, the History Channel, parent to H2, also went in search of the Roanoke colony on its previous historical adventures series, *Digging for the Truth*.[4] Wolter, however, pointedly ignores the older History Channel series in developing his own take on the "real" history of the Roanoke colony, which is all to the worse since the older show did a much more credible and thorough job of it, as did the 2009 PBS version of *Time Team*. In 2006, *Digging*'s Josh Bernstein reported the results of a DNA test that suggested a match between living British members of the Henry Payne family who came to Roanoke and a Payne living in America, suggesting—though not proving conclusively—that at least one colonist survived and intermarried with the Croatoans.

Let me begin by stating upfront that I have absolutely no personal interest whatsoever in the lost colony of Roanoke; my interest is in ancient history, and I had incorrectly assumed that Scott Wolter could not possibly screw up a discussion of such a well-documented period as the sixteenth century. The events on Roanoke occurred in the Early Modern period, well after the European discovery of America, so even accepting alternative claims at face value would have no impact on the "hidden" history of America, unless aliens abducted them or something. So it was an uphill battle for me to pay attention to this fairly padded hour of television, at least until Wolter started getting royally pissed off. Then, for a few minutes, the show finally got good.

We open with Scott Wolter entering pushpins into a map of America, connected by red thread, like the sort of charts obsessed police detectives (or serial killers) use on forensic crime shows. We focus in on a Polaroid (who has those?) with the word "murder" written across its white frame in black permanent marker, and then we cut to the opening credits. No murder will be discussed in the hour, so this is all just for show. Instead, the opening graphics tell us that the lost colony of Roanoke is "America's oldest cold case," further drawing parallels to crime scene procedurals. Wolter shows us the "Dare Stones," those rocks allegedly carved by a colonist named Eleanor Dare with messages about the lost colony's fate. Found between 1937 and 1940 in three locations along a single route between Roanoke and Atlanta, we've seen that scholars quickly determined they were hoaxes, which *America Unearthed* actually mentions since this cannot be denied. Because it undermines Wolter's thesis, he fails to present any of the evidence for hoaxing assembled over the past seventy years, simply dismissing all of the evidence as part and parcel of an academic conspiracy against the truth. But even if the stones are authentic, it changes nothing about the history of America and would provide at most a tiny footnote to the story of European colonization.

Wolter examines the first of the Dare Stones, Virginia's and Ananias's headstone, and says that the geological evidence from this stone suggests the authenticity of all of the stones. Sadly, his evidence is once again the same microscopic analysis that has led him astray on other artifacts, based on his visual identification of weathering patterns. I'm not sure Wolter is truly able to distinguish between three hundred years' weathering and one hundred or thirty. He does not, for example, compare the weathering on the Dare stone to that observed on rocks in the locales where the stones were found, and he is well aware that the amount of weathering is highly dependent on local conditions. He does not examine the later Dare Stones with the same care, nor does he report whether there are differences, as the clear evidence of hoaxing found by qualified scholars indicates that there would be. Instead, he makes a dumb argument that the differences in rock type between the various groups of Dare Stones suggest authenticity because it would mean they were carved *in situ* rather than all at once. One might equally well suggest that the hoaxer(s) simply carved them as he or they traveled from Roanoke to Georgia, or at locations of convenience where they lived and worked.

What follows is a truly extraordinary scene.

Wolter goes to meet author Scott Dawson, a local innkeeper who runs a museum on Hatteras (formerly Croatoan) island and has been active in promoting the history of the Roanoke colony. Dawson tries to patiently explain to Wolter all of the archaeological evidence for English occupation at Croatoan Island and what happened to the colony after they abandoned Roanoke for Croatoan Island and vanished. Dawson waves his hand over a presentation of the evidence and explained that *all the evidence* supports the Croatoan Island theory *except* for the Dare Stones, so either the Dare Stones are real and *every piece of evidence ever collected* is wrong, or the evidence is right and the Dare Stones are a hoax. Wolter, visibly agitated, insists on another explanation. The colony simply split up into competing tribes, like on *Survivor*!

"All of that is just speculation," Dawson reminds Wolter.

"The only thing I can do is testify as to factual evidence," Wolter says, again quite agitated, stating that the standard of proof should be what's allowable in "a court of law." "When the facts stand in the way of speculation, then the facts win," he says, arguing that claims of a hoax are just that, claims, supported by appeals to "romanticism." Wolter may want to dismiss the "romanticism" of the 1930s as irrelevant, but his show has purposely left out the *factual* evidence collected in 1941 that the stones were a recent hoax, including the linguistic problems, the evidence of exactly who hoaxed the stones and how, the continued hoaxing after exposure, and Eberhart's confession.

This confrontation was so upsetting that, in a scene filmed in November 2012 (based on the date visible on an email Wolter reads) at the St. Paul airport but presented as though it happened just moments later in North Carolina (complete with Wolter in summer shorts), Wolter calls his wife (!) on camera (!!) to complain about the close-minded attitude of Scott Dawson for refusing to agree with Wolter's speculations. Wolter insists that Dawson was blind to the "geological" evidence, but as we saw earlier, Wolter never conclusively dated the stones, merely suggesting that they "looked" weathered and old. (Nor does he consider that the first stone may be genuine while the others could be fake; he considers them all of a piece.) To date them, as he well knows, they'd need to be compared to stones in the locations where they were found to evaluate the weathering involved.

So, to recap: Wolter, on sketchy evidence, closed himself off to all possibly explanations except legitimacy for *all* the stones and is upset that someone else evaluated the evidence and has a conclusion that differs from his own.

After this episode aired, Scott Dawson spoke out about his experience on *America Unearthed* in an interview with his twin brother, Ryan Dawson, posted on YouTube.[5] In the interview, Scott Dawson explains that Committee Films reached out to his wife in order to request an interview about the history and archaeology of Croatoan. Instead, Dawson says that in an eight-hour shoot, Wolter and his producer focused exclusively and relentlessly on the Dare Stones. "I was just completely dumbfounded that they wanted to, just stayed with that, and anything that didn't fit that agenda was just edited off the show, and it was horrible," Dawson said.

Dawson spent a significant portion of his time with Wolter explaining the island's archaeology off camera "because I didn't want to embarrass the host. ... I didn't want to make him look stupid." Dawson stated that he was never told that the program would be about the Dare Stones, and he feels that Committee Films arranged the interview under false pretences. When Dawson refused to discuss the Dare Stones, which he believed (rightly) to be false and therefore misleading to present as true, Wolter became insistent and badgered Dawson to discuss the stones. According to Dawson, Wolter told him that he was unfamiliar with the literature on Roanoke and never read the primary sources related to the lost colony. All of the research Wolter showed Dawson came from secondary sources. "I wasn't going to discredit myself," Dawson said. "I've dedicated a good portion of my life to studying this, and I'm not going discredit all of it by supporting something that's a known hoax."

While Dawson acquitted himself so well that the producers were unable to find a single line they could edit to support Wolter's claims, the challenge failed to faze Wolter. He continued on his quixotic quest to find the lost colony. To that end, Dr. Stephanie Pratt, an art historian at Britain's Plymouth University, shows us an old map of Virginia drawn by Roanoke's governor, John White, sometime between 1585 and 1590, called the Virginea Pars map. In 2011, it was discovered that beneath a patch placed on the map at the time of its creation, the map features a hidden four-pointed splotch that is similar to the ground plan of the first Roanoke fortification used at Fort Raleigh. I'm not really sure what this is meant to prove other than the possibility that there was once an English fort farther inland than originally suggested. Wolter believes this means that the colonists moved inland rather than south to Croatoan, and he suggests this was part of a conspiracy by Sir Walter Raleigh. I suppose this is possible, but it's really irrelevant to the Dare Stones question since the colonists could not have built a large defensive earthwork given the terrible conditions described by the Dare Stones. The map has been repaired, and the fort symbol was covered up, either because the fort ceased to exist, was never built, or because it was drawn on the map in the wrong place.

While in England (or, rather, in another segment from the production's British Isles tour) Wolter learns that early colonists came to America to find sassafras, believed to be a cure for syphilis. (Sir Walter Raleigh had Samuel Mace collect sassafras at the Roanoke site in 1602 in hopes of selling it to avoid losing money investigating what happened at Roanoke.) Wolter suggests that finding a place that matches evidence from the map of the inland fort, conforms to the narrative of the Dare Stones, and features sassafras, will give us the lost colony of Roanoke. This place is Scotch Hall Preserve golf course.

The golf course is built atop the place the hidden section of the map indicated a fort either once stood or was planned. A golf course spokesman tells Wolter that no evidence of a fort was found during the construction of the course. Wolter concludes that the fort was planned but never existed. Despite this, he's thrilled to find out that the first Dare Stone was found near the golf course, suggesting to Wolter that "my theory is right" and some of the colonists fled here. I fail to see how the fact that the fort *did not exist* somehow confirms that the colonists escaped to its location. The logic seems to be that Eleanor Dare hoped that her father, John White, would come to the planned fort site in search of her when he returned to build the fort. This is possible, I suppose, and if the first Dare Stone is authentic, perhaps more than possible. But the lack of any evidence of English occupation other than the Dare Stone is troubling.

Wolter seems to think he found the lost colony, though he has no bodies. He also finally recognizes that finding rocks *in situ* is important for evaluating whether the Dare Stones are legitimate; however, he stops after finding the same type of quartzite nearby. (Do the other states not count?) He does not check to see how and whether such stones were weathered to learn about the weathering in the area in order to evaluate how long the Dare inscriptions had been exposed, or whether their weathering was consistent with these rocks. Wolter may claim the stones' inscriptions look old to him, but in 1941, the experts consulted by Boyden Sparkes for the *Saturday Evening Post* thought they seemed fairly recent (except, perhaps, for the first). Surely Wolter ought to have evaluated the un-carved stones before declaring the Dare Stones real, since geology, like any "hard" science, requires controls.

So, overall, there is perhaps a kernel of truth buried in this episode, if the first Dare Stone really is what it claims to be (which is, of course, extremely uncertain), but this episode's lack of critical thinking and incomplete (to the point of being deceptive) presentation of the facts surrounding the stones' discovery makes this a case far from proved.

EPISODE EIGHT

Chamber Hunting

Airdate: February 8, 2013

Episode Summary

Scott Wolter investigates a small stone chamber built over a spring in Pennsyl-vania. He links this chamber to what he claims are ritual baths taken by Free-masons and Knights Templar, and he investigates whether similar chambers were built by medieval Irish monks. He concludes that some chambers are me-dieval Irish but that the Pennsylvania chamber is colonial Freemason.

Historical Background

Т he Freemasons have been the subject of conspiracy theories dating back nearly to their origins, largely because the decentralized or-ganization cloaked itself in secrecy. The general consensus, from existing documents, is that Freemasonry originated in the guild practices of medieval stone masons who worked with "freestone," that is, stone that had to be chiseled by artisans for decorative purposes. For example, in 1506, "freemasons" were employed in decorating Windsor Castle with "free-stone," according to contemporary records, and many scholars un-derstand the origin of the word *freemason* to be tied to freestone.[1] The guilds had their own organizing myth, as did all Christian organizations of the time, tracing their origins back to the Bible, specifically to Jabal, son of Lamech and half-brother to the inventor of blacksmithing, Tubal-Cain. His knowledge passed to Euclid and thus to Egypt, and from Egypt to Isra-el during the Exodus.[2] In time, the benefits of the guilds were expanded into broader mutual benefit organizations of the seventeenth century, first by adding "accepted" (non-practicing) masons and then by allowing "speculative" masons who had no connection with the stone trade at all. At this point, probably around 1700, the modern Freemasons were born.

Modern Freemasonry traces its birth to the founding of the first Grand Lodge in London in 1717. This Grand Lodge became the first organizing body for formerly independent lodges. In 1736, the first Grand Lodge was formed in Scotland, and sometime in those years the English, Scottish, and Irish Grand Lodges founded daughter organizations in the American colonies, the first known entry of Freemasonry into America. The establishment of the first American lodge, in Philadelphia, was an event Benjamin Franklin's *Gazette* noted on December 8, 1730.[3] The Grand Master of England, the Duke of Norfolk, appointed a Daniel Coxe for two years Provincial Grand Master of New York, New Jersey, and Pennsylvania, a position he exercised in the colonies for all of two months in late summer 1730, the rest of the time being spent elsewhere. It is only with Benjamin Franklin joining the Masons in 1731 that Freemasonry begins to take off and become a fad among the colonial elite. In 1734, a new Grand Master was appointed from England for all of North America, and from there the history of Masonry in the United States is well and thoroughly documented.

As a pastime of many of the elite—many Founding Fathers were Masons—the craft was openly practiced, in prominent lodges in the center of most colonial cities, numbering perhaps 150 by the outbreak of the Revolution. As proof against Masonic conspiracy, the much talked of roll call of Founders who belonged to Masonic lodges was easily matched by a similar constellation of stars among Loyalists as well as opponents of Revolution in England, including Benedict Arnold, the traitor; indeed, those on opposite sides of independence sometimes dined together during the war at their lodges. Nevertheless, the Masons earned a bad reputation when some of their number committed crimes ranging from arson to the possible murder of a man named William Morgan to protect the secrets of the craft from outsiders. Such actions helped to foment anti-Masonic feelings, incurring nationwide protests. When Andrew Jackson, a Freemason—and a believer in a lost white race that once rule America before Columbus (!)—

became president, opponents launched an anti-Masonic party, whose influence was great enough to force Jackson's other opponents to similarly denounce Masonry, sparking the modern anti-Masonic movement and its attendant conspiracy theories.

This state of affairs was not helped by the Romantic impulse among the Masons to embroider their history with a fanciful pedigree. Apparently, descent from mere stonemasons was not highfalutin enough for the nobility who came to join the craft in England and Scotland, so a new, aristocratic heritage was concocted, descending from Solomon's Temple to the noble Crusaders of the Middle Ages. The key figure in this myth making was the Chevalier Andrew Michael Ramsay (1686-1743), a Catholic convert who hoped to secure the Church's blessing for Freemasonry. Ramsay fancifully but counterfactually suggested that if the first Masons were the builders of Solomon's Temple, then it followed that the Crusaders would have brought back the secrets of the Masons from their time ruling Jerusalem. In his famous oration of 1737, he said:

> At the time of the Crusades in Palestine many princes, lords, and citizens associated themselves, and vowed to restore the Temple of the Christians in the Holy Land, and to employ themselves in bringing back their architecture to its first institution. They agreed upon several ancient signs and symbolic words drawn from the well of religion in order to recognise themselves amongst the heathen and Saracens. These signs and words were only communicated to those who promised solemnly, and even sometimes at the foot of the altar, never to reveal them. This sacred promise was therefore not an execrable oath, as it has been called, but a respectable bond to unite Christians of all nationalities in one confraternity. Some time afterwards our Order formed an intimate union with the Knights of St John of Jerusalem. From that time our Lodges took the name of Lodges of St John. This union was made after the example set by the Israelites when they erected the second Temple, who whilst they handled the trowel and mortar with one hand, in the other held the sword and buckler.
>
> Our Order therefore must not be considered a revival of the Bacchanals, but as an order founded in remote antiquity, and renewed in the Ho-

ly Land by our ancestors in order to recall the memory of the most sublime truths amidst the pleasures of society. The kings, princes, and lords
returned from Palestine to their own lands, and there established divers
Lodges.[4]

At the fame of the Knights of St. John (the Hospitallers) declined and
that of the Poor Fellow-Soldiers of Christ and of the Temple of Solomon
(the Templars) grew, Ramsay's origin story was reassigned to the Templars, possibly due to the introduction at this time of a new degree of Masonry, the Knights Templar, supposedly a "revival" of the medieval order
of crusader knights who had occupied the Temple Mount in Jerusalem and
were rumored to be privy to the secrets of Solomon. Ramsay himself is
often credited as the originator of this degree, supposedly as part of a plot
to help create support for the Stuart pretender in Scotland, but at any rate
Masonic Templarism did not exist before the 1740s. Masons themselves
recognized that it had no connection to the medieval order, which had
been disbanded in the early 1300s when the King of France became envi-
ous of their fabulous wealth and power. Leaders of the medieval group
were accused of worshiping a demon named Baphomet, performing homo-
sexual rituals, and other offenses. Several were executed, and the remaining knights were allowed to join the Order of St. John, providing the ten-
tative connection later writers would use to link Ramsay's assertions back
to the Templars as the forebears of the Freemasons.

Several other neo-medieval degrees of Masonry were also created
around the same time, including orders "reviving" the Knights of Saint
John and the Knights of Malta, as part of the increasingly aristocratic cast
of the craft and the revival of medievalism in the eighteenth century—
something clearly reflected in the rise of Gothic literature and neo-Gothic
architecture in those same years. It is this neo-medieval revivalism that
allows anti-Masonic writers and alternative historians like Scott Wolter to
claim that the Masons are a "revival" of the original Knights Templar. This
extremely tenuous connection drove a claim Wolter made to me a week
before "Chamber Hunting" aired, a claim that sheds light on the episode:

Before you scoff, have you compared the four Midéwin rituals with the Masonic Knights Templar degrees the earliest missionaries and fur traders said the Natives were practicing when they got here? They are identical and I will be publishing this research in my forthcoming book.[5]

Remember: The Masonic Knights Templar degree was not created in Europe until the mid-1700s. The Midéwin or Midewiwin were the rites of an Ojibwa "secret" society called the Midē´ Society that practiced shamanism and through which members rose by rank, translated into English as "degrees." However, these were not symbolic gradations like Freemasonry but rather closer akin to academic degrees, with each level representing a new body of medicinal knowledge and practice. Among the Ojibwa, pictures of the ceremonies were recorded on birch bark "scrolls" that were copied and recopied across the generations; the originals of course have long rotted away. Anthropologists believe that since the Ojibwa "secret" society has no clear parallel to the east, it likely arose in the late seventeenth century—during the Contact Period.[6] The Ojibway themselves believe in an earlier origin, but like so many oral traditions, this is an example of the slippery timelines used by traditional cultures. They believe the knowledge imparted by the ceremonies to have originated from the gods and ancestors; therefore, it must be ancient, according to traditional views. In reality, a ritual can be retroactively declared ancient by virtue of its sanctity. Think of America's Thanksgiving, which is claimed to date from 1621 but in reality was only celebrated after 1863, and only became a fixed holiday in 1942. The Ojibwa ritual incorporates some traditional knowledge and shamanic aspects that may derive from as far back as the Hopewell, but the ritual itself is apparently very recent.

The earliest claim I can find that the Midē´ shamanistic society was related to Freemasonry occurs in the Masonic publication *The Builder* for April 1922. In it, a brother named A.B.S. answered a reader's question about whether any Native Americans were Freemasons:

Among the Ojibway the secret society known as the Midewin is highly developed, and possesses ceremonies, rituals, and rites of initiation and raising very similar to that described in my article "Little Wolf Joins the Mitawin," in the October, 1921, number of THE BUILDER; in fact, many students of ethnology believe that it is among the members of this tribe that the oldest form of the rites occurs. Unfortunately, although considerable time and money have been devoted to the study of this very organization among the Ojibway, the scientists who have hitherto done the work have not been Masons, and hence much of the most significant facts have escaped attention. The late Mr. W. J. Hoffman has written a monograph entitled "The Midewiwin or 'Grand Medicine Society' of the Ojibway," based largely on studies made among the Red Lake and Leech Lake Indians, and published in the Seventh Annual Report of the Bureau of American Ethnology of Washington, D.C. in 1885-6. He, however, entirely failed to grasp the significance of what he saw and heard, and, if I remember correctly, got no inkling of the true meaning of the underlying ritual, or the myth of the death and resurrection of the ancient founder of the lodge.[7]

The author goes on to say that despite living with the Ojibwa he himself was "blind to the facts" until he became a Mason, and he also claims that some other tribes have rites that "are much farther from Masonry as we know it than the others." The obvious implication is that after one accepts Masonry as ancient and supreme, one can then "read backward" into other rites a corruption of these original, pure rites.

Hoffman's report appears to be the description of the first four degrees of initiation that Wolter is referring to, but it contains little that relates to Masonry and is in fact frequently cited as a classic description of Native shamanism and the education of shamans.[8] So far as I can tell, the similarity is no greater than with any other secretive or mystery society, like the Eleusinian Mysteries or the Dionysian Mysteries, which also involved degrees, sequestration in secret chambers, chanting rituals, revealing mystical secrets, etc. An obvious difference is the fact that during the initiation into Midewiwin, the candidate is primarily concerned with learning the lore of medicinal plants, which to my knowledge is not a part of Freemasonry in general or Masonic Templarism in particular. (The use of medicinal and possibly psychotropic plants was likely part of the Eleusinian Mysteries, however.) Another difference is that Masonry has three primary degrees (originally just two), not four; traditionally the degrees labeled 4 through 33 in Scottish Rite Masonry (including the special Templar degree—and not consistently found in other versions) were considered supplemental to the essential three, while Midewiwin's four degrees are essential, though few attained the highest degree, Hoffman wrote, because, like Scientology, each degree of advancement required costly payments that took years to assemble.[9] A third difference is that men and women could both become members of the Midē′ Society, while only men are allowed to be Masons.

Also, the purpose of the rites is very different from Masonry. The Midē′ Society is designed to train future shamans (medicine men) to engage in healing and intercession with the spirit world. Freemasons do not, so far as I know, claim to wield supernatural power.

Based on the anthropological data on the Midewiwin—which, I stress, does not derive entirely from Hoffman but from many anthropologists who have studied and continue to study this shamanic rite—there doesn't seem to be any greater structural or functional similarity between Midewiwin and Masonic rites than between any two secret or mystery groups. But at any rate, so long as the best data indicates that this secret society only developed after the Contact Period, this has no bearing whatsoever on the question of whether Europeans reached America earlier.

Nevertheless, Wolter's belief that Native Americans prior to European contact had knowledge of Freemasonry is tied directly to his belief that stone buildings in America, like the chamber explored in this episode, could conceivably be evidence that medieval Europeans, specifically the Templar offshoot he imagines preserved their heritage until the rise of Freemasonry, came to America in the Middle Ages—a story he will develop more fully in the season's last few episodes, as we shall see.

The Episode

I grew up in upstate New York, an older part of the country whose settlement dates back to the colonial era. Although I lived in the city of Auburn, I spent a great deal of time traveling across upstate New York's farm country, and I've visited plenty of farms whose structures dated back to the early 1800s, and more than a few that had origins in the 1700s. I've seen pretty much every type of farm building used in those days, and a goodly number of outbuildings, root cellars, spring houses, powder magazines, and other buildings that were built using the dry stone technique brought over from England. This is a rather longwinded way of saying that the mysterious "chamber" Scott Wolter investigates in "Chamber Hunting" is "mysterious" only to those who've never spent much time visiting farms or studying the lives of people who were not part of the cultural, religious, or political elite that Wolter favors. As a society, we've lost quite a bit of knowledge about agrarian life in the transition to a predominantly urban society.

The episode opens with overhead footage of a semi-wooded area, with an on-screen graphic telling us that eight hundred mysterious stone sites exist in the northeastern United States. They are "mysterious" because the show does not ask anyone knowledgeable about them what they really are—nearly all have been studied and explained. Some manipulated intercut footage is made to look like grainy VHS tape of the stone sites, a trick borrowed from low-rent horror movies to give a touch of conspiracy to the program, especially when the graphic tells us that "many" of the stone sites are not open to the public. That would be because many of them are colonial era root cellars or spring houses, Victorian boundary markers, etc. currently on private land.

The manipulated video shows a man in contemporary dress (so the video isn't old—it was filmed within the year) entering what appears to be at first glance a late eighteenth or early nineteenth century stone storage chamber with a small aqueduct feeding water from a natural spring to a tiny, possibly concrete, basin within. The water flows into the chamber and then immediately out again. Why, I wondered, did the producers purposely degrade the footage? The manipulation shows that the producers are playing fast and loose with the "truth" of the video, and it makes me question what else they're willing to manipulate alongside the video.

I should probably pause here to explain that in colonial times down to the nineteenth century, farmers built "spring houses," which were wooden or stone buildings constructed over the outlet of a natural spring in order to use the cold underground water to cool the air within the chamber and preserve the food stored within. The chamber on display here is very much like every known colonial spring house in America and Canada. One in West Virginia is even on the National Register of Historic Places (the Tomahawk Spring spring house), so they are not exactly unknown. Similar structures, without springs, served as cold cellars, and Wolter previously investigated the stone "caves" Jonathan Pattee used as cold cellars at Mystery Hill, which featured very similar stone architecture. No one on this show, I predicted in its first five minutes, would spend even a moment contemplating the historical record to discover whether early Americans ever built atop springs.

The opening credits roll, and we're off.

We open at Scott Wolter's lab in Minneapolis. Wolter receives an email from the discoverer of the spring house and immediate runs off to investigate since the email says that the site "seems old." A staged phone call shot with dramatic lighting wastes some extra time as we fly out to Chad Snyder's land in Tionesta, Pennsylvania, near the site of the stone "chamber." Wolter meets Snyder and another man, and they examine pictures of the stone chamber. The workmanship on display is completely typical of eighteenth and nineteenth century dry stone construction methods, widespread throughout the northeast in farm country. It is unlike the architectural styles used in Antiquity or the Middle Ages. Even Wolter seems aware of this, and no one mentions that the basin into which the water flows appears to be poured concrete.

Wolter immediately leaps to secret societies, claiming that the Knights Templar and the Freemasons use "ritual bathing" in their rites and therefore "could have a connection to this chamber." Neither the Knights Templar nor the Freemasons are known to use ritual bathing, which immediately made me wonder why he brings it up. There is method to the madness, however. The entire claim rests on the fanciful idea that the Templars adopted the ancient Essene practice of ritual bathing as part of their secret continuation of rituals associated with protecting the Holy Bloodline of Christ. A link between the Templars and the Essenes was suggested as early as the eighteenth century, itself part of a conspiracy theory that held that the Templars were initiates into Syrian secret societies descended from the Essenes. Modern conspiracy writers believe that the Essenes preserved covert knowledge of the secret child of Jesus, the Holy Bloodline Wolter believes in, and that Joseph of Arimathea was an Essene who spread this message. This, in turn, builds on the work of the Prussian theologian Karl Friedrich Bahrdt. He felt German Freemasonry was a poor imitation of the British, so he became a Mason in London in 1777 and was later active in creating a German secret society to affiliate with English Freemasonry, the German Union. He argued from 1784 onward that the Essenes were a secret society—the model for later societies like the Templars and Freemasons—who used Jesus to create a false religion. Jesus was an Essene, and they helped him fabricate miracles and fake his death in order to launch a religion through which they could rule the world (several hundred years later). The Prussian government took a dim view of this, and in 1788 when Bahrdt satirized the government's edict on religious scholarship, they threw him in jail, where he spent the next year writing pornography. His work, which was almost entirely fiction and presented in the form of a dialogue, is almost entirely forgotten—except by modern Jesus conspiracy theory writers. And thus we have Wolter's "ritual bath," with all the back story that hides behind so simple a statement.

Meanwhile, back in reality Snyder and his friend offer that the stone chamber site might have been a root cellar, but Wolter will have none of it because root cellars don't have water, and no one seems aware of spring houses. He says such stone chambers have been found since colonial times, implying that they existed prior to Columbus. Since he says Native Americans don't build in stone, they must belong to European people who came in the Middle Ages. This seems wrong, especially since spring houses can be constructed and forgotten in as little as a single season, especially if the farmer should happen to die, as in a particularly cold winter. I'd need to see more evidence that they were older than the colonists who reported them.

We then watch the video from the beginning of the show, shot by Snyder and the other man, and we can see that there is no grain in the tape, nor is there static as it leaps from scene to scene, exposing the producers' overdramatic manipulation of the video.

Wolter chips away at an outcropping of stone and explains how long it takes to build a chamber. He wants to see the chamber, but the land owner (who is not Chad Snyder) informed Snyder off camera that Wolter's television production is not allowed on the land, which everyone involved assumes is aimed squarely at Scott Wolter himself, who was not a famous television personality when this was shot in late 2012. Wolter grows angry (even though he must have known before arriving that no filming permission was granted) and snarls that "this kind of shit has happened to me before, and the fact that they won't let me on means that either they're hiding something or they're afraid to know what the truth is." No, there's another option: The land owner knows full well that this site is a colonial spring house and has no interest in turning his or her land into a circus for alternative speculators, especially since it's highly unlikely that Committee Films is going compensate anyone for shooting on the land.

But Wolter does an end run around the site owner by taking advantage of the fact that the owner has opened the land for public hunting. He sends Snyder across the property line in bad faith, posing as a hunter, to gain access to the site. Either this was all staged for the camera to make Wolter look heroic, meaning that no access was really denied, or Committee Films knowingly chose to engage in trespassing, or no one ever actually crossed the property line. Either way, this is terrible and a gross violation of ethics in one way or another.

After the break, we see the same "shit" statement again to reestablish the conspiracy, but the wording is different. This time Wolter speaks of "bullshit" and "crap." I wondered how many takes this self-described "documentary" series makes of events it supposedly was capturing as they happened (as opposed to narration or explanation for which several takes would be expected). The manipulation of "reality"—even this show's reality—is awful.

So, Snyder dresses up as a hunter, complete with gun, thus conspiring with Wolter to fraudulently gain access to the land and to trespass thereon. Is this photographic evidence of a crime? Or is the entire scenario created *ex nihilo* to make Wolter look like the victim of a conspiracy? The landowner, Industrial Timber and Lumber, and its local management company, Chagrin Land L.P., did not return my request for comment. Wolter explains over and over that someone doesn't want him to know what's going on. He sounds paranoid. But we never actually see Snyder cross the property line, so we have no way of knowing that he actually went to the chamber or took the alleged measurements he returns with.

I think it's interesting that at this point Wolter seems to recognize that the chamber is not very old. Now he begins attributing it not to the Knights Templar, as in the beginning of the show, but to the Freemasons, in the eighteenth century, thus conceding that it is a colonial-era structure. This means that the earlier speculation about pre-Columbian stone chambers is now moot. Therefore, the only question left to address is whether this colonial-era spring house also featured in Freemason rituals in an era when the Freemasons had their own Masonic halls and were practicing openly. The conspiracy was so deep that even the president, George Washington, was a Freemason and was *clearly* being oppressed by the federal government!

Wolter states his belief that the water in the chamber *must* have been used for ritual bathing because it's the only thing "I can think of." Drenched as he is in alternative history Jesus conspiracies, I can understand why he had no other option in mind and why he did not bother to do even cursory research into colonial architecture and farming practices. Farmers are often forgotten in televised history because they weren't the elite and weren't in possession of gold and glory, but farmers outnumbered cultists and conspirators and are much more important to understanding daily life than the few hundred people involved in any given "secret society."

Using measurements the show claims were taken by fraud from the "mysterious stone chamber," Wolter concludes that the chamber is aligned to sunset on the summer solstice, a time of day of no particular relevance to any of the secret societies Wolter has investigated. He then hires someone to build a model of the chamber from these measurements by deriving the chamber's shape and size from the video and some rough sketches. Accuracy, of course, can't possibly be proved and any conclusions are highly suspect, especially when claiming an accuracy of millimeters, as any astronomical alignment would require—as we established back in Wolter's investigation of Oklahoma's Anubis Cave.

While the model is being built, Wolter travels to Gungywamp Archaeological Site in Groton, Connecticut, the site of some stone ruins whose origins have not yet been definitively established but which are believed to be colonial-era root cellars, based on their close similarity to known root cellars in use in the area. Archaeologist Ken Feder, a card-carrying member of the anti-alternative conspiracy and a friend of mine, has identified the stone circle at the site as a bark mill used in colonial leather making. The reason for the confusion is that Native American artifacts and petroglyphs have been found here as well. Archaeological investigation has found that Native Americans placed stones around the lodges they are known to have built in this area (and the remains of which still exist and have been excavated). Native Americans are not mentioned, and this show seems to have a serious blind spot when it comes to Native peoples; they simply exist as furniture decorating an empty continent. In fact, in the show's first season, only a single non-white person was interviewed, archaeologist Alfonso Morales. Surely Native Americans have an important viewpoint on their own history. Instead, we hear that the Irish and any number of white people came here to build these root cellars. One root cellar is claimed to be a calendar "measuring" (I suppose they mean recording) the equinoxes, which is presented as a mystical event. Wolter fails to mention that on the equinoxes the sun rises due east, so *any* building well-aligned to the cardinal directions will "measure" the equinox. Instead, Wolter concludes that the root cellar was built by Irish monks on the model of Newgrange, a Neolithic stone tomb aligned to the winter solstice (note: not the equinox). But Native Americans were also well-aware of equinoxes and solstices and marked them with calendars made of standing wooden poles, as at the Mississippian mound site of Cahokia, or "medicine wheels" of standing stones. Europeans are not necessary for this "amazing" feat.)

On this strength, Wolter makes the "early Irish candidates for construction" of these stone sites. Wolter has simply decided to go with the hypothesis that the chambers are ancient and of non-American origins. Not once does he do *any* research into colonial-era construction even though in an earlier scene *he already said the Pennsylvania chamber was from the colonial era!*

Wolter travels to Ireland to learn about St. Brendan the Navigator, and he meets with Tim Severin, a nautical adventurer who is famous for recreating ancient voyages. I know him best for the 1984 *Jason* adventure, in which he attempted to recreate the voyage of the *Argo* from Greek myth, traveling from Greece to the Black Sea in a Mycenaean-style ship. In that trip, Severin failed to recognize that the story of Jason and the Argonauts was not static (he recreated Apollonius' version) and that the oldest versions of the tale had a completely different itinerary, with the Black Sea never mentioned. Severin has a tendency to take myths at face value and then try to explain them literally on the theory that they "might" be true, not a good sign for an "expert" in the field. Therefore, I have little faith in his opinion on the reality of Brendan's voyage. Severin proved that the Irish *could* have sailed to America, but we already knew that because the Vikings did the same thing five hundred years later; knowing something *can* be done is not the same as proving that it actually happened.

A medieval Latin text called the *Navigatio* tells of Brendan's voyage to the Isles of the Blessed in the West, but I find it silly to assume—with no evidence—that this mythological text tells of a real event, or that we could separate fact from fiction if it did. Some people think this story refers to a trip to North America, but I just don't see how. Supposedly, on this trip Brendan encountered an island populated solely by blacksmiths who throw slag at his crew, obviously modeled on the fuming Polyphemus and Talos of Greek myth. They also find a volcano—not something available on the east coast of America, though they can be found in Iceland—and one of their party is taken to Hell. So, Hell is real? There is nothing in the *Navigatio* that correlates in any way to North America, not the island of sheep Brendan found, nor the (white) monk he found, etc. It's a religious allegory, very similar in form to other nautical-themed popular entertainments of its period, including the earlier *Voyage of Bran*, which was its likely model and probably the direct source for some passages.

We then meet Alan Butler again (first seen in Episode Two), described this time as a "Megalithic Era Historian," and he is no more helpful than when he speculated wildly about cliff dwellings, or when he tried to sue me for reviewing his alternative history book about megaliths. Wolter and Bulter examine Newgrange, but neither can quite explain how it is that a pagan tomb from 3200 BCE should be reproduced by Christian monks in 500 CE on another continent while no similar examples from that period exist in Ireland or anywhere in between. Wolter simply asserts the continued existence of an astronomy-based Irish cult for 3,700 years without any proof of continuity. In fact, the published texts of the early Middle Ages make quite plain that the Catholic Church did whatever it could to wipe out any remnants of continuity from pagan times. That's part of the conspiracy, of course.

Wolter returns from Ireland to review a model of the Pennsylvania chamber, which, as I've noted, simply cannot be taken as accurate but only as a very rough approximation of the chamber. To discuss alignments in any detail, one needs more than a "precise" angle for the chamber entrance; one needs a careful survey of the site to know the exact measurements of the chamber's interior. So, the light he shines into the model is cute, but useless. He moves the light around the trace's the sun's path and find some point in the day when it enters the chamber. Nor did he survey the land around the chamber to see whether the sunlight would have reached the chamber, which is set into a hill and appears to be surrounded by hills and a forest. The light, even by Wolter's measurement, enters the chamber only at some unspecified point during the day on the solstice, not at the key moment of sunrise, the period most commonly believed to be the essential moment of the solstice in esoteric lore.

I find it strange that Wolter is seen asking Snyder trespass again on the summer solstice to prove the alignment. He called this "going back," implying the program was filmed prior to June 20, 2012, the date of the summer solstice that year, but the exterior shots seen in the episode were filmed in the autumn rather than spring, as indicated by the autumn leaves on the trees and the ground. This means that the timeline given in the show has no real relationship to reality, and most of the episode was filmed in fall 2012, long after the June 20, 2012 solstice footage was supposedly shot. As a result, Wolter and company knew of the video footage *before* creating the unnecessary model of the "alignment" and then pretended to send Snyder back for dramatic effect.

From this experiment, Wolter concludes that the Freemasons built the site to symbolize "the fertilization" of the earth "by the male" principle of sunlight. I am not aware of any sun-earth pagan fertility rites in Freemasonry, though maybe I'm just part of the conspiracy. Nineteenth-century anti-Masonic activists argued that the square and compass symbol of the Masons was an esoteric sexual symbol of the pagan god Baal and his consort, Astarte. In fact, the "sun-earth" fertilization claim is taken nearly word-for-word from Victorian anti-Masonic tracts (misrepresenting Masonic symbolism under the assumption that the Masons preserved Ancient Egyptian fertility rites) and repeated in modern conspiracy books and websites. It isn't true, but it was part of the anti-Masonic hysteria of the time, which Wolter has apparently bought into because it ties in so well with his belief in the secret Jesus Bloodline and the goddess-based "sacred feminine" religion he will investigate later in the season.

After repeatedly calling the chamber's builders "ancient" throughout the hour, Wolter concludes the show by conceding that the building "dates back to colonial times"—hardly ancient—and is therefore utterly irrelevant to rewriting American history. So, while this place appears to be a colonial-era spring house, even if this one was a Freemasons' chamber (for what purpose?) it changes nothing. George Washington was a Freemason in the same period; the Masons had well-known lodges in that period, and though they did have some secret rites and hidden sites, I can't see that they needed a tiny "secret" chamber out in the backwoods of Pennsylvania—except insofar as a Freemason bath house contributes toward "proving" the Freemasons were really Templars and the Templars were really Essenes—and all were involved in the Jesus Bloodline conspiracy.

Motive for Murder

February 15, 2013

Episode Summary

Scott Wolter investigates whether Meriwether Lewis, the leader of the famed Lewis and Clark expedition, was murdered to keep secret the existence of a tribe of Native Americans of medieval Welsh descent, people whose prior claim to American land could threaten American sovereignty. After testing Lewis' Masonic apron for DNA, Wolter concludes he was murdered.

Historical Background

T he story that there was a tribe of Native Americans whose ancestors were from Wales has a very long and complex history, intimately tied to the politics of the colonial era and the early American Republic. Although this claim has its roots in the imperial struggle for control of North America, the myth thus generated continues down to the present day in a different form.

Let's begin with the most interesting aspect, at least for me, of the recent claims for Welsh exploration of the American interior. In this episode of *America Unearthed* we will hear that the Welsh supposedly arrived in America in the sixth century CE. This is astonishing because the traditional claims for Welsh exploration are dated to 1170 CE (some sources say 1160), when Welsh nationalists claim that Prince Madoc sailed westward from Wales and discovered America. The earliest reference to the story was told by Maredudd ap Rhys in the fifteenth century (before the discovery of America, and including no details recognizable as America). In

Maredudd's poem, Madoc is referenced in a single line as traveling "to the sea." Scholars conjecture that an oral version, perhaps based on the *Navigatio* about the voyage of St. Brendan, once existed. Only after English colonization began did the Elizabethans begin expanding on the Madoc story, giving rise to the legend of Welsh colonization.

The Tudors, as it happens, were considered "Welsh" monarchs of Britain by the Welsh, and it was in their interests to promote the exploits of a fellow Welshman, especially insofar as a claim that Madoc reached America long before Columbus could be used to help undermine the claims of Spain to the whole of the New World. The Welsh of the time undertook a massive effort to rewrite the early history of Britain in the image of Wales, particularly after the Tudors fully integrated the principality into the legal and political framework of England. Thus, King Arthur—the "Welsh" king—became hailed as the progenitor of all British kings, and another man of Welsh descent, the infamous occultist and advisor to Queen Elizabeth, John Dee, seized upon the story to support British imperial claims. Several versions of the tail were in print in the 1580s, beginning with George Peckham's *True Reporte*, but Dee took this much further, stating that Madoc had done no less than rediscover Atlantis itself, America!

> The Lord Madoc, sonne of Owen Gwyndd prince of North Wales, leaving his brothers in contention, and warre for their inheritance sought, by sea (westerlie from Irland), for some forein, and—Region to plant hymselfe in with soveranity: wth Region when he had found, he returned to Wales againe and hym selfe wth Shipps, vituals, and men and women sufficient for the coloniy, wth spedely he leed into the peninsula; then named Farquara; but of late Florida or into some of the Provinces, and territories neere ther abouts: and in Apalchen, Mocosa, or Norombera: then of these 4 beinge notable portions of the ancient Atlantis, no longer—nowe named America.[1]

Dee later presented this information as part of a "Title Royal" awarding Queen Elizabeth all of Madoc's lands. This claim was meant to directly rebut that of Francisco López de Gómara, a Spanish historian, who had claimed in 1552 that the Spanish-controlled Caribbean and Mexico were Atlantis, and that this ancient land was the rightful possession of England's rival, Spain: "But there is now no cause why we should any longer doubt or dispute of the Island Atlantide, forasmuch as the discovering and conquest of the west Indies do plainly declare what Plato hath written of the said lands."[2] Dee knew of this text from a 1555 English translation made by Richard Eden, and on the strength of Dee's claims the occultist won a charter for vast territories in North America, but nothing came of them after the failure of the Roanoke Colony.

As a direct result of Dee's work, in 1568 a Scotsman named David Ingram made the first claim of meeting Welsh-speaking Natives, in the Caribbean, though his claim was not published until 1582. The first Welsh-speaking person to make such a claim was One Stedman, who met supposedly Welsh-speaking Natives somewhere on the eastern seaboard in 1670. These Welsh, however, were apparently not related to the Madoc expedition or anything earlier, since they allegedly told Stedman about their ancestry from what they called by the Welsh name for Great Britain, a term not used until after 1603. Subsequent encounters with "Welsh" Indians occurred in South Carolina in the mid-1600s.

Queen Elizabeth and her Stuart successors cared little about this, however, and as Britain's geopolitical needs changed during the seventeenth century, the claims for Prince Madoc were abandoned until a Welsh cultural revival in the late 1700s, specifically in large measure due to the work of Edward Williams (Iolo Morganwg). He, in turn, was notorious in committing fraud, including his invention of a fake Welsh alphabet, which we will encounter later in this episode when Scott Wolter finds it on the Brandenburg Stone in Kentucky. Williams made plans to travel to Missouri to seek out the Welsh Indians, who he thought would have preserved a "pure" medieval Welsh culture that could be used to revitalize Wales.

Although he was not able to make the trip himself, an associate named John Evans, a fellow Welshman, did make the journey in 1793, arriving in the Spanish city of St. Louis (Spain controlling the Louisiana Territory in those years), where the governor imprisoned him as a British spy because he believed the Welsh Indians were merely a cover story for a covert mission. He managed to turn things around, and with the help of John McKay, a Scotsman, he earned a commission from the Spanish government to search the Louisiana territory for, among other things, Welsh Indians. He thought he might have found them when he encountered the Mandan people, as an earlier French expedition had claimed, but he later determined that they did not, after all, speak Welsh: "I am able to inform you that there is no such People as the Welsh Indians," he said.[3]

A fellow Welshman, Morgan John Rhys, came to America to found a Welsh-language colony. He followed with interest the work of Evans; he was more skeptical of the survival of Welsh Indians but had no doubt a lost race of white Caucasians existed somewhere in America. In 1795, he wrote a letter explaining his beliefs: "It is a confirmed fact that there are white Indians on the Missouri and in many places far west of the Mississippi. I have seen deer and buffaloe skins with various other articles dressed by them in a most capital manner. [...] Every part of this continent affords sufficient proofs of a more civilised people having existed here than the present Indians..." I have reproduced the whole letter in Appendix One.

Morgan John Rhys communicated with Thomas Jefferson at the time of the Lewis and Clark Expedition, and this is what gives us Scott Wolter's "Motive for Murder." There is one complicating factor, however. Wolter doesn't trace the Welsh to Prince Madoc, as had everyone from the Tudors to today; instead, he traces them to the sixth century CE. So why move them to the sixth century when there is no literary or historical warrant? One reason is that this is the alleged time of King Arthur, who is often claimed to be Welsh and who is recorded as having sailed to the west (to Iceland[4]) in Geoffrey of Monmouth and therefore is a much more famous sponsor of the Welsh than Madoc. The second reason is that in the 1960s the Vikings were confirmed archaeologically to have been in America, at L'anse-aux-Meadows, around 1000, predating Madoc's alleged voyage by nearly two centuries. Welsh partisans have to move them back in time to maintain their primacy, despite the lack of any sixth-century evidence;

and Wolter needs them there to help support the later Jesus Bloodline timeline whereby Europeans had to be colonizing America prior to 800 CE in order to pave the way for the Holy Grail to come to the future United States and transfer God's blessing from Scotland to America.

The Episode

"Motive for Murder" begins with a disclaimer that on this "special episode" the murder investigation forensic geologist Scott Wolter is about to undertake contains images that "may be disturbing." Insert your own joke here. We proceed to a reenactment of Meriwether Lewis sitting at his desk writing in his journal about his famous expedition across America, which the on-screen graphics state includes "secret" information that had been suppressed. We then see Lewis commit suicide with a pistol. The "disturbing" image is the blood splattering on a map hung upon the wall. The on-screen text tells us that Lewis died of multiple gunshot wounds, calling into question the suicide theory. Then we see the opening credits.

Lewis's suicide at Grinder's Stand in Tennessee is widely accepted by historians, but questions about whether he was murdered have been discussed since the 1800s. There is nothing exciting here, to be honest with you, for the exact nature of Lewis's death doesn't really change anything about American history. If you're a fan of the History Channel, though, you already know where this is going because you've seen this story before, in 2010, when it was called "Secret Presidential Codes" and was the second episode of *Brad Meltzer's Decoded*. In that episode, we also went through the claims that Lewis had been murdered rather than committed suicide. Meltzer's show suggested Lewis had been assassinated because he possessed President Thomas Jefferson's secret codes. Scott Wolter is going to go in a different direction, however.

Wolter arrives at former TV journalist Don Shelby's home in Minnesota to discuss the "missing" pages of Lewis's journal. Shelby, a retired local TV news anchor, believes (without evidence) that Lewis was murdered and the pages stolen to suppress facts that were "frightening" to "that day and age." What are these facts? Shelby is very interested in why Thomas

Jefferson asked Lewis to look for evidence of Welsh colonization of the Louisiana Territory. He believes Lewis found this and that the government suppressed the fact because it would take "the whole idea of American colonial history, our very foundation, and toss it out the window."

He knows nothing of history. No mention of Welsh Indians occurs in Jefferson's instructions to Lewis, dated June 20, 1803 (see Appendix One). As Jefferson and Lewis planned the expedition to explore Louisiana, neither made any mention of Welsh Indians. In fact, it is not until 1804, when the expedition was underway, that any mention of Welsh Indians occurs. On January 22, 1804, Jefferson wrote to Lewis that a Welshman named Mr. (John) Evans had explored the St. Louis region in search of Welsh Indians and that his map would be helpful. And he does so because of John Morgan Rhys. Jefferson wrote to Lewis:

> In that of the 13th inst. I inclosed you the map of a Mr. Evans, a Welsh-man, employed by the Spanish government for that purpose, but whose original object I believe had been to go in search of the Welsh Indians, said to be up the Missouri. On this subject a Mr. Rees of the same nation, established in the Western parts of Pennsylvania, will write to you.

I have reproduced the entire letter in Appendix One. It is Jefferson's only known reference to Welsh Indians in his papers.

Note that Jefferson is either uncertain or unconcerned whether Evans had been in search of Welsh Indians. Instead, his concern is to get Lewis a useful map that will help the expedition. It is reasonable to conclude from this letter that in order to obtain the map, Jefferson agreed to let Rhys write to Lewis about his pet subject, the Welsh Indians. However, Jefferson doesn't seem at all interested in the subject, and is content to let Rhys write under his own name (i.e. unofficially) about any such inquiry. Sadly, Rhys's letter does not exist, or else was never sent. He died suddenly in December of 1804. The subject, though, appears to have captured the fancy of Lewis and Clark. Here's exactly how much of a state secret they considered it: John Whitehouse, an expedition member, wrote about it his journal, and he intended to publish the journal for a profit upon his return from the expedition (some secret!), but gave up on the idea after putting together a final draft and preface in 1806. These journals were not published until 1904. Any conspiracy against Lewis somehow missed Whitehouse. Here's what he had to say (with original spelling) about a mysterious tribe they encountered:

> we take these Savages to be the Welch Indians if their be any Such from the Language. So Capt. Lewis took down the names of everry thing in their Language, in order that it may be found out whether they are or whether they Sprang or origenated first from the welch or not.

Similarly, Sgt. John Ordway recorded the same:

> these natives are well dressed, descent looking Indians. light complectioned. they are dressed in mo. Sheep leather Deer & buffalow robes &C. they have the most curious language of any we have seen before. they talk as though they lisped or have a bur on their tongue. we suppose that they are the welch Indians if their is any Such from the language.

I've reproduced Whitehouse's and Ordway's journal entries on the Welsh Indians in Appendix One. As is evident, the borrowed language indicates the men conferred and discussed the issue and had no concern about writing down such speculation—hardly the hallmark of a conspiracy entrusted to Lewis.

Jefferson expressed no belief in Welsh Indians in his letters to Lewis (though like his contemporaries he wondered if it could be true), and he makes no explicit instruction that Lewis should look for Welsh Indians. All of the standard books I consulted about Jefferson's instructions to Lewis make no mention of a directive to find Welsh Indians, except for Stephen Ambrose's *Undaunted Courage,* which provides no source. Ambrose mentions that Jefferson supposedly told Lewis in 1802 (before the Louisiana Purchase) that an expedition might find the fabled Welsh Indians, though this was not an explicit objective, more of a statement of curiosity. *America Unearthed* is therefore wrong in claiming an 1803 "presidential mandate" to find Welsh Indians. Instead, we see the expedition members bringing their own knowledge to bear.

What Jefferson did ask for was a list of vocabularies of the various Native tribes west of the Mississippi, which he hoped would help him prove that the Native Americans descended from Asiatic peoples of Russia, a subject he had discussed years before in his *Notes on the State of Virginia*. Indeed, the word list Whitehouse saw Lewis take was exactly this type of vocabulary list. Jefferson's preliminary finding was that many Native American words were similar to languages spoken in eastern Russia, implying a Bering Sea entry point from Asia for the first Americans, and he hoped to find more. Unfortunately, he wasn't able to do this because the trunk containing these vocabulary lists was stolen from him in 1809 en route from Washington to Monticello, and the thief, unable to read the Native words, thought it worthless and simply threw them all in the James River! (Or was it part of the conspiracy? Dun-dun-dun!)

According to the *History of the Expedition under the Command of Lewis and Clark*, in 1764 (nearly three centuries after European contact) a French trader discovered "white" Indians with beards on the Missouri (it was actually 1738, according to modern accounts), referencing the Mandan people, who were later in regular contact with Canadian and French explorers, none of whom noticed anything particularly odd about their complexions. In 1805, William Clark's servant York (an African-American) apparently went around telling people that he and the expedition had found a tribe of white Indians, but York was famous for his wild tall tales, and he was apparently exaggerating from the somewhat fairer complexion of the Mandan Indians, whom Lewis and Clark had met in 1805 (and whom Whitehouse had described as possibly Welsh), and who were quite taken by York's dark skin. York's stories ended up quoted as fact in the *New York Medical Repository* in 1806 and helped resurrect the legend of the Welsh Indians.[5] Native peoples, of course, are not uniformly of one color, and they vary greatly in the shades of their skins depending on genetic and environmental factors.

In the America of 1809, theories about white colonists of the pre-

Columbian age were all the rage, and the myth that white colonists predated the Native Americans eventually became the official policy of the
United States government (under the Freemason Andrew Jackson!), in
large measure as a way of justifying the seizure of Native American land.
Not only would the U.S. government of the age have *welcomed* evidence
that white people predated Native Americans, they would have trumpeted
it from Georgia to Maine as proof that land seizures were justified, since in
those days it was often assumed that Native peoples had been on the land
only a few centuries. When the United States gained independence from
Britain, all prior British claims—including those of the Welsh—transferred
to America's sovereignty. Therefore, the discovery of Welsh interlopers in
pre-Columbian America would have had no effect whatsoever on America's sovereignty. Even the discovery of Welsh land claims in Louisiana
would be rather useless since there was no Welsh occupation between 600
CE and 1800, meaning that the land had long been considered "abandoned" under international law.

Wolter seems to think that Welsh Indians would have given the Welsh
the right to the American land, which is ridiculous since the title to Louisiana had passed through Spanish and French hands before becoming
American, and the British made no move to contest the transfer on the
grounds that they owned Wales. The British were well aware of claims of
Welsh colonization, which the original British colonists had been making
for a hundred years; they surely would have asserted such claims against
Spain or France had they thought anything of them, on even the flimsiest
grounds. You might also be interested to know that many British authors
of the era asserted that the Welsh actually founded the Aztec Empire and
were themselves the Aztec. Again, Britain did not dispute Spain's control
of Mexico on this basis, nor did they claim that the Spanish conquest of
the Aztec was illegitimate as a result of the racial makeup of the Aztec;
indeed, as we have seen Spain itself *sponsored* the McKay-Evans expedition
specifically to find the Welsh Indians. Obviously, Spain had no thought
that these people posed a threat to their control of the Louisiana Territory.

Now why is that? Well, in the case of the United States, it's because

Britain wouldn't have had a leg to stand on. The governing law in this case is the Treaty of Paris (1783) signed between the United States and Britain to end the Revolutionary War. In that treaty, America and Britain agreed upon terms demarcating the dividing line between the United States and British North America. The treaty was quite explicit that Britain surrendered all claims formerly held by the Crown to the new country within its territorial boundaries:

> His Brittanic Majesty acknowledges the said United States, viz., New Hampshire, Massachusetts Bay, Rhode Island and Providence Plantations, Connecticut, New York, New Jersey, Pennsylvania, Delaware, Maryland, Virginia, North Carolina, South Carolina and Georgia, to be free sovereign and Independent States; that he treats with them as such, and for himself his Heirs & Successors, relinquishes all claims to the Government, Propriety, and Territorial Rights of the same and every Part thereof.

The treaty then spells out the boundaries of the new country, which included all the territory south of Canada, north of the Spanish dominions, and east of the Mississippi. This includes all the land that the Welsh were believed in those days to have explored, including South Carolina, Virginia, and—if you were to believe the Brandenburg Stone—the land now called Kentucky. Everyone alive in those days believed that any Welsh exploration began in the eastern United States and expanded westward (as it must have done since one must travel through the east to get west of the Mississippi if one first travels from Wales across the Atlantic). Consequently, with the passage of all "territorial rights" of "every part" of the former colonies to the American government, any Welsh claims to territory west of the Mississippi passed therefore to the United States since they would have been an extension of any original Welsh claim to territory stretching from South Carolina westward.

Further, this is entirely contingent upon the recognition of any Welsh Indians as legitimate heirs and descendants of the Welsh. To start, let's get a few basic facts: Wales was an independent principality until 1228, when England conquered it and made it part of the Kingdom of England. At that point, all Welsh territory and claims passed to England. In 1535-1542, England integrated Wales into the English legal system, and all Welsh laws thereafter conformed to English law. There is no record of Wales granting a charter to any American colony, let alone one that permitted them to legislate for themselves, so the "Welsh" settlement in America would presumably have been either (a) governed by Welsh and then English law, or (b) independent of Wales and therefore subject to the right of conquest. Let's start with the first option.

By 1809, it is highly doubtful that any court would have ruled that the alleged Welsh Indians were legitimate heirs since the first generation was not likely conceived in a legal, recognized marriage (and none after the death of last clergyman on the expedition) and therefore illegitimate and unable to inherit property under English law. This issue is complicated a bit due to common-law marriages and Welsh bastard laws. Common-law marriages were forbidden by the Catholic Church after 1215, reinstated by the Protestants, and abolished again in England in 1753 and Wales in 1800 but legal in the United States. Theoretically, common-law marriages would have been valid in "Welsh" America before 1215, but not after, since the Welsh who arrived in 1170 would have been, by definition, Catholics and subject to the canon law. Thus, legally, there would have been a break in marriage continuity after 1215 (there being no legally appointed Catholic bishop to consecrate new priests to announce marriages), though I have no idea what allowances civil law would have made for their ignorance of the changes in canon law. (The revised date of the sixth century for the Welsh in America complicates this slightly since there is an outside chance of pagan/Druid travelers, but Christianity was by and large the religion of Wales by 600, and is at any rate the only faith Wolter contemplates.)

Further, Wales had a special illegitimacy law that allowed for Welsh fathers to pass property to any child, bastard or not, whom he formally acknowledged. This right was in effect in 1170, but it expired in 1535-1542, when England incorporated Wales into the English legal system. England would not have recognized Welsh bastards as legitimate heirs (except for first born bastard sons who could inherit if and only if a second son was born in wedlock) until 1926, when retroactive legitimization was enacted by Parliament. Again, I don't know what allowances were made for the ignorance of the Welsh colonists, but upon the conquest of Wales, all Welsh dependencies passed to the English Crown.

That brings us to the second option: Perhaps the colony considered itself independent of Wales. In that case, its land claims would not have passed to England, but neither would the colony itself. As an independent state, it would have lost all claims to the land upon the failure of its government. Even if the Mandan were the legitimate successors of the independent Welsh-American state, they would have been subject to the same right of conquest as any other Native polity, just as actually happened. Their historical claims would have carried no more weight than those of the Cherokee, the Iroquois, or any other group. The defunct Welsh-American state would have had the same legal standing as the fallen city of Cahokia, the Anasazi ruins, or Poverty Point: none.

While we think of Europeans as simply conquering Native peoples without respect to their rights, the Europeans actually made a show of following a strict legalism involving reading out proclamations, signing treaties, etc. in order to legitimize their conquests, even if the Natives had no idea what they were hearing or signing. Consequently, from an 1809 legal point of view, if the Mandan (or any other tribe) were the legal successors of the Welsh-American state, they had no more right to a land claim than any other Native group and could be deprived of any and all lands by treaty, as eventually happened.

But in support of Wolter's misreading of history, we look at the Brandenburg Stone, found in Kentucky, for a long time housed in Indiana, and now again in Kentucky, another disputed artifact covered in badly-written scratch marks that are supposedly Welsh. Wolter examines the stone using his best geological analysis and concludes it can be no more recent than 1492. According to a translation made by the Arthurian Society of Wales, it reads "Toward strength (to promote unity), divide the land we are spread over, purely (or justly) between offspring in wisdom." It was found in 1912, during a widespread outbreak of fake artifacts, and nothing on the stone would have been impossible to fake in 1912. The show is honest enough to let Shelby explain that the stone's writing can date no earlier than the eighteenth century (because, Shelby says, it's fake pseudo-Welsh writing invented by a known hoaxer, our friend Edward Williams, in the 1700s!), calling into question Wolter's geological credibility since he just finished asserting that the stone is unlikely to be newer than 1492 based on his extensive geological training. (More than fifty similar stones have been found, and none has passed archaeological muster.) Wolter also talked about the provenance of the stone and how that was needed to really date it, which is a laugh since he didn't care about that at all when it came to the Dare Stones. Note carefully: Scott Wolter's own show conclusively demonstrated that his microscopic technique for dating rocks—his so called "new" science of archaeopetrography—produces false results that are off by centuries. We can safely ignore his dating claims now that a real-life test of his technique has proved him wrong.

However, Wolter challenged my evaluation of his results shortly after this episode aired. In a posting on my website, he wrote:

> In your haste to try and discredit me, you are getting careless. If you had listened carefully you would have heard me say the weathering of the Brandenburg Stone COULD pre-date Columbus. In the next sentence, I said because the provenance of the artifact was unknown, and therefore the weathering environment it was exposed to is unknown, we cannot say how old the inscription is. You obviously thought you heard something different, but I invite you suffer through the episode one more time to check the facts.

Therefore, in the interest of scrupulous accuracy, I transcribe below Wolter's discussion of the Brandenburg Stone, proffered in three separate segments of the episode:

Wolter

This is the first time I've ever looked at this stone. These are limestones, probably oolitic limestone. If you look very closely, you'll see what looks like little sand grains. They're actually sand of limestone, and they're called oolites. When I look down into the grooves, I can see some of those ooids, so that's an indication of weathering. Based on everything I've seen, we're not lookin' at a hoax here. Does anybody know what this inscription says? [Discussion of the content of the "Welsh" message.] This could actually call into question the whole legitimacy of the United States!

[commercial break followed by recapitulation of previous segment]

Wolter (V.O.)

I examined this clue and saw evidence of weathering that takes (emphasis) a long time. But now, I need to see where it came from, a place called Paradise Bottom.

[Wolter travels to Paradise Bottom to match the type of rock, not its weathering pattern, and the segment shows him examining rocks. He interviews a man at the quarry who asserts that the Welsh arrived in the sixth century CE, and that the stone may be from this period.]

Wolter (on phone)

I've had a chance to look at the Brandenburg Stone, and it's very interesting. It does show some evidence of weathering.

[commercial break]

Wolter (V.O.)

My analysis of the stone's weathering suggests it could have been carved before 1492, but there is no way to get a more precise date because it was taken out of its original environment, and its provenance isn't clear.

I hope you can see how I concluded that Wolter thought the stone was carved before 1492. First, he concluded that the stone was not "a hoax" (therefore genuinely ancient). Second, he spoke with an "expert" who claimed that the Welsh occupation of America occurred in the 500s CE, which Wolter does not contradict. Third, he repeats that the weathering took a long time, emphasizing the word *long*. Finally, he states that the rock "could have been carved before 1492," with the conjunction "but" used to link that thought to the second, that there was no way to "more precise." The use of the term "more precise" implies that it refers to "before 1492" as the antecedent, so any more precise date would be before 1492. Therefore, I had no choice but to conclude from the grammar of the sentence that Wolter believed that 1492 was the *terminus ante quem* for the stone's carving. The fact that the only other date offered for it was in the sixth century CE seemed to establish a *terminus post quem*, meaning that until the final segment of the show, the stone's proposed date was sometime between c. 550 CE and 1492. This is why we do not do science by television. It requires more than a single sentence to convey the full range of possibility and all the qualifications needed in presenting a conclusion.

As we know, the stone was actually carved much, much later. It is written in Coelbren y Beirdd, a hoax Welsh alphabet created in Wales in 1791 by Edward Williams (Iolo Morganwg), but not widely popularized outside of scholarly circles in Wales until years later when his son Taliesin began publishing his father's works in 1826. The alphabet was widely published in the 1830s and 1840s, and whoever forged the Brandenburg Stone (it was not actually either Williams, who were never in Kentucky) almost certainly used such publications, possibly Taliesin Williams's widely-read book about the alphabet, in forging the stone. The younger Williams's popular book was published to scholarly acclaim in 1840 (having won a prestigious prize two years before) and the alphabet was exposed as a hoax in 1893 (though suspicions had been raised earlier, until Taliesin successfully combated them), which makes it *much* more likely that the stone was actually carved between 1840 and 1912, though a date as early as 1792 cannot be excluded. In the United States, libraries had dozens of different volumes on Coelbren y Beirdd, including the *Iolo Manuscripts* (1848), *Bardaas* (1862 and 1874), etc., but I am not able to find evidence that the alphabet itself would have been widely available in rural America prior to Taliesin's book. However, it is possible that some of Edward's specialist publications imported from Britain were available in some places.

After 1862, the largest collection of the Williams forgeries was in print and the alphabet was at the height of its popularity. Thus, the latter nineteenth or early twentieth century seems the best candidate for the time of forgery. *America Unearthed* is a bit deceptive on this point in an attempt to make the stone seem as old as possible. Given this, even if we accept everything Wolter claims as true, he still can't tell the difference between a stone that was carved a scant century ago and one that is 200, 500, or 1500 years old.

After the Brandenburg Stone, we also hear that the Mandan tribe of Native Americans was Welsh, a claim resuscitated by the painter George Catlin in 1832 but one that the Victorians had debunked. A thorough review of the linguistics of the Mandan tribe finds no connection to Welsh but rather to other Native languages, specifically Siouan. No DNA studies have ever found a European connection. Their bull boats, supposedly identical to Welsh coracles, are not unique to the Mandan and are the result of the technical limitations of building skin boats in the absence of wood. But did you know that the Mandan still exist and number among the six thousand people now considered the Three Affiliated Tribes (the Mandan, Hidatsa and Arikara)? (Technically, the last full-blooded Mandan died in 1971, and those living today have ancestors from two or more of the affiliated tribes.) They're living in North Dakota right now, but we don't hear from them on *America Unearthed*; instead, we see nothing but a single, romantic painting of a Mandan by none other than George Catlin. Perhaps they have a valuable point of view about whether their culture is nothing but the corrupt castoff of Welsh colonists? If they do, *America Unearthed* doesn't want you to know.

Wolter engages in some conspiracy-mongering, eventually tying Lewis's supposed murder to his status as a Freemason, and he raises no objection when the Masons he interviews explain to him that the Masons only originated in their modern form in the 1700s—a direct contradiction of Wolter's assertion that Masons descend directly from the Knights Templar. Wolter wants to test blood stains found on Lewis's Masonic apron at the time of his death, but I don't see how the blood could possibly explain whether Meriwether Lewis was murdered. If the blood is his, it could be due to either suicide or murder, and if it is not his, it implies nothing since there is (a) no claim that the shooter was injured and (b) there is no way to know when the blood was deposited on the apron. I also don't want to be indelicate here, but the "family member" used for comparison after two centuries might not actually be a direct descendant of Meriwether Lewis. For example, infidelity, adoption, etc. can contaminate the bloodlines. A positive match can prove a connection, but no match is not negative evidence due to the aforementioned complications of human relationships. Worse, no precautions are taken during collection of the sample, and contamination is not just possible but likely.

An interesting vignette occurs at the end of the episode when Shelby explains to Wolter how his geology has failed in the face of the fact that the Brandenburg Stone is an obvious hoax, and that the claim of medieval Welsh Indians was in all likelihood invented to help Britain establish a prior claim to America to supersede Spain's fifteenth-century claims. Wolter, instead of defending his science, instead turns toward the Masonic apron and the murder-mystery, all but abandoning his entire thesis about Welsh colonization in the hope of distracting viewers from his complete and total failure as an "archaeopetrographer," on which he stakes his reputation and makes his living. What a crock.

Wolter is very excited that DNA testing reveals that Lewis's Masonic apron has two sources of blood, and Wolter believes that the blood was that of one or more murderers because Masons keep their aprons clean and therefore the blood must have been deposited on the night of his death. Of course, it's been two hundred years; it could have found its way there at any time, including during the handling of his body and effects after his death, or through contamination from Wolter's own skin or fluids during collection of the sample. Even the DNA specialist was hesitant to describe the sample as anything more than suggestive.

Wolter suggests that Lewis was killed to cover up a Welsh land claim from the Middle Ages. His evidence for the cover up? A "presidential mandate" to find Welsh Indians that doesn't exist and a "Welsh" land claim stone that is a hoax. The truth? Lewis's own expedition wrote more than once about the Welsh Indians, and its members made no secret about their speculation that the Flatheads, Mandans, or others might be they. The story of Welsh Indians was printed far and wide in newspapers and newsletters, and it was widely repeated for decades afterward. For example, in 1843, a British subject, Sir W. Stewart, published an account of discovering "Welsh" Indians in the Rocky Mountains, and England made no objection to Mexican control of them (eventually ceded to the United States in 1848) based on this "Welsh" land claim. In 1876, the governor of the state of New York, Morgan Lewis, published an influential book advocating the discovery of America by the Welsh in 1170. Again, England raised no objections despite this endorsement by an American official.

Any conspiracy that sought to assassinate Lewis to "cover up" the fact did a terrible job, since both Ordway and Whitehouse lived on with the knowledge and the incriminating documentary evidence, and by 1830 Andrew Jackson was using the possibility of pre-Columbian white colonization as part of the U.S. government's official policy of removing Native Americans from the eastern United States, the same U.S. government Wolter thinks was engaged in assassination to cover up the "true" history of prehistoric white Americans. All of this caused me to wonder if he had spent even a single moment reading about the actual ideas and opinions of the dead people for whom he claims to speak?

EPISODE TEN

The Desert Cross

Airdate: February 22, 2013

Episode Summary

Scott Wolter investigates a cache of lead artifacts found near Tucson, Arizona in the 1920s. He concludes that these artifacts were created by a precursor organization to the Knights Templar, exiled to America following the Muslim invasion of eighth-century Europe. He concludes that Templars and Freemasons hide this secret in a conspiracy reaching to the Exxon oil company.

Historical Background

Archaeologist Marc A. Beherec has argued that in "The Mound," one of horror writer H. P. Lovecraft's tales ghostwritten for Zealia Bishop, Lovecraft alluded to the 1924 discovery of alleged artifacts in Arizona proving the existence of a lost medieval Jewish-Roman colony in Arizona called Calalus.[1] While the tale tells of a prehistoric civilization hidden beneath a mound in Oklahoma, there isn't anything about "Roman" Arizona in "The Mound," and the only reference to Arizona is an unsourced quotation from H. R. Wakefield's "He Cometh and He Passeth By" (1928). I suppose one could read the whole story as a reference to a "lost" civilization in the West, but there were plenty of claimants to that title. Anyway, the Lovecraft claims come into play because in this episode Scott Wolter travels to Arizona to complete "microscopic" analysis of some of the lead artifacts dug up in 1924 and now known as the Tucson Artifacts, the Silverbell Artifacts, or simply the lead crosses. Wolter claims that under the microscope he found mineral deposits consistent with deposition in the desert sands for a thousand years or so. Mainstream scholars who have examined the finds have unanimously declared them fake on historical, archaeological, and linguistic grounds.

The story of the artifacts can be summarized in a few words. In 1924, Charles E. Manier and his family claimed to have discovered a cache of thirty-one lead artifacts, primarily swords, crosses, and spears, on Silverbell Road seven miles from Tucson that supposedly chronicled in Latin and Hebrew the history of a medieval European colony called Calalus, founded around 775 CE when Jews and Romans somehow landed in the Americas. No other evidence of occupation—no pottery shards, no buildings, no bodies—was ever found, even though the artifacts claimed that the colony lasted for a century or more. The cache contains dates down to around 1000 CE and conveniently supports Mormon claims about Jewish migrations to medieval America. Despite some initial support from Arizona State Museum archaeologists, as more investigations occurred, scholars increasingly recognized the lead artifacts as a hoax.

One key to recognizing the hoax was the very poor quality of the inscriptions, which were plagiarized from earlier authors, written with terrible grammar, and contained anachronisms. The very poor Latin on one lead cross reads, in translation:

> We were carried (or sailed) by sea to [error for "from"] Rome Calalus ["to Calalus" probably intended, but the case is wrong], an unknown land. They came in the Year of Our Lord 775, and Theodorus ruled of [error for "over"] the people.

The Anno Domini dating system was not widely used before 800 and is not well attested outside the Carolingian heartland until around 1000. Most medieval inscriptions also tended to abbreviate rather than write out the Latin. Worse, the specific phrases used to construct the bad Latin have been traced by Frank Fowler and others to standard Classical Latin texts available at the Tucson Public Library when the artifacts were found. In the journal of the *New England Antiquities Research Association*—an alternative history publication and hardly a skeptical source!—Marshall Payn, an engineer and a believer in some alternative history, explained that thirty-four (!) specific Latin phrases appearing on the crosses could be traced to a widely-used 1881 Latin primer, *Latin Grammar* by Albert Harkness.[2] Scott Wolter is familiar with the NEARA. The group commissioned him to examine a rune-bestrewn rock in Massachusetts in August of 2003, and Wolter has spoken at NEARA conferences. Their publications therefore cannot be a surprise to him and should have been available in researching these claims.

Consider the coincidence of the following sentence appearing word-for-word in both the Harkness book and on one of the lead artifacts:

Catilina in prima acie versari, omnia providere, multum ipse pugnare, saepe hostum ferire.

(Catiline was active in the front line, he attended to everything, fought much in person, and often smote down the enemy.)[3]

Harkness took the sentence from Sallust's *Conspiracy of Catiline* (60.4), a Classical text from c. 50 BCE of some repute, but one which it would have been nearly impossible for a functionally illiterate medieval scribe to have quoted verbatim out of context. Studies of plagiarism have determined that after six identical words the probability of accidental duplication approaches zero. Even in a language more limited in vocabulary than English, the chances of thirteen identical words reproduced in a row—including the proper name!—are vanishingly small. Having it happen thirty-four times boggles the mind.

The most zealous advocate of the artifacts' authenticity is Cyclone Covey, a former history professor at Wake Forest University, who wrote a book called *Calalus* (1975) about the "lost" Jewish colony he intuited must have existed based on these artifacts. (Covey also believes that Egyptians came to prehistoric America, among others.) That said, when Covey was shown the Latin plagiarism, he had no response. He simply ignored it, at least down to 2004, when he deigned to comment. That's when Covey argued that the bad Latin is actually a sign that the artifacts are genuine rather than a hoax since a modern copyist wouldn't make so many errors. Covey, for example, wrote that the errors indicated a Latin novice: "Confusing *ad* and *ex* by a novice in Latin compares with present-day speakers in English who reverse *ante* and *post, terminus ad quem* and *terminus a pro,* induction and deduction. We have all heard such solecisms."[4] No, it's really not. It's like confusing "to" and "from," which is what *ad* and *ex* mean in Classical Latin, Vulgar Latin, and the Romance languages.

In 775 CE, the supposed immigrants from Rome would have by definition needed to be fluent in *sermo vulgaris* or *rustica lingua romantica,* Vulgar Latin, the common tongue from which the Romance languages developed. No matter where in Covey's proposed mix of Romans, Britons, and Gauls the immigrants came, they would have needed a basic understanding of prepositions to communicate. Romans obviously spoke Latin. The Britons, I can only imagine, had to communicate somehow with the Romans and Gauls, and I doubt the Romans spoke Old English. Since Old French did not develop until around 800, Vulgar Latin would have been the preferred language for the former residents of Gaul. Now, you might argue they spoke Gaulish, but that language went extinct under the Empire, and Old Low Frankish, a Germanic tongue, was associated with Franks (Germans), not Gauls. That said, we know that in 772 CE Boniface complained that he could not understand the pope's Latin, and in 813 CE the Council of Tours ordered priests to preach in vernacular because common people could not understand Latin. This did not extend to basic prepositions, however, which remained (with gradual modifications through time) part of Vulgar Latin, Old French, and modern French.

Oh, and more importantly: There is not a single archaeological trace of a colony of Europeans anywhere in Arizona. No trash middens with European artifacts, no foundations of European-style structures, no graves with European artifacts. Nothing.

Perhaps most humorously, the artifacts tell a remarkably complete story that specifies that the Jewish-Roman people who came to Arizona recognized the Natives ruling all Mexico and the southwest as *Toltezus,* i.e. "the Toltec," obviously derived from the Nahuatl word Toltecatl, which gives us the modern name for the Toltec people. The word derives from the Aztec (Nahuatl) formation of the words meaning "inhabitant" (catl) of Tollan, the Toltec capital. While "Toltec" is what the Aztec called the people of Tollan, we do not know what the Toltec called themselves, though they were Nahuatl speakers. The Toltec flourished from 800 to 1000 CE, but perhaps tellingly the "Toltez" term is attested as a modern (mis)spelling of Toltec, which I was able to find dating back, though infrequently, to 1910, when Toltec Gorge in neighboring New Mexico was thus misspelled by the Delta Sigma Delta dental fraternity. At any rate, the "z" is very rare for Latin; it was used only for transliterated Greek words in Classical Latin and to represent the sound of "di" as in *diaconus* or an initial "i"—sounds that were on their way to becoming the medieval "j." According to Isidore of Seville, by the mid-600s, "z" had replaced "di" throughout Italy[5]—but not the letter "c," as on the lead cross. Since the lead artifacts aspire to formal Classical Latin, my guess is that the forger could have misread an italicized "c" in Toltec, such as appears in William Prescott's *Mexico* (1900) or in Latinized scientific uses of "toltecus" as species descriptors, in which in an italic serif typeface a "c" can look like a "z.")

So how do we get the Toltec to Arizona? The answer, for Cyclone Covey and other supporters, lies at sites like Wupatki, one of the ancestral Pueblo (Anasazi) ruins. Both of these sites feature evidence that Mexican peoples influenced, traded with, or immigrated to this area of Arizona. The Hohokam territory extended deep into northern Mexico. Nevertheless, while Mexican features appear at Snaketown (including luxury trade goods and platform mounds after 800 CE), it does not amount to what Covey describes as "Toltec domination of Snaketown" in the eighth century. The Hohokam could be Mexican all on their own, and they were incorporating and localizing broader Mexican cultural traits. Wupatki's "Toltec" connection derives primarily from the fact that it has the northernmost example of Mesoamerican ball courts (also found among the Maya and most Mexican peoples), a feature Wupatki shares with (and probably borrowed from) the Hohokam.

Now, to tie this all together with a bow, let's briefly consider the Hopi,

Zuni, and Navajo legends about the ruins of Wupatki. The Hopi believe that the people who lived and died in the ruins continue to haunt the site as spiritual guardians. This story of the spirit guardians perfectly parallels H. P. Lovecraft's "The Mound," in which the ghostly forms of long-dead residents of a lost civilization patrol the titular edifice. This would have been a great way to tie together all these threads, except that Zealia Bishop actually suggested that much of the plot from a romantic imagination and a love of conventional ghost stories, and the titular mound itself was based on real mounds (and a natural hill) that actually exist in and around Binger, Oklahoma and had nothing to do with the Toltec.

As for the Arizona artifacts themselves, the evidence is fairly straightforward. Covey argued that the rocky substance in which the artifacts were found covered, called caliche, a precipitate of calcium carbonate, takes centuries to form so the artifacts must be genuine. But Payn reported that a mining geologist, the late James J. Quinlan of Tucson (1924-2001), formerly of the U.S. Geological Survey, examined the site where the artifacts were uncovered to determine how fast the caliche formed. Quinlan first identified the strata in which the objects were found. He and a team consisting of a paleontologist and an archaeologist determined that the stratum was Pleistocene, dating back between ten thousand and two million years. Therefore, the objects could not have been naturally deposited and slowly covered over by gradual accretion of soils since no one was speaking Latin ten thousand years ago.

Payn takes up the story from here, noting that the objects were found at the site of a modern kiln in use at the time of the objects' discovery:

> Quinlan showed me two rock samples. The first he hacked out of the site's caliche. It was encrusted and very hard (caliche varies from that which crumbles at the touch to that which resists a pick-axe). The second he made. He bought some quick-lime (the product made at the kiln) from a hardware store and mixed it with sandy soil, small rocks and water. He then inserted into this concoction a piece of lead and allowed it to set for a day or so. The resulting rock was quite similar to the first rock and I could not extract the piece from his newly formed "caliche."[6]

Since the caliche could be recreated in just hours, and the objects were found embedded in million-year-old rocks that long predated Latin, the only conclusion geology could reach is that the objects were purposely embedded into the rock using quick lime.

This information was available to Cyclone Covey, who ignored it. It was also available to Scott Wolter—a geologist who worked with the NEARA!—who purposely omitted it, or else is so incompetent at his own job that he is completely unaware of it. With this information, I think it's fair to say that the Tucson Artifacts are unequivocally fake, but nevertheless Wolter devoted an hour to rehabilitating the hoax. Why? Because of the Jesus-Templar myth.

The Episode

This episode didn't play fair, and it ended up outright lying, even about its own lies, in pursuit of what I can only describe as a hidden agenda, one designed around Wolter's apparent fixation on a Templar-Freemason conspiracy around the Bloodline of Christ. (Yes, it's the *Da Vinci Code* plot, as made explicit in Episode Eleven.) Did you know there really was a hidden culture of ancient Jews in the American Southwest? It's true. They were not, however, the Mormon master race who first peopled America, nor the alleged Judeo-Roman hybrids of the Calalus literature. Instead, they were a group of *conversos*, Jews who converted to Christianity under the threat of expulsion from Spain but maintained Judaism in secret, under a veneer of Catholicism. Known as the crypto-Jews, a group left Spain for the New World, eventually settling in New Mexico, where they kept a vigil on Friday nights (the Jewish Sabbath) and abstained from eating pork. For five centuries these Latino crypto-Jews retained Judaic practices, and a few remaining crypto-Jews still do down to the present day, though many have lost most other traces of their ancestors' Judaism.[7]

This would have made an excellent episode of *America Unearthed*, looking for a real example of a "lost" culture that could be reconstructed only from the scant traces it left behind in the later practices of its successors. Its origins certainly predate the Roanoke colony that was the subject of Episode Seven, so it ought to fall under the show's purview. But, sadly, that's not what we got. Instead, we're treated to another "investigation" of how a group of supposed lost white colonizers blazed a trail across America, left behind nothing except some highly dubious luxury goods, and vanished in large measure due to cultural contamination from the uncouth savages with whom they practiced miscegenation. (See also: Roanoke colony, Minnesota Vikings, Welsh Indians, Oklahoma Celts, New England Phoenicians, etc.) I don't think anyone involved with this show is actually racist, but it's hard to believe they could be blind to the clear implication of nearly *every* episode that advanced white culture inevitably succumbs to the savagery and sensuality of surrounding dark-skinned primitives. Heck, in this episode Wolter even blames swarthy Mideast Muslims for "forcing" the pure white people out of Europe! Does he even know the artifacts state that these Templar superheroes were Gauls and Romans, with Jewish names and Hebrew writing? It's hard to ignore the fact that this narrative has attracted such a large following in this particular time in United States history, as a particular demographic of white Americans is experiencing anxiety about the country's multicultural future, when, in short measure, white Americans will become a plurality rather than an outright majority for the first time since the colonial era.

The episode opens in Tucson with a recreation of events from 1924, when a cache of "artifacts" was unearthed. This scene is oddly filmed from the artifacts' point of view, with unnamed men uncovering, moving, recovering, and staring at them in sepia-toned video, concluding with Scott Wolter opening a box in 2012 in his Minnesota lab and looking dramatically into the box, which could not possibly be the actual box from Arizona despite the implication since the artifacts are safely housed at the Arizona Historical Society. Then we cut to the opening credits. The show proper starts with a long tracking shot of the Arizona desert over which a graphic informs us that ritual objects and a lead cross were unearthed in 1924 on which was the date 800 A.D. Here is the first omission: Another cross is actually dated 775 CE (and other artifacts still earlier), but that doesn't conform to the narrative. The program uses a meaningless graphic saying, in scare quotes, that Christopher Columbus "discovered" American in 1492, implying this is a lie. Well, yes, it's a lie in that the Vikings were in North America in 1000 and the Native Americans "discovered" America some 15,000 or more years ago. This does not, however, have any relationship to whether Romans were in Arizona in 800 CE. (I will be using the modern dating terminology of BCE and CE to talk about dates and the older A.D. system when speaking of the date on the cross itself.)

Scott Wolter is bringing his son Grant with him to view the artifacts inscribed in very poor Latin, and Wolter calls this an "important" group of evidence—of what, I wonder? At the Arizona Historical Society, Wolter reviews some paperwork and photographs documenting the unearthing of various lead artifacts found by Charles Manier and Thomas Bent, and he meets with Chuck Bent, Thomas Bent's grandson. Chuck suggests that there was a secret surrounding the artifacts and says that they were kept hidden in his grandfather's house. Chuck says that Thomas doubted the explanation offered by "these academics" (as Wolter scoffs) that the crudely-formed swords were faked and planted in the ground as a hoax. Wolter is indignant that academics weren't "all over" the artifacts, which bear no resemblance whatsoever to any medieval weaponry or symbolic ritual artifacts. They look like what they are: crude modern approximations of medieval material.

I suppose it goes without saying—not that Wolter would say it—that lead, being one of the heaviest elements, produces swords that weigh far too much for everyday use, nor is it common to find ritual artifacts made of lead in Europe. I'm not able to find any discussion of the use of lead for making ritual objects, swords, and military standards, which were almost always made of gold, silver, bronze, or iron. According to standard encyclopedias, medieval lead was used for cast objects (which the swords were not), small decorative badges for pilgrims (which these were not), and far after our period cast reliefs and coffins (which these were not). I can't find anything about swords. Wolter once again asserts that historians are unwilling to "rewrite history" to account for Wolter's own discoveries.

So, Wolter and Bent travel out to the site where the artifacts were dug up to look at the rocks from which they were extracted. He hopes that the caliche (hardened rock formed of calcium carbonate) will match traces on the artifacts and thus prove the rocks dripped calcium carbonate over the artifacts for a long time, which is not as clear an indication of age as Wolter suggests. The rate of caliche formation is largely dependent on the amount of water present, which can cause it to form in mere months or years rather than centuries, and the presence of plants other than cacti at the site suggests enough water to have a fairly quick-forming process. Many people have seen their drainpipes fill up with caliche in short order and would not be surprised by this, and as we have seen, geological work conducted at the site in 1996 determined that the stratum in which the artifacts were found was ten thousand or more years old. Wolter is silent on this geological fact, nor does he mention that quick lime produces instant caliche and was in abundance at the kiln next to where the artifacts were found.

At the Arizona Historical Society, we see the various lead artifacts, and we see some very quick looks at the inscriptions on the crosses. No Hebrew inscriptions are shown, only the Latin ones. Why is that? We never find out. Wolter is smart enough to realize that the A.D. dating system on the crosses might not have been used in 800 CE but tables the discussion for later. Grant Wolter "translates" the text on the cross, but while he seems to have a general notion of Latin, he seems to be reciting someone else's translation because—as discussed—the Latin is atrocious and requires a good understanding of Latin to figure out its intended meaning. Ignoring the problems with the Latin, the two Wolters simply agree that it describes a voyage to America, omitting who made this voyage or what they did when they got here. This is a lie by omission.

It bothers me that Scott Wolter does not discuss the content of the inscriptions on the artifacts, probably because the story they tell of the century-long adventures of Jews, Romans, and Toltecs is so stupid and fails to support his Bloodline of Christ *Da Vinci Code* Templar fantasy, expounded in Episode Eleven. Wolter leaves all this out because it would imply the existence of a colony for which no buildings, no trash middens, no artifacts of any kind remain. This is intentionally deceptive and leaves out an important factor in considering how to evaluate these artifacts. Worse, by leaving out the Jews it only reinforces the idea that this show is obsessed with finding Christian Caucasians in America. The entire connection to ancient Mexico (the Toltec) is also left out, the defining narrative of the artifacts. This is another unforgivable lie by omission and one understandable only in the context of trying to hide anything testable. There are no Toltec artifacts in Tucson either.

Scott Wolter seizes upon the appearance of the name Theodorus on the cross to jump to the conclusion that this was the same Theodorus who was allegedly Charlemagne's lieutenant in the 770s. I am not able to find any reference to a Theodorus among the entourage of Charlemagne; the closest I could find was a Theodorus of the Huns who visited Charlemagne in the 780s, or Theodulf of Orleans, an ally of the Frankish king's in the 790s. A Theodoric (not Theodorus) was a commander under Charlemagne, but continued on past 775. In fact, I can't find any reference to this Theodorus outside "alternative history" discussions of the Arizona artifacts themselves. When Wolter claims that "some" say Theodorus came to America in 775 CE, he is actually quoting another of the Arizona lead crosses (the one I translated above on page 130), one which he had declined to feature on the show because its wretched Latin is so obviously a fake. He's quoting *the artifacts themselves* as evidence *for the artifacts!*

One artifact has a dinosaur drawn on it. A dinosaur. This bothers even Wolter, and we will return to it anon.

Wolter looks at the artifacts under a 3-D microscope, which he claims will help him to use "archaeopetrography" (his self-created "new" science) to date the crosses. That went so well with the Brandenburg Stone. At any rate, petrography of course refers to rocks, and the crosses are made of lead, so the crystallization of the minerals on the rock is what will pass for stone. Wolter notes that the deposition of the minerals on the crosses could take as little as decades but perhaps centuries. He fails, however, to consider the amount of water at the site where these were unearthed or the presence of quicklime, thus meaning that his findings are speculative and have no real value since we can't know how fast caliche was forming in the place where they were deposited without knowing about the water table, capillary action, rainfall, etc. Needless to say, he ignores the possibility that quicklime could produce the same results, and he never thinks to check the age of the strata in which the artifacts were embedded—strata that exclude the possibility that they are genuine, if the scientific team that investigated in 1996 is right.

Wolter becomes very excited after discovering an image of the Cross of Lorraine on one artifact, the symbol of the Knights Templar. This cross, also called the Patriarchal Cross, looks like a standard Latin cross with a smaller crossbar near the top representing the plaque nailed to Christ's cross at the crucifixion. Do I even need to say that the Knights Templar weren't formed until the 1100s? If they hadn't decided to dig for the Ark of the Covenant on the Temple Mount, no one would have cared at all about them at all. Nevertheless, Wolter says that the same symbol represented the dragonfly to Native Americans so both groups "shared" it. There's a connection all right, but only in the sense that Hitler, the Hopi, and Helena Blavatsky "shared" the swastika. Similar symbols do not imply cultural connections. The Cross of Lorraine on the artifact appears to be surmounted by a stereotypical crown, with large, rounded drapery between supporting arches—a style of crown not used until the modern period. Medieval crowns were bands of gold or helmets. (It might be an episcopal crown.) Another artifact shows what appears to be a "church" complete with a Gothic arch, an arch not used until the High Middle Ages.

Next up we go looking for the source of the artifacts' lead, but this is a wild goose chase. It makes no difference to the story whether the artifacts were made from local or non-local lead; any result Wolter would interpret as evidence of "Romans." If it is local, the Romans were mining; it not, they brought it from home. A careful shot of the crossed X's in the Exxon Mobil logo is meant to imply a modern connection to the Templars via the Cross of Lorraine.

Wolter calls up a friend, Canadian author William F. Mann, identified as a "Masonic historian." He's actually a Freemason and Templar conspiracy theory author who is not a trained historian; instead, he is a landscape architect by trade. Mann published a book claiming Thomas Jefferson was in a Freemasonic conspiracy to hide ancient knowledge that would unite all world religions, one that claimed Lewis and Clark were secretly tasked with finding the Templar Jesus Bloodline treasure (but we know they *really* sought Welsh Indians!), and a third claiming that Henry Sinclair, whom we will meet again in upcoming episodes, brought the Holy Grail—the Bloodline of Jesus and Mary Magdalene—to America in 1398 with a clandestine contingent of Knights Templar who had a secret base in Nova Scotia—the one Wolter will explore in the season finale, Episode Thirteen. But *America Unearthed* isn't ready to reveal its end game this early. It's still setting up the final Templar revelation, so all of this goes unmentioned.

Wolter and Mann launch into a weird conspiracy theory about how the Knights Templar gave rise to the Freemasons, but this is rampant speculation with no basis in fact whatsoever, as we saw in my historical background to Episode Eight. There is no evidence of any Templar activity from the fourteenth century to the rise of Masonry three hundred years later. This idea's inclusion here is out-and-out conspiracy-mongering. Wolter thinks that the artifacts display "Masonic" symbols, part of a 1,500-year-long cult. But both Wolter and Mann are more interested in the Exxon Mobile logo! Mann, as a so-called "expert," explains that the red and white logo represents the Templars' red and white colors; the crossed X's are the Cross of Lorraine, and the blue bar under the logo is the Atlantic Ocean, across which the Templars sailed to establish their secret club hideouts.

In the real world, we know that the colors come from the fact that Exxon (and Mobil) were once part of Standard Oil, whose colors were the American red, white, and blue. The crossed X's were put in place to symbolize reliability, according to Exxon. The X's weren't added until 1966 (when the current Exxon name was adopted), and an actual document exists showing the many draft versions of artist Raymond Loewy, from which the one with crossed X's was finally chosen. Among the logos are a few that look something like the Masonic square and compass, as Wolter immediately notes. Even if Loewy did this on purpose, the entire corporate executive suite would have to be in on it, or else oblivious to it. There is no conspiracy here, much less any truth to Wolter's claim that it is "accepted as fact" that Freemasons are Knights Templar. There is no continuity whatsoever in this. But what difference does any of this make to crosses from 800 CE?

As we barrel toward a conclusion, Wolter tests the caliche and finds that the caliche matches the limestone surrounding the artifacts. No fooling. As I noted before, he failed to check for groundwater, capillary action, rainfall, and other factors that influence rate of deposit, and he failed to examine the quicklime evidence from the nearby kiln. Instead, he simply declares that there is no evidence of hoaxing, which is not the case. Since Wolter failed to examine the Latin on the crosses, or to even tell viewers about the story told by the artifacts—much less its clear evidence of hoaxing—the only one hoaxing anyone is the fakery the show is pulling on the audience by lying through omission to turn what was originally a hoax about a Roman-Jewish colony in America into a Templar fantasy.

Wolter entrusts his son Grant to determine whether the Anno Domini dating system was used in 800 CE. "It does work because they were using A.D.," Grant says, and that's the last word. No one even bothers to check to see how and when the system was adapted gradually and incompletely across medieval Europe. As a point of fact, "Romans" from Rome (as the Latin on the artifacts state—not that you'd know from this show) did not adopt the A.D. system until much later, after 1000. Under the medieval popes, they used the *ab urbe condita* (A.U.C.) system in combination with the reigns of the popes, even despite Charlemagne's only partly successful attempts to impose A.D. in Germany. At any rate, in 775 it would be even less likely than in 800 to have an A.D. date.

We return to the bad drawing of a stereotypical early twentieth century image of an Apatosaurus (brontosaurus) or diplodocus, and Wolter declares that the forked tongue makes it a lizard. No lizard looks like this, with a humped back, tapering tale, and long neck, and the drawing is, to my artistic eye, quite obviously a modern forgery made by someone with as little knowledge of biology as he or she had of Latin. I would like to counter the assertion that this is a lizard by offering up the fact that many people of the early twentieth century believed dinosaurs had forked tongues and therefore would have faked a dinosaur drawing in just such a way. First, let's remember that dinosaurs were thought in those days to be giant lizards, which would have shared reptilian characteristics with lizards, including forked tongues. Second, paleontologists hadn't yet clearly separated the various types of large lizard-like creatures into true dinosaurs, large sea creatures, pterosaurs, etc., so all of these long-necked, long-tailed monsters were seen as closely related. But let's not take my word for it. In 1917, Charles Hazelius Sternberg, the amateur paleontologist, wrote a book about hunting for dinosaur bones in western Canada. Discussing *Gorgosaurus libratus*, a type of tyrannosaur, he wrote: "Fierce indeed must he have looked, when he slunk up on his prey, his eyes flashing cruelty, with glistening teeth also, and forked tongue."[8]

Victorian depictions of dinosaurs reveal the same forked tongue on a range of dinosaur images, and these would have been just like those a forger would have come across. Now for the *pièce de résistance*: In the July 1911 edition of the *American Review of Reviews*, reproducing earlier engravings, we see two reconstructions of the diplodocus, a long-necked dinosaur discovered in 1877. There is an almost exact match to the diplodocus on the Tucson Artifacts. One of the reconstructions features the same long neck and humped back, while the other offers the long neck culminating in a protruding tongue![9] It is entirely possible that the Arizona drawing was meant as a really poor representation of an indigenous lizard like the *teiidae*, the fringe-toed lizards, brush lizards, or some such. But none of them match the picture half so well as the early twentieth century reconstructions of diplodocus and brontosaurus (know called Apatosaurus), especially give the prominent hump on the back, long neck, and thick feet. Since a forked tongue is no bar to fakery, I feel comfortable concluding this drawing was badly copied from one very much like the *Review* illustrations.

But I'm not only one to think this. Here are the words of A. E. Douglass, the Arizona State Museum archaeologist who reviewed the find in 1925: "The distinctive mark on the sword was a representation of a long necked, long tailed, four-legged animal resembling in a striking way restorations of the Diplodocus."[10] Interestingly, Douglass had in his papers an early pamphlet on prehistory called "The First Story Ever Told," and that pamphlet contained a near-identical drawing of a diplodocus.

But none of this is of interest to Scott Wolter. Instead, Wolter concludes that a "precursor" to the Knights Templar came to America as religious refugees—a precursor organization for which not a lick of evidence exists in Europe. Wolter reminds us again about his work on the Kensington Rune Stone, which the show simply presents as settled fact despite the widespread criticism of his geology, and this somehow "proves" that Wolter is right about the "precursor" group, which makes no sense since accepting the Rune Stone implies nothing about anything that happened prior to 1362. Even Chuck Bent seems confused that Wolter concluded the artifacts were genuine when Wolter comes to tell him, probably because he knows what the Latin inscriptions say and is dumbfounded that Wolter hasn't paid any attention to that in crafting his Templar fantasy. The heavy editing of the scene makes it hard to judge just what Bent was really thinking. The critical questions he asked suggest that he was less certain than the show makes him seem about accepting Wolter's verdict.

"Who were these people, who made the artifacts, and where did they come from?" Wolter asks. Well, the artifacts actually *say* (their version, anyway), but since you didn't bother to *read*, you don't know. They say that a group of Romans, Gauls, and Jews came over and interacted with the Toltecs. Wolter is purposely hiding this information in order to preserve the mystery, create false connections to the Knights Templar, and avoid the real problems with the inscriptions, not least of which is the completely absent "colony" of Calalus that the artifacts assert actually existed. Instead, Wolter wants us to believe that "some Muslim group" "persecuted" the "precursors" of the Knights Templar—a story completely contradicted by the artifacts he created this story to support! I thought this was simply an incongruous reference to the Islamic conquests of the seventh and eighth centuries CE. But in researching Vinland for more background on the Viking occupation of Newfoundland, I came across an interesting reference in Sir Daniel Wilson's 1892 essay "The Vinland of the Northmen" that I think sheds some important light on this throwaway line and the thought process behind it. The results are surprising and somewhat disturbing. Wilson wrote:

> Another tale comes down to us from the time of the Caliph Walid, and the invincible Musa, of the "Seven Islands" whither the Christians of Gothic Spain fled under the guidance of their seven bishops, when, in the eighth century, the peninsula passed under the yoke of the victorious Saracens.[11]

Although he does not give a reference, I was able to track down a fuller version of the story. In most accounts it is not Seven Islands but rather an Island of Seven Cities, better known as Antillia. One version is recorded on Martin Behaim's 1492 Nuremberg globe:

> In the year 734 after the birth of Christ, when all Spain was overrun by the miscreants of Africa, this Island of Antillia, called also the Isle of the Seven Cities, was peopled by the Archbishop of Porto with six other bishops, and certain companions, male and female, who fled from Spain with their cattle and property. In the year 1414 a Spanish ship approached very near this Island.[12]

Johannes Ruysch tells the same story on his 1507 map, in nearly the same words, adding that the people spoke "the Hispanic language" when they were first contacted but had since vanished. Scholars believe such stories were modeled on the *Navigatio* of Saint Brendan. The story is further retold by Antonio de Herrara in the 1601-1615 *Décadas*, in which the Island was home to the Portuguese

> at the Time when Spain was overrun by the Moors in the Reign of King Roderick, for that seven Bishops, flying from that Persecution, embark'd with a great Number of People, and arriv'd in that Island, where each of them built his Town, and to the end the People might not think of returning, they set fire to the Ships.[13]

It appears in several other places as well, with slightly different details.

The story of "pure" Christians escaping the infidel rather than submit is almost certainly mythical, akin to the Sleeping King myth and more generally the Returning Hero motif of folklore, for these "lost" people were believed in medieval times to be perpetually on the verge of returning to rescue Spain from the Muslim yoke. This is very similar to the British myth of King Arthur and his knights asleep on the far-distant Isle of Avalon until England should have need of them again. Nevertheless, in time Antillia became identified with America. By 1729, Gregorio Garcia could assert in the *Origen de los Indios* that the eighth-century "Spanish" had fled Moorish Spain and settled in Mexico—tying in with the then-popular belief that the Toltecs and/or Aztecs were the descendants of a lost race of "white" Europeans.

The Islamic writer and traveler al-Idrisi of Sicily was rumored to have recorded a variant of the legend, at least according to alternative history writers like David Childress. This Idrisi claimed to have sailed as far as the Canary and Madeira islands and to have recorded all the lands of the world on a silver globe made for King Roger II of Sicily. The globe was soon lost, and a single Arabic description of it remained, translated into Latin in 1691. Here, Idrisi locates among a confused report of the Canaries and Azores an additional island, Sahelia, which he describes as having "three cities of equal size, much peopled, the inhabitants of which were now all slain by civil wars."[14] This island was almost certainly one of the Canaries, but it was roped in to support the Spanish story of the Seven Cities despite significant differences, not least of which was the fact that Sahelia maintained constant nautical contact with the mainland, while the Seven Cities cherished isolation.

Now here is where things get interesting. Holy Bloodline writers make much hay of the fact that St. James the Just, often called the brother of Jesus in the Bible,[15] was particularly revered in Spain. Catholics do not recognize Mary as having given birth to any other children (the perpetual virgin), so Bloodline writers think this means that any group venerating

James must therefore be aware of secret holy bloodlines and the "true" history of Jesus and his kids. It is an article of faith among later Bloodline writers, especially Laurence Gardner, that James the Just was actually Joseph of Arimathea, and thus since James was believed to have traveled to and lived in Spain, Joseph must have brought the Holy Grail and the Holy Bloodline there with him. (As far as I know, the claim does not appear in the cult's *ur*-text, *The Holy Blood and the Holy Grail*.) Gardner, of course, also believed Jesus was descended from gold-hoarding, bloodthirsty extraterrestrials bent on world domination, an alien other derived from Zecharia Sitchin's *Twelfth Planet* aliens from Nibiru, themselves unconsciously repurposed by that Jewish author from anti-Semitic stereotypes.

If any of this be true (and it is not), then it follows that when the Arabs conquered Spain, the bishops who departed to found a colony in the mysterious lands to the west had to have been in on the secret and traveled to America to preserve the truth about Mary Magdalene's and Jesus' descendants.

What I thought was simply a throwaway line on *America Unearthed* turns out to be much more likely an expression of a conspiratorial mindset that sees all of European history entwined with the Jesus Bloodline—and part and parcel of Scott Wolter's master narrative, one that governs his approach to history. I honestly thought it was just an offhand reference to medieval history, but in light of these revelations, it looks more and more like Wolter was referencing the deeper levels of the Jesus Bloodline conspiracy he apparently believes in so strongly. Now we see why he wanted to dump the story of the Romans, Gauls, and Jews told on the supposedly eighth-century Tucson Artifacts in favor of a proto-Templar group unattested in the inscriptions on any of those hoaxed lead crosses and weapons. It all ties together with a hubristic faith in a hidden history where America plays a starring role as the refuge of God's elect. An episode that seems so silly on the surface unintentionally reveals the whole game plan of the series.

Tracking the Templars

Airdate: March 2, 2013

Episode Summary

Scott Wolter reviews his research into the "hooked X," a character found on the Kensington Rune Stone, and concludes that this symbol represents the penis of Jesus, the uterus of Mary Magdalene, and the fetus implanted within. He argues that the Holy Grail is the secret bloodline of Jesus and Mary Magdalene and that the Knights Templar protected that secret.

Historical Background

When this episode aired in March 2013, it had been almost exactly ten years since Dan Brown sparked a new interest in the mythology of the Holy Grail with his *Da Vinci Code*. In it, Brown weaved a badly-written conspiracy thriller in which a globetrotting hero in a made-up field of study (symbology) put together a series of ambiguous clues to reveal that the Holy Grail was actually an esoteric symbol for the bloodline launched when Jesus Christ married Mary Magdalene and had a secret child with her. In "Tracking the Templars," another globetrotting protagonist, show host Scott Wolter, who also operates in a self-created field of study (archaeopetrography), follows the same clues and also goes in quest of the fruits of Mary Magdalene's womb.

However, the Holy Grail originally had nothing whatsoever to do with Christ. In fact, it does not date back far enough to do so. The first appearance of the Holy Grail is in the *Perceval* of Chrétien de Troyes, written around 1190 CE. There, a "golden serving dish" descends before Perceval in the castle of the Fisher King, but Chrétien does not call it holy or call any more attention to it than to an equally sacred lance. A century later, Wolfram von Eschenbach made the Grail into a stone in his poem *Parzival*, guarded by *Templeisen*, the unfortunately-named "temple soldiers" or Templars, who occupied the Grail's sacred temple. Robert de Boron told a different tale in the twelfth century, that Joseph of Arimathea had received the Holy Chalice that caught Christ's blood and spirited it away to Great Britain and founded a line of knights to guard this sacred vessel. The stories of the Holy Chalice and the magical Grail merged, and suddenly a myth arose that a line of sacred knights guarded the magical cup of Christ called the Holy Grail. Medieval people understood Robert's poem to be courtly fiction, not a report of actual fact.

The name Holy Grail derives from Old French for Holy Cup, *san graal* or *sangreal*, derived via Latin from the Greek *krater*, or drinking-vessel. Medieval writers, discussing how the Holy Cup held Christ's royal blood (since he was of the royal line of David), played on a pun, writing *san greal* as *sang real*, or Holy Blood. Thus, mystically, the Royal Blood and Holy Grail were one and the same, the cup standing for the divine blood it contained. This is very much in keeping with medieval religious symbolism, and most scholars accept that the magical powers of the holy cup derive from a mixture of Christian symbolism, particularly that of the newly-instituted ritual of communion, and Celtic (more broadly, Indo-European) myths of the immortality bestowed by magic cauldrons.[1] Many appear in Celtic lore, though I am more familiar with the cognate cauldron used by the Greek witch-queen Medea to restore the hero Jason (or his father Aeson) to youth, another version of the same Indo-European magic cup myth. (The story also is the origin of the witch's cauldron of fairy tales and Shakespeare.)

The trouble is that modern speculators are not content with the idea that medieval people had mystical or religious symbolism that wasn't tied to facts on the ground. Beginning in the Romantic Era, writers began to see a parallel between the storied Knights Templar and the Grail Knights, part of the increasing respect afforded the pageantry and drama of the

Middle Ages in that era. The Knights Templar, officially the Poor Fellow-Soldiers of Christ and of the Temple of Solomon, existed from about 1119 to 1312. They were a practical military order based at the Temple Mount in Jerusalem during the Crusades. Involved in banking, they became very wealthy, leading the French king and a compliant pope to accuse them of idol worship and heresy in 1307 in order to suppress the order and gain their money. They were never famed in their own time for any particular religious piety beyond that of any other crusading group. Since then, writers have tried to imagine a less mundane reason than money for their demise. Often, this effort descended into wild claims about alternative religions, derived from the original accusation of the heretical worship of a demon-idol named Baphomet, an Old French corruption of the Islamic prophet Muhammad.

To this whiff of Islamic apostasy Richard Price added in his 1824 preface to the *History of English Poetry* that the Grail myth was influenced by "esoteric doctrines" brought from the heathen East,[2] though he accused no specific group; but this was simply part of the standard anti-Catholicism of the era, which saw the Catholic Church as too influenced by ritual and ceremony. Price specifically accused the early "Romish Church" of perpetuating the doctrines and rites of the "heathen temple."[3]

The first connection between the Templars and the Freemasons came from the Enlightenment-era German critic Gottfried Lessing in the 1770s. He was a Freemason and read backward into the Grail Romances the Masonic tradition, on the authority of the Scottish Freemasons, who had adopted the Templars as honorary predecessors as part of their fabricated mythic past. As I noted previously, in the background to Episode Eight, in 1737, Freemason Andrew Michael Ramsay gave a speech in Paris claiming that the Knights of St. John gave rise to the Masons, in symbolic association, derived from his belief in the One True Religion of which all pagan cults were decadent aspects: "Our Order [was] founded in remote antiquity, and renewed in the Holy Land by our ancestors in order to recall the memory of the most sublime truths among the pleasures of society." This became confused with the Templars after the speech was adopted into Masonic lore, probably because after 1314 the pope had allowed the ex-Templars to join the Knights of St. John, also called the Hospitallers. By the 1820s, anti-Masonic activists were using the confused Templar connection to paint the Masons as a revival of the idol worshipping pagan Templars. The Austrian Joseph von Hammer-Purgstall specifically claimed that the Masons revived the Templar heresy, the worship of the idol Baphomet, and that Templar images of Baphomet's head were cast in the form of a Greek *krater*, the very origin of the blasphemous Holy Grail. He also implied that the Grail Knights were Templars.[4]

Claude Charles Fauriel, in 1832, was the next to seriously argue that the Knights Templar (named for the Temple Mount in Jerusalem) were the Grail Knights when he described the Grail as preserved in a temple in the Pyrenees, from which the Knights took their name: "Titurel [the Grail King] instituted for his defense and his guard a militia, a special Order of Chivalry, which is called the Knighthood of the Temple, whose members are called Templiens or Templars. ... I have already hinted, and I can say here explicitly, in this religious Grail guard is an obvious allusion to the Order of the Templars."[5] He had no evidence other than a shared chivalry between the groups and the fact that one Grail romance described the knights as *templien* (French) or *Templeisen* (German), or "temple-guardians," not Templars as in the Knights of Solomon's Temple. But Fauriel was proposing a *literary* theory—that the Grail Romances symbolized the Templars—not a *historical* theory that they encoded an actual Holy Grail. Later scholars, such as Alfred Trübner Nutt, agreed that the Grail stories were intended as *political* documents, designed to provide a mythic history for the Angevin Kings of France, thus paralleling the Knights Templar; mainstream scholars, however, never thought the Templars had an actual magic cup, or anything else that actually belonged to Christ.

The development of this idea is chiefly the work of the mid-Victorian French scholar E. Aroux, who believed that the Holy Grail must have been the secret doctrine of the Templars, an alternative Gospel, for which they were condemned for heresy. A German named Dr. Simrock—a mythologist prone to seeing ancient connections in every similarity of symbol—took up the story, reporting the work of his Austrian predecessor:

> Baron von Hammer-Purgestall, who gives the most detail on the connection of the Templars with the Holy Grail, by tracing its history from the identity of hieroglyphs which he found on the old churches and buildings in the Danubian Provinces. He unfortunately is for ever trying to find the most unsavoury interpretation for all the ancient symbolism; with his views we are not concerned, but to the work of research which he carried on with such ability we are profoundly indebted.[6]

By 1900, the idea that the Holy Grail story had *symbolically* represented the Knights Templar had become a given, and one that became associated with anti-Masonism and Theosophy, that strange Victorian cult that mixed Eastern mysticism, Western occultism, and a belief that earth life was governed by aliens from other planets. The Theosophical writer Isabel Cooper-Oakley produced a book called *Traces of a Hidden Tradition in Masonry and Medieval Mysticism* (1900) that forever linked the Grail, the Templars, and the Freemasons in service of the alien-worshipping Theosophists, who believed the Templars were privy to extraterrestrial secrets imparted by the Ascended Masters from other planets. She, in turn, was again drawing on Simrock, who divined (without proof) a secret order that had preserved Templar secrets from the fourteenth to eighteenth centuries.

And that's about where things stood for most of the twentieth century. There was no evidence of any Grail-Templar-Freemason connection outside of some disconnected symbolism, some anti-Catholic assumptions, and a confusion between the Templars—suppressed because the French king wanted their money—and the Cathars, who believed in dualism and flourished around the time of the Templars, though no evidence links the groups. The Cathars provided the final pillar of this theory, the worship of the "sacred feminine." That weird concept derives from works like those of the Freemason and Rosicrucian Hargrave Jennings, who believed all religion was penis-worship, and Otto Augustus Wall, whose influential book *Sex and Sex Worship* (1919) claimed that all religion was the worship of sex organs, particularly the penis. The triangle, circle, or lozenge, due to their resemblance to the female pubic region, was in Wall's view symbolic of the woman and thus the feminine counterpart to the true object of universal veneration, his—er, *the*—penis. It would, however, be modern writers who introduced Wall's sex-worship theory into the Grail mythos.

The pseudo-archaeologist Graham Hancock, in *The Sign and the Seal* (1992), thought that the varied descriptions of the Grail as a vessel and as a stone suggested that it was a symbol of the Ark of the Covenant, a vessel containing the stones inscribed with the Ten Commandments. In this reading, the Grail Knights were of course the Knights Templar, who had conducted secret digs on Jerusalem's Temple Mount in search of the Ark. Never mind that the Knights Templar were not British, as Robert de Boron insisted that the Grail Knight must be. But Hancock was merely piggybacking on the success of an earlier book, *The Holy Blood and the Holy Grail* (1982) by Michael Baigent, Richard Leigh, and Henry Lincoln. It is impossible to summarize this influential and ridiculous book in a few words, but its central thesis is that in 1099 a secret society called the Priory of Sion formed to guard the "Holy Grail," which was the bloodline of Mary Magdalene and Jesus, currently represented by the dethroned Merovingian royal house of France. The Priory created the Knights Templar and continues working today to reestablish Merovingian rule over all Europe, following the anti-Semitic *Protocols of the Elders of Zion*, which the authors believe was not a hoax but the Priory's master-plan. It was this book that tied together Theosophy's Masonic conspiracy, Wall's "sacred feminine" sex worship, and Fauriel's literary view of the Templar-Grail connection— all theories for which there was little direct evidence. Compounding speculation upon speculation did not strengthen the results.

The Priory of Sion was a hoax created in 1956 by a delusional French draftsman named Pierre Plantard who fabricated its entire history to support his false claim to be the last descendant of Christ and the rightful universal monarch of the world prophesied by Nostradamus. Despite the exposure of the hoax, Laurence Gardner, the late genealogist to the self-proclaimed pretender to the Stuart royal line in Britain,[7] wrote a book called *Bloodline of the Holy Grail* (1996) recapitulating all of this and ascribing the Christian bloodline to his patron, the Stuart pretender. He then wrote a follow-up called *Genesis of the Grail Kings* (2002) where he explained that the secret society guarding the grail originated with Zechariah Sitchin's aliens from Nibiru, and their alien-hybrid human descendants maintained immortality by consuming refined white gold and human menstrual blood.

In 2000, Andrew Sinclair and Timothy Wallace-Murphy connected the imaginary Bloodline of Christ to Rosslyn Chapel, the Sinclair (St. Clair) family chapel in Roslin, Scotland. They believed the chapel had been built as a model of Solomon's Temple in Jerusalem (even though the ground plans do not match in any way) and that the chapel contained Templar and Masonic symbolism, a claim denied by both experts in the Templars and the Masons themselves. (Some Masonic symbols were added later, and others are actual mason's marks used by stonemasons in building the chapel.) In this reading, the Norman-Scottish Sinclair family was in fact the Scottish branch of Jesus Bloodline, guarded by the Templars, who after their disbanding became Freemasons. (They did not, of course, as mentioned above. Freemasonry did not erupt for more than four hundred years after the end of the Templars, too long for any real connection.) Then, to tie it up with a bow, the faker Pierre Plantard once went by the fake name Saint-Clair.

Dan Brown then canonized the entire story by using elements of all these modern versions in *The Da Vinci Code* (2003). Thus was the modern idea of a Grail-Templar-Freemason-Bloodline myth born from the accidental asides of a range of earlier ideas, including literary theory, anti-Catholicism, anti-Masonry, Theosophy, sex worship, New Age mysticism, and fraud. Quite the pedigree. Scott Wolter simply accepted all of these as more or less true in his book *The Hooked X* (2009), where he sees a mason's mark at Rosslyn Chapel featuring an **X** with a line through it as identical to the "hooked X," an otherwise unattested rune found on the Kensington Rune Stone. They are not morphologically the same, as I discussed in the introduction to this book.

The Episode

We start the episode in New England in 1984 with a giant boulder called the Narragansett Rune Stone with "fourteenth century" carvings that the show asserts contained a "hooked X," a symbol used by "only one group at that time," the Knights Templar. The boulder was stolen, so there is nothing to look at it. Instead, we get mood shots of an airport, where Scott Wolter takes a phone call from Paul Roberti in a quite obviously staged discussion of the stolen stone. "I've got to handle this right now!" Wolter shouts, as though he had authority to do anything. The stone was actually stolen sometime in the early summer of 2012, and Wolter commented on the affair in August of 2012,[8] but the airport scene, filmed in the autumn—as shown by the colors on the trees and Wolter's heavy clothes—pretends it just happened and he just learned of the theft. "This stone is one of the very few artifacts that *proves* the Templars came to America," Wolter asserts. It does not. There is no evidence that the Templars ever used a hooked X, and Wolter over the course of the hour provides none. State officials recovered the stone on April 16, 2013.

As I mentioned in the introduction, in 2009 the History Channel—and Wolter—had a documentary called *The Holy Grail in America* which already covered this material. As I described before, the entirety of Wolter's claim for the "hooked X" derives from its appearance on the Kensington Rune Stone, before which it is unattested in any medieval literature. It exists in only six places on earth—five in America and, as mentioned above, once in a very different form at Rosslyn Chapel in Scotland—not enough to draw any conclusions. Other American rocks featuring this same symbol only appeared *after* the discovery of the Rune Stone, suggesting that the inscriptions were copied from the Rune Stone by recent hoaxers. No museum specimen or ancient text from prior to the 1890s features this "mysterious" symbol despite Wolter's attempt to tie it to European symbols of differing shapes. The "hooked X" at Rosslyn chapel differs in two key respects from the one on the Rune Stone: Its crossbar (the hook) appears on *both sides* of the upper right stave of the X, not on just one; and the lower two staves are connected with a small "V," forming a lozenge-shape not found on the Rune Stone "hooked X." It is quite obviously a mason's mark, very similar to other mason's marks of various shapes found on *every* medieval stone building. It isn't special, or sacred.

There is an inscription with the "hooked X" on the Narragansett rock, but it is therefore almost certainly a modern hoax. Yet in this episode, Wolter suggests that the Narragansett stone was stolen due to its occult connection to the Templars. This is not, however, what he told Chris Church of the *Independent* the previous August: "Wolter suggested the boulder was removed by a neighbor who was tired of people coming to the neighborhood to search for the stone."[9] It's interesting that his ideas changed upon filming the episode. Therefore, Wolter and Roberti commiserate about the loss of the stone, and Wolter repeats information provided just minutes ago about his study of the Kensington Rune Stone. Wolter describes the Rune Stone as reporting a "land acquisition journey" in 1362, though he does not explain why the Templars, an order disbanded in 1312 and largely composed of a core of French knights, would be writing fifty years later in Scandinavian runes. Nor can he explain how he sees a connection between the Knights Templar in 1312 and Rosslyn Chapel almost 150 years later—without leaving a single "hooked X" of any kind in any other record before or between the two dates.

Wolter next drafts Christopher Columbus into his conspiracy, arguing that Columbus used the "Templar Cross" (a standard red cross used by many European orders), signed his name with a "hooked X," and married into the Sinclair (St. Clair) family. Columbus's monogram signature is written in a combination of Greek and Latin characters, XPOFERENS, using the Greek Chi-Rho, standing for Christ, followed by an "o" and the Latin gerund *ferens*, meaning "bearing," referencing the etymology of his name, Christopher, the Christ-bearer. It does use a small, rounded "hook" atop the stroke forming the lower-left to upper-right line of the X (actually the Greek Chi), but it also has one in the lower left as well, and on the lower left leg of the "M" and the top right leg of the "Y," which Wolter thinks has no special significance. It is obviously a handwriting tic, almost certainly due to the constraints of writing with a quill and needing to have the ink flow smoothly. Innumerable writers of the period made similar marks when writing with quill and ink on parchment. Oh, and as for the claim that Columbus married into the Sinclair family? That's hot air, too. His wife, Filipa Moniz Perestrelo, had a brother who married the aunt of Tistao vaz Teixeira, the first husband of Catarina vas de Lordelo, whose *second* husband was the grandson of Henry Sinclair. Even Maury Povich and Jerry Springer wouldn't see a close family connection there.

In reviewing Templar history, Wolter claims that the Templars fled Europe to practice their religion and to "protect" a secret—the Holy Grail —which, of course, is the fictional bloodline of Christ that I discussed above. Confusing ancestors and descendants in his spoken remarks, Wolter seems to think that Jesus's kids gave rise to the Templar hierarchy (a departure from the *Holy Blood* claims about the bloodline being the Merovingian kings). Wolter then discusses the "symbols" of males (Λ) and females (V) derived from the Victorian sex-worship theorists, and he chooses to revise the Holy Trinity to represent the family of Christ: Jesus, Mary Magdalene, and their kid ... Boots? Esmeralda? Scott? Thus, the small bar on the "hooked X" is the baby in Mary's V-shaped womb above Jesus' Λ-shaped penis. The entire symbol (X) is, for Wolter, the very act of holy penetration and impregnation, sex made stone. That would be news for the Norsemen most alternative believers claim carved the Kensington Rune Stone. I'm also unsure how the French Knights Templar, fleeing France, decided to start speaking Old Swedish, the language of the Kensington Rune Stone.

The "proof" of this theory, according to Wolter, is a sculpture made in the 1500s in which Mary Magdalene appears in bulging, flowing robes. This Wolter and Roberti interpret as evidence of Mary's pregnancy. I am not quite sure I understand, though, how the statue connects to the Templars that Wolter had just asserted fled from Europe to America two centuries earlier, on Saturday, October 14, 1307. Who was left to carry on the Templar heresy in Europe and become Freemasons if all those not condemned to death went to America?

Wolter's next piece of "evidence" is a "dot code" on the Kensington

Rune Stone that supposedly indicates which special runes to read to find the word "Grail," or *gral* in Swedish (so he says), though that form of the word is actually German, from the French *graal* or *greal*. In fact, the word *gral* is not found at all in any genuine Old Swedish document.

One of the marked runes is the hooked X itself. There has been a great deal of controversy over whether these dots were intentional, and I have no particular interest in litigating this dispute. I am not sure how Wolter can translate the hooked X as the letter A if there are no other examples of a hooked X to know what letter it is meant to represent, but most who have viewed the Rune Stone are content that the rune was meant as an A. Wolter uses 3-D microscopic analysis to determine that the marks are genuine, but his former colleague Richard Nielsen,[10] who accused Wolter of dishonesty, has also conducted microscopic analysis and found that, when accepting Wolter's standard for what constitutes a punch mark (i.e., a "dot") two other runes feature the same dot in between those representing the G and the R, forming the nonsense word GTERAL, not GRAL, and ruining the Grail code.[11] At the very least, the evidence is much more ambiguous than Wolter claims.

As we cross the halfway point in the episode, Wolter suggests that a purported first-century CE ossuary (burial box) featuring the name of Jesus was (a) really that of Christ and (b) concealing a hooked X as a sacred symbol of Wolter's imaginary trinity. This "Lost Tomb of Jesus" was the subject of a 2007 documentary of that name, promoted by Canadian filmmaker Simcha Jacobovici, who claimed that because two ossuaries marked "Jesus" and "Mary" contained remains whose DNA proved were unrelated, they were therefore a married couple, the Jesus and Mary Magdalene of the *Da Vinci Code* conspiracy. A forensic archaeologist who Jacobovici initially claimed confirmed the marriage of the two denied he did any such thing, noting DNA cannot test for marriage. Additionally, the archaeologist who first excavated the Talpiot Tomb in 1980 confirmed that the "Jesus ossuary" was not found in the tomb when it was opened but had been added into the tomb at a later date, backed up by site reports that failed to record any evidence of the Jesus ossuary in 1980. By most scientific accounts, the Jesus ossuary was a fake, with a new inscription added to a genuinely old ossuary. But even if it were there, Jesus and Mary were two of the most popular names of the era, making the chances of these boxes belonging to the Biblical figures vanishingly small.

But that is the real world. In the fictional conspiracy world of *America Unearthed* Jerry Lutgen, whose only credential seems to be that he runs a website about the Talpiot Tomb, claims that the odds are 175:1 in favor of this being Jesus' tomb, a number derived from several assumptions about the statistical prevalence of certain Biblical names and the uncritical acceptance that the Jesus bone box is legitimate, something most archaeologists do not accept because of significant problems with it. In the real world, scholars know that the name Jesus (Yeshua), when not referring to the Jesus of Christian fame, appears in almost one hundred different records, including twenty-two ossuaries, while Mary (Mariamne) appears seventy times, including on forty-two known ossuaries.

Wolter is happy to accept Lutgen's figures and claims as true, and he points to one of the marks on the so-called Jesus ossuary, a very loose X with a curve (not a hook) at the end of the lower right stave, as an "early" hooked X. I don't see it myself; it looks like a random curve, certainly not an intentional crossbar. Wolter seems to have started from a conclusion and is working backward to pick out evidence.

Then we see something so profoundly stupid that it made me laugh: Wolter asserts that a Templar coin from c. 1200 contains an image of the front door to the Talpiot Tomb because the geometric shape surmounting the man on the coin's face, probably meant as headgear, has a triangle with a circle in the center, which he thinks looks like the triangular pediment of the Talpiot Tomb with its circular medallion set beneath. He also asserts that the face on the coin is that of Jesus himself. As soon as the episode aired, Simcha Jacobovici immediately concurred that this coin was the "smoking gun" connecting the Templars to the Jesus tomb.[12]

At no point does it occur to Wolter to check with a numismatist to find out what the coin actually depicts, or even to read the writing on the coin to see if it has any relevance; that would all just be part of the conspiracy anyway. Various combinations of chevrons and circles appear on several coins of the era, and on this coin by chance the chevron appears above the circle. More commonly, the chevron (or triangle) is placed between two circles, as in several well-known examples. However, it's important to understand that the Knights Templar were not recognized as sovereign and therefore did not have the power to mint coins. The specific coin that Wolter identifies as Templar is actually clearly labeled "JOHANNES REX" (King John) and was minted by John of Brienne during the Frankish occupation of Damietta in 1219. John had been titular King of Jerusalem by marriage since 1210, but actual control of the city had been permanently lost to the Muslims by the treaty signed with Saladin in 1192.

The first Latin king of Jerusalem wore no crown because he considered it inappropriate to wear a golden tiara where Jesus had worn but thorns. His successors, however, were under no such compunction. The headgear we see John (or Jesus in his stead, following Byzantine coin conventions) wearing on the coin is almost certainly a Byzantine-style crown, which featured a conical or round gold helmet with long golden chains (pendilia) dripping down both sides, dangling over the ears.[13] Such helmet-style crowns were common in the East, but differed from the open-style crowns of the West. Other Crusaders, like Guy de Lusignan, used the same style on their coins.[14] The Byzantines themselves were in exile at Nicaea, and the Crusaders in charge of Constantinople, but a comparison of John's headgear to that of the contemporary Greek emperor at Nicaea, Theodore I Komnenos Laskaris, finds an almost perfect duplication of John's tiara, complete with the prominent round center jewel and jeweled gold tassels dangling on either side of his bearded face. In fact, this crown had been depicted on Byzantine coins and murals for nearly five hundred years, including in images of the emperor at the time of the First Crusade, Alexius I Komnenos, and was familiar to the Crusaders. The only real difference is that the Byzantine imperial crown was rounder than John's, possibly due to the heavy stylization on John's coin. It is perhaps no surprise that within a few years King John would become emperor-regent at

Constantinople in full Byzantine-style pomp.

The only connection between John of Brienne and the Knights Templar is that the Templars (along with the Hospitallers) served under him during his 1210 trip to Acre. But even this was not his doing. Pope Innocent III paid for their services on the recommendation of King Philip Augustus of France and arranged for them to support the then-Count John of Brienne so he could go to Acre and marry the seventeen-year-old Queen Mary of Jerusalem—which is how he got to be King John in the first place. Dedicated to the Temple Mount in Jerusalem and to ridding the Holy Land of Muslims, the Templars fought under King John to reclaim the Kingdom of Jerusalem. When King Philip Augustus's French forces returned home from Acre, King John had no one left but the Templars and the Hospitallers, which prompted him eventually to return to Europe to seek more soldiers. Sadly, the queen died, prompting a succession crisis when John continued to call himself king while the Holy Roman Emperor insisted that the claim passed to him. What follows is beyond our scope except to say there was no room for a conspiracy here since the alleged conspirators were at each other's throats.

Ignoring or ignorant of all this, Wolter next asserts that his proof that the Templars became Freemasons was the hooked X, which is circular logic since he earlier asserted that the Templar-Freemason connection was what led him to his understanding of the hooked X. Oh, well. It doesn't matter because the Rosslyn Chapel "hooked X" isn't one, and the Knights Templar didn't speak Old Swedish.

Wolter also claims a connection to a "hooked X" appearing on the Copiale Cipher, an alleged Masonic document. It is believed to be either a coded set of German Masonic ritual instructions or a pseudo-Masonic document created in the 1740s by a group of Catholics after the pope banned Catholics from becoming Masons. The "hooked X" again differs from the Rune Stone version in having a crossbar *through* the right upper stave, and a *circle* attached to the left upper stave. Bookbinder Joe Rose tells Wolter that he is very excited about the symbol and its secrets. "It's like an eighteenth-century James Bond movie!" Wolter enthuses.

And just because we're not far enough down the rabbit hole, we have to look at Nicolas Poussin's *Shepherds in Arcadia*, the infamous painting supposedly offering a connection to the Priory of Sion and the Holy Grail. (It illustrates a moment from Pliny's *Natural History* when the first artist sees his shadow and thus discovers the art of painting by tracing it.[15]) As I mentioned above, the Priory of Sion is a modern hoax. We see a stone carving of the painting in Britain known as the Shugborough Relief, but nothing much comes of this other than some speculation about hidden codes. We hear that some mysterious letters carved on the stone version can be read as a code indicating 2,810 miles (English, presumably) between the relief and Oak Island, the site skeptic Joe Nickell identified as a Freemasons' initiation center and Wolter will claim in Episode Thirteen was a resting place of the Holy Grail. The Shugborough Relief dates only from the mid-eighteenth century and is therefore far too late to have anything to do with the Bloodline of Christ that would have left Europe five hundred years earlier; and even if the relief were a Freemasonic code (which it is not), it falls within the historic period of Freemason activities and therefore does not imply anything about the missing centuries between 1312 and the eighteenth century.

Wolter leaves us with a cliffhanger: He promises to travel next to the Newport Tower! But at this point in the series, Wolter's true purpose becomes obvious: *America Unearthed* thinks of itself as a miniseries building toward a *Da Vinci Code* climax, and Wolter sees himself as making a case for a deeply-held, near-religious belief that he will find the Holy Grail. It really gives new meaning to the term "cult archaeology."

America's Oldest Secret

Airdate: March 9, 2013

Episode Summary

Scott Wolter investigates the ruins of a round stone structure in Newport, Rhode Island. Based on astronomical alignments and architectural similarities, he concludes that the so-called Newport Tower was built as a church by the Knights Templar in the 1300s.

Historical Background

The Old Stone Mill in Newport, Rhode Island, better known to aficionados of the occult as the Newport Tower, is more famous as a ruin than it ever was as a working building. A nearly-circular tower supported on eight not-quite equal arches, the ruins of the tower sit in a park in Newport, where they failed to much excite anyone's attention from the time of the building's construction down to 1839, when the first "alternative" theories about it emerged. The known facts about the Newport Tower can be summarized rather simply.

The first record of the tower comes in the will of Gov. Benedict Arnold, colonial governor of Rhode Island in the mid-seventeenth century, just four decades after the settlement of Rhode Island, previously inhabited by Native Americans. On December 24, 1677, he described it in his will as marking the place where he wished to be buried, on a "parcel of ground containing three rod square being of & lying in my land in or near the line or path from my dwelling house leading to my stone built wind mill in ye town of Newport above mentioned." He died the next spring, on June 19.

His will remained public record (escaping British destruction of Newport's records in 1779) and was widely consulted by antiquarians down the centuries. Arnold left the mill to his daughter, Freelove Arnold Pelham, along with warehouses, a mansion, and a farm. Freelove tried to bequeath the land to her children, but her brother successfully sued for control in 1730, arguing that a woman was not allowed to decide how to dispose of real estate under English law.[1] At no time did anyone mention, describe, or refer to the stone windmill as anything else, and neither child of Arnold expressed the least doubt that the mill had been built by their father. It continued to be described as a windmill throughout the eighteenth century in colonial and early Republican documents, including a 1776 map of Newport.

In 1836, a magazine called *Penny Magazine* from Britain included an illustration of the Chesterton Windmill, a 1632 stone-built windmill in Chesterton, England (still extant today), that is remarkably similar to the Newport Tower in size, shape, and design. It was located close to where some of the colonists at Newport had once lived in England, including George Lawton. This Lawton lived less than twenty miles from the Chesterton mill before coming to the colony, where he became the go-to man for designing windmills. In fact, tower-shaped windmills had increased markedly in popularity in England between the thirteenth and seventeenth centuries; when the colonists came to Rhode Island in the years after 1638, it only made sense that their mill would take the form of the latest (and therefore best) in English style.

Between the 1630s and the 1730s, no one doubted that the Newport Tower was exactly what everyone could see it was: A functioning windmill. Things began to change when it fell into disrepair, possibly due to damage from being used as a powder magazine. Left as a ruin, it sparked the romantic interest of local residents, who saw in it an analog to the romantic stone ruins of Europe, then a popular subject in engravings and paintings. America, having few ruins of its own, had to make do with what it had; in at least one painting, the Tower featured in a romantic pastoral scene, serving the same purpose as a castle keep in European art.

Nevertheless, down to 1838, no one batted an eye at the idea that this building—which had been functional in living memory—was a windmill. As late as 1834, for example, the *American Magazine*—which modeled itself on and borrowed from the *Penny Magazine*—still described this building as a "wind-mill, an old stone tower on the top of the hill."[2] This is especially surprising, for had it truly been a pre-Columbian, Continental European church, as later claimed, it would have been a great piece of propaganda during the Revolution, a symbol tying the new United States to its greatest ally, France—the very home of the Knights Templar—and cutting at Britain's legal and moral right to sovereignty. And yet the Freemasons in the new American government—those supposed heirs to the Templars—said nothing about it. Archaeologists have conducted several excavations around the tower (notably in 1948 and 2006-2008) and have found no artifacts predating the seventeenth century. In 1848, an analysis of the mortar found that it matched other mortars from area buildings of the 1640s. In 1984, radiocarbon testing tied the Tower to the seventeenth century.

So where did the alternative view come from?

In 1820s, the Danish antiquarian Carl Christian Rafn became convinced, based on his readings of medieval literature, that the Norse had crossed the Atlantic and that the Vinland of the Norse sagas had been a real place. This inspiration was in fact true, as the 1960 excavation of L'anse-aux-Meadows in Newfoundland would prove, but it was still a contested idea in the 1820s. To prove his case, Rafn decided to gather together every possible scrap of evidence that the Norse had been in the Americas. But he didn't know about climate change or that Newfoundland had once been warm enough to grow grapes—the *vín* or "wine" in Vinland—during what we now call the Medieval Warm Period. So he aimed too far south and assumed the Vikings had colonized what is now New England, the northernmost place known in those days to be capable of sustaining viniculture. (Historians do not know if Vinland really had grapes—explanations range from Leif Erikson making it up as a marketing tool to a transcription error substituting *vín*, or wine, for *vin*, or meadow.) To that end, he tried to assemble the best available evidence of Viking occupation in 1831 in the *Antiquitates Americanae,* a monumental book written in Latin. Some of it would turn out to be right, and a lot of it would be wrong; among the wrong material were ambiguous petroglyphs (like the Dighton Rock) he thought were Norse runes, based on reports provided to him by Thomas H. Webb, M.D. of New England.

Americans devoured the book and went looking for more "proof" of Norsemen in America. No "hooked X" rune stones were known in those days, despite every effort to find Norse runes in America. This is a pretty good indication that many of the so-called "rune stones" were fabricated much later.

Rafn's enthusiasm had gotten the better of him. He began corresponding with New England antiquarian societies for information about "Norse" artifacts. In May of 1839, Thomas H. Webb wrote again to Rafn with exciting new information. Webb, an ardent bibliophile and one of the founders of MIT's library, wondered whether the Newport Tower was not what all agreed it was—a mill—but something else. He based this on his own erroneous belief that no round windmill had ever been built of stone, and therefore a stone building of that size and shape had to be something more important. As we have seen, stone mills of this type were well known in England. Webb made a description of the Tower and asked Frederick Catherwood, the artist best known for his romantic images of the Maya ruins, to draw some images of it to send to Rafn. These images were highly romantic, and they made the Tower look much more regular and finished than the actual rough-hewn building really is. "The drawings sent may be relied upon as accurate in all essential particulars," Webb told Rafn.

From that false assertion and the romantic imagery, Rafn spun a fantastic tale, which I have excerpted at length in Appendix Two. He compared the shape of the Tower to Cistercian baptisteries, and he suggested that the arches were Romanesque and therefore medieval. Since he had never been to America, his evidence was nothing more than a superficial similarity between Catherwood's romanticized drawing of the Tower and selected elements of Northern European architecture. There was nothing more to it than that. He published his ideas in an English-language *Supplement* to the *Antiquitates Americanae* in 1839. Henry Wadsworth Longfellow was impressed, including the Norse origin of the Tower in the "Skeleton in Armor." Articles and books for and against the Norse hypothesis proliferated in the late nineteenth century, with historians often expressing bafflement at the diffusionists who insisted that a windmill was a church or a lookout tower. In 1942, the archaeologist Philip Ainsworth Means, working backward from the conclusion, tried to "prove" that the tower was of Norse origin, though his evidence was faulty—he did not, for example, know that stone windmills often had fireplaces, so the presence of one at Newport was no argument against its original purpose.

But in time the Norse were no longer interesting enough. Several people tried to claim that the Tower was built by the Portuguese, but on no better evidence. Gavin Menzies claimed that the Chinese built it, but his claim that the tower matched Chinese architecture of the fifteenth century held no water. Finally, Andrew Sinclair decided in 1992's *The Sword and the Grail* that the Tower must have been built by Henry Sinclair at the head of a voyage to America by medieval Scottish Knights Templar. But his evidence was nothing of the sort. The claim derives from the infamous Zeno map and narrative—a sixteenth century hoax.

In 1558, a Venetian named Nicolò Zeno published a book and an accompanying map claiming that his ancestors, Nicolò and Antonio Zeno, brothers of the naval hero Carlo Zeno, had made voyages of equal importance to Columbus, and a century earlier to boot, earning Venice a place at the pre-Columbian table and a triumph over its rival Genoa, home to Columbus.[3] The book supposedly summarizes the correspondence of the two brothers about their adventures—correspondence which was conveniently destroyed before scholars could examine it when the younger Nicolò Zeno tore the original manuscripts to pieces.[4] Oddly, the book freely mixes supposed quotations from the letters and first person narration by the later author, all cast in the same first-person voice, as though one writer took on three personalities. I have reproduced the best-known English translation of the Zeno Narrative in Appendix Three.

According to the younger Nicolò's book, one of the Zeno bothers (also called Zeni in the plural, or the Zen in the Venetian dialect), Nicolò, sailed to England in 1380 (which is true) and became stranded on an island called Frisland (which is not true), a non-existent North Atlantic island larger than Ireland. In the book, the elder Nicolò claims to have been rescued by Zichmni, a prince of Frisland. Fortunately for him, everyone he meets speaks Latin. Nicolò invites his brother Antonio to join him in Frisland, which he does for fourteen years (Nicolò dying four years in), while Zichmni attacks the fictitious islands of Bres, Talas, Broas, Iscant, Trans, Mimant, and Dambercas well as the Estlanda (Shetland) Islands and Iceland.

Later, after Nicolò had died in 1394, an expedition lost for twenty-six years arrives and reports having lived in a strange unknown land filled with ritual cannibals, whom they taught to fish. In fact, rival island groups fought a war in order to gain access to the travelers and learn the art of fishing. Worse, despite being the Arctic "they all go naked, and suffer cruelly from the cold, nor have they the sense to clothe themselves with the skins of the animals which they take in hunting."[5] Antonio Zeno is still there and joins Zichmni on a voyage to the west in search of these strange lands. They encounter a large island called Icaria, whose residents' speech Zichmni understands. Finally, they travel to Greenland, where Zichmni remains with a colony while Antonio returns to Frisland.

Nothing in this story was true. The real Nicolò Zeno (the elder) had been a military governor in Greece from 1390-1392 and was on trial in Venice in 1394 for embezzlement. He lived until at least 1402, despite having "died" in Frisland in 1394. Later attempts to verify the Zeno story with an appeal to a summary in Marco Barbaro's undated manuscript *Genealogies* also fail because Barbaro's work cannot be show to be complete before 1566 (a date Barbaro gives in his genealogy of Marco Polo), despite widely-repeated claims (originated by Cardinal Zurla in 1808 and repeated by Major) that it was written in 1536 and thus predates the 1558 publication of the Narrative.[6] Barbaro probably worked on the manuscript for many years at midcentury, but the Zeno passage cannot be firmly dated. Here is what Barbaro said:

> He wrote with his brother, Nicolò the Cavalier, the voyages of the islands under the Arctic Pole, and of those discoveries of 1390, and that by order of Zicno, King of Frisland, he went to the continent of Estotiland in North America. He dwelt fourteen years in Frisland, four with his brother Nicolò, and ten alone.[7]

The text seems closely dependent on the Zeno Narrative, but makes explicit the connection to America only implicit in Zeno. Further evidence against its age is that Barbaro explicitly describes Antonio Zeno as the discoverer of "America," a term not applied to the northern continent until 1538 when Mercator so described it. Prior to this "America" referred only to what is now Brazil. Even among those who accept the 1536 date for the majority of Barbaro's work, some believe that Nicolò the younger interpolated the reference into the manuscript, as the Barbaro and Zeno families were related. In 1536, Marco Barbaro was twenty-five and Nicolò Zeno twenty-one; even accepting the 1536 date tells us only that the Zeno family concocted the story a few years earlier.

On the surface of it, the story seems ridiculous—any survey of the Atlantic admits many of the islands are fakes (though defenders suggest Nicolò the younger misread references to Icelandic settlements as referring to islands since Iceland is called Islande)—but it was one of the most successful hoaxes in the history of exploration. The sixteenth century mapmakers Orelius and Mercator reportedly used it as a source, and Sir Martin Frobisher took it with him on his voyage to the Arctic.[8] One part of the reason for this is that the Zeni were real people, and they really did undertake voyages in the north. There was a foundation on which the younger Nicolò drew in fabricating the story. The other reason for the success is the infamous Zeno Map, also called the Zeni Map.

The map in question was drawn by the younger Nicolò, supposedly from his ancestors' now-vanished charts, and was for a long time considered the most important chart made in the 1390s, showing the North Atlantic in stunning accuracy for its day, despite the appearance of several islands that simply do not exist. Even those who denied its authenticity noted it was extremely accurate even for 1558. Of particular note is the accuracy of the shape of Greenland, better than any other fourteenth century chart. Of course, no copy of the map exists prior to its appearance in Nicolò Zeno's 1558 book. But even from the first, there were several troubling issues. For one thing, the map showed latitude and longitude, something not included on medieval maps. Some scholars dismissed these as a later interpolation. Second, the accuracy of the map varies wildly from land to land. Greenland's shape is highly accurate, while Iceland's shape is very much inaccurate. Frisland—which does not exist—has been identified with the Faroe Islands, but only at the cost of sacrificing any claim to the map's tremendous accuracy, since the two lands look nothing alike.[9]

Martin Frobisher, in exploring the Arctic in 1577 in search of the Northwest Passage, relied on the hoax map, and as a result of its mistaken latitudes—listing Greenland's south tip at 65° north latitude instead of 60°, he mistook Greenland for Frisland—twice!—in 1577 and again in 1578, and extolled how accurately the map of Frisland matched the coast he reached, which was really Greenland![10] John Davis, on his subsequent trip to the Arctic in search of the same Northwest Passage, at least recognized that the Zeno Map's Frisland did not match the coast he found, so he claimed to be the discoverer of the new island of Desolation. Sadly, it was again Greenland, which he completely misunderstood because he was using a hoax map to guide him. The island of Desolation, which never existed, was then placed on Jodocus Hondius' great chart of the world and the Molyneux Globe. The fictitious passage between Desolation and Greenland was named Frobisher's Strait, and Henry Hudson though he found it when he sailed up the east coast of Greenland at 63°, believing himself still south of Greenland proper. Also, when Spitsbergen was discovered, it was mistaken for part of Greenland for the same reasons![11]

Modern scholars, having researched the map, concluded that it is derived from a haphazard compilation of earlier charts, including Olaus Magnus' *Carta marina* (1539), printed in Venice; Cornelius Anthoniszoon's

Caerte van Oostlant (1543); and derivatives of Claudius Clavus' early map of the North (c. 1427), including Greenland, which appears nearly identical in shape and orientation on the Clavus-derived 1467 map of Nicolaus Germanus as it does on the Zeno Map. Many believe that the younger Nicolò Zeno faked the voyage of his ancestors to help give Venice a prior claim to the discovery of the New World, older than that of Genoese rival Columbus. Some still hold that Zeno merely garbled his ancestors' real-life voyage to the north, exaggerating or misreporting real events. Literary analysis, however, finds a clear dependency of the Zeno text on literary works of the period, including Olaus Magnus' *History of the Northern Peoples* (1555), from which the narrative derives its weird references to volcanoes, transposed from Olaus' Iceland to Zeno's Greenland.

The reason any of this is relevant is because this story is the only text that supports any claim that the Knights Templar came to America. As we shall see when we examine him in more detail in our next chapter, in 1379, Sir Henry Sinclair, Admiral of Scotland, was made Earl of Orkney by the King of Norway. The family lost the Orkney earldom under James III of Scotland, but picked up one in Caithness. Sir Henry Sinclair's grandson was the William Sinclair who built Rosslyn Chapel. This is important because in 1784 the debt-ridden Johann Reinhold Forster, a German from a dispossessed Scottish noble family, identified Henry Sinclair as Prince Zichmni. His claim, obviously, had an emotional pull, especially since it served to show up the German-descended royal family of England, who had brought Scotland into political union with England in 1707, not to mention England in general, the ancient enemy of Scotland who were responsible for dispossessing Forster's lordly forebears. Forster saw specific place names in the Zeno Narrative as being similar enough to place names in and around Orkney to justify identifying the fictional island of Zichmni with Orkney, and the word "Zichmni" as a corruption of "Sinclair." Here's how he explained it in a footnote:

> Though this *Friesland,* together with *Porland* and *Sorany,* appear to be countries which have been swallowed up by the sea in consequence of

earthquakes and other great revolutions in the above-mentioned element, yet I cannot help communicating in this place a conjecture, which has struck me whilst I was employed on this subject. Precisely in this same year 1379, *Hakon*, King of Norway, invested with the Orkneys, a person of the name of Henry Sinclair, who was one of the descendants in the female line from the ancient Earls of Orkney. This name of Sinclair appears to me to be expressed by the word Zichmni. The appellation of *Faira*, *North Fara*, *South Fara*, or *Fara's Land*, have probably given rise to that of *Friesland*. *Porland* must be the *Fara Islands* (the *Far-ver*, or *Farland*) and *Sorany* is the *Soderoe*, or *Soreona*; i. e. the western islands. Add to this, that the names of the *Shetland* Islands correspond with many of those conquered by Zichmni in Estland: *Bras* is indubitably *Brassa Sound*, *Talas* appears to be *Yell*, or *Zeal*, *Broas* is *Brassa*, *Iscant* is *Uuft*, *Trans* is probably *Trondra*, and still more similitudes of this kind affording yet greater foundation for these conjectures. Nay, the amazing quantity of fish that was caught yearly off the Orkneys, or, according to Zeno's account, off Friesland, and with which Flanders, Britania, England, Scotland, Norway, and Denmark were supplied, and the inhabitants of Friesland greatly enriched, relates doubtless to the herrings that are caught here every year in great abundance. *Iceland* was too powerful for *Sinclair* (or *Zichmni*) to conquer. *Nicolo Zeno* visited likewise *East Greenland*. But Estatiland and Drogio, which were discovered afterwards, appear to be some country that lies to the southward of Old Greenland. Perhaps *Newfoundland*, or *Winland*, where some Normans had settled previous to this, who likewise, in all probability, had brought with them from Europe the Latin books which were at this time in the King's library there.[12]

The nineteenth-century English translator of the Zeno narrative, Richard Henry Major, picked up Forster's suggestion and made it the centerpiece of his explanatory essay prefacing his influential translation. (In fact, the preface is five times the length of the translation, making the book rather a pseudo-historical argument with an appended translation.) He claimed that Zichmni's Porlanda must have been the Pentland Firth astride Orkney, conflated with the land by ignorant Italians (who nevertheless correctly named every other island). His claim was that the Italians had such poor handwriting that confusion over spelling yielded all the variant names in the text. He also pleaded that the Zeno narrative had been significantly rewritten by its later editor, thus accounting for the otherwise unbridgeable differences between the life of Henry Sinclair and Prince Zichmni—special pleading that also sapped away any reason to accept *any* part of the Zeno narrative as real. A more troubling problem is that the Zeno Narrative, if taken at face value, describes Zichmni's voyage to *Greenland* and founding of a colony there, not in America. Worse, the text says Zichmni stayed in Greenland.

Based on Forster's conjecture that Zichmni reached Vinland, later writers took this to mean that Henry Sinclair *must* have visited America in the 1390s (or, later, following Frederick J. Pohl's calculations, the specific date of June 2, 1398). Because in the eighteenth and nineteenth centuries Vinland was assumed to have been New England—since scholars weren't aware of climate change and did not know grapes could grow much farther north during the Medieval Warm Period—the secondary literature began referring to Henry Sinclair as having traveled to New England.

Writers like Christopher Knight—the writing partner of *America Unearthed* guest Alan Butler—claimed that Henry Sinclair was a member of the Knights Templar, an order disbanded half a century before Sinclair's birth, for reasons we shall explore in the next chapter. Worse, the Sinclair family is on record as having testified *against* the Templars at their trial in 1309, clear evidence they were not of the order. The only actual connection is that the Scotland's first Grand Master of Masons, William St. Clair, shared a name with the noble Sinclairs. He was made Grand Master in 1736, having been a Freemason for less than one year. An apocryphal history was concocted from spare parts by mythologizing Masons retroactively making the Sinclair family the "protector" of Masons since the 1440s, but this rested on nothing more than Sir David Brewster's assertion in *Lawless's History of Freemasonry* (1804) that it was so, which even in the nineteenth century was recognized to be a fabrication.

Why is any of this important?

It's important because the two strands of Henry Sinclair claims combined to produce the narrative seen in Episode Twelve: that the Templars came to New England and that they built the Newport Tower. The *only* connection between the Tower and the Templars is the fictitious voyage of Henry Sinclair, without which none of this speculation could exist. In 1992, Andrew Sinclair picked up Forster's admitted speculation, ran with it as truth, and declared the Tower to be Templar. And the entire thing started because Carl Rafn had a good idea, pursued it beyond the facts, and speculated without warrant from Catherwood's romanticized drawing about superficial similarities. And that's how we come to this episode of *America Unearthed*, which demonstrates far less understanding of the source material than the brief sketch I just provided, but is much more confident in its ignorant assessment than Webb, Rafn, or Forster ever were.

The Episode

"America's Oldest Secret" begins with a summary of last week's episode before opening with a staged scene of show host Scott Wolter dramatically peering over Gerardus Mercator's 1569 world map with a large magnifying glass intercut with shots of the Newport Tower digitally altered in postproduction with a teal filter. The camera focuses in on the word "Norombega," better known as Norumbega, a legendary settlement in New England, first recorded in the sixteenth century, but which is widely believed to be a figment of European geographical imagination, like Antillia and Brasilia. The show won't tell you this, but in 1542, French explorer Jean Allefonsce found what he described as the inhabitants of Norumbega:

> The river is more than 40 leagues wide at its entrance and retains its width some thirty or forty leagues. It is full of Islands, which stretch some ten or twelve leagues into the sea. ... Fifteen leagues within this river there is a town called Norombega, with clever inhabitants, who trade in furs of all sorts; the town folk are dressed in furs, wearing sable. ... The people use many words which sound like Latin. They worship the sun. They are tall and handsome in form. The land of Norombega lie high and is well situated.[13]

As with the case of the "Welsh" Indians, this report appears to be a case where a European explorer, unable to speak a Native tongue, heard in it what he wanted to hear, just as the Greeks misunderstood the Median word *yazona* to be a reference to their hero Jason (Iason). In fact, Norumbega, originally *Oranbega*, is an Algonquian word referring to quiet waters. Only much later, in the nineteenth century, did this geographical anomaly become tied to the Vikings, after Rafn's claims, and for the same reason: ignorance of the Medieval Warm Period led to placing Vinland far too far to the south on the assumption grapes could only grow in lower latitudes.

Oddly, Wolter ignores Norumbega altogether and never mentions it once in the episode.

After the credits, we travel to the Newport Tower in Rhode Island, which Wolter calls one of America's "biggest mysteries." He asserts that the Tower is constructed of "thousands of intricately placed stones," though this is highly deceptive since *any* stone construction of the seventeenth century also features "intricately placed stones," a prerequisite for creating a stable stone structure. He also asserts that "nobody knows who built" the Tower, "or when, or why," though as described above, this is only the case if one discounts the entire historical and archaeological record from Gov. Benedict Arnold down to the 2008 excavations, which, of course, Wolter does. He never mentions any of the historical record in the episode, another instance of failing to play fair with the facts.

Wolter asserts that the Tower cannot be a windmill because he believes that it looks nothing like "colonial architecture," again discounting the clear analog with the Chesterton Windmill, as well as other stone-built colonial structures. That said, he also failed to recognize stone-built spring houses as colonial back in Episode Eight and stone-built cold cellars as colonial in Episode Six, so it is entirely possible that he has no knowledge of colonial buildings. At no point in the episode is even a hint of the known historical record of the Tower mentioned.

Over some previously-filmed footage of actors playing the Knights Templar, Wolter summarizes their history and his idea that the Holy Grail came to America with the Templars after their order was suppressed following the French raid of 1307. Interestingly, while the previous episode made the Grail into the Bloodline of Christ, in this episode it is reintroduced merely as the Cup of Christ from the Last Supper, with only a hint that it may have "symbolized" something more. Once again, Wolter offers a scoffing reference to "academics" who are butting heads with Our Hero in his quest to find the Holy Grail. He meets with a fellow alternative historian, Jim Egan, the proprietor and curator of the private Newport Tower Museum. Egan does not believe that the tower was a windmill; instead, he thinks it is the first and most sophisticated English structure in Rhode Island, built in 1583, based, again, on the fact that it simply doesn't look like a windmill to him. He believes that John Dee planned a secret colony for Rhode Island, that the Tower was its first building, and that the colony failed, leaving behind, conveniently, no trace of its existence archaeologically or historically. His evidence is only architectural, for he claims that the Tower functioned as a camera obscura and as a calendar, which he believes only John Dee could have constructed, although buildings serving both those purposes were well-known in Europe. However, he is certain that it is not medieval in date.

Wolter asserts that the Newport Tower is "exactly identical to what they built in the twelfth century" because of the "equally spaced" pillars, round centerpiece, and (missing) "ambulatory." The pillars are *not* equally spaced but are in fact slightly irregular. There is no evidence of a stone ambulatory as shown in the computer reconstruction (though some possible post holes uncovered in 2008 suggest there could possibly have been a wooden structure around the tower at some point). Worse, there is nothing "exactly identical" to the Tower among the medieval churches of Europe. Even Carl Christian Rafn, the very first to make this connection, could turn up none that exactly matched; he could only talk of how *elements* of the Tower resembled *elements* from various medieval buildings. He compared the arches from Romanesque churches but the round shape of various churches without arches; none had *all* of the elements in the Tower in the same organization and order. The closest he could come was an *octagonal* structure at Mellifont Abbey in Ireland, but which is significantly different in construction, ornamentation, and design. The only European building that is almost "exactly identical" is the Chesterton Windmill. Wolter, however, merely asserts that "identical" European churches existed, but in his very next sentence backtracks and instead suggests only that such churches merely "incorporate" "elements" also found in the Newport Tower, contradicting his own assertion (and computer reconstruction) of ten seconds previous.

It becomes very obvious his material is derived from secondhand summaries of Rafn's 1839 speculation when he cites Mellifont Abbey and the Danish round churches of Bornholm, both key pieces of Rafn's evidence. They don't look the same, or even close. He claims that the Tower is an "exact duplicate" of Cambridge Round Church, which it is not. Cambridge Round Church (more properly the Church of the Holy Sepulchre, Cambridge) has a stone ambulatory, and the Tower does not. Cambridge Round Church has an arched clerestory triforium, and the Tower does not. The Church has ornately carved capitals on its columns, and the Tower has no capitals. During the period when the Templars supposedly came to America to build the Tower, the Round Church had already been significantly altered from its original design, having had a chancel and aisle added a full century earlier. (The Church as seen today was rebuilt in the 1840s based on assumptions at that time about its original design—that's why in 1839 Rafn didn't think anything of it.) The Tower has no evidence of an aisle. In sum, the resemblances are entirely superficial.

Wolter next asserts that Geradus Mercator's 1569 world map depicts the Newport Tower. What we see is nothing of the sort. We see Norumbega and Mercator's symbol for a settlement, a pair of towers connected by a wall, the small number of towers representing the small size of the settlement, as reported by Allefonsce. It is no different than his symbols for other settlements around the world, all drawn in the same Renaissance style no matter the culture or age, or actual architecture. Needless to say, of course, the Newport Tower is singular and not plural. In fact, Mercator offers an even closer approximations of the Tower when representing the cities on the edge of the Sahara desert in Western Africa—a place where no such European-style round tower ever existed. It's just Mercator's map symbol, not a secret drawing spirited back from America by the Templars. There is therefore no evidence that Mercator depicted the Tower, and an edited sound bite from Egan shows that Egan, too, recognizes that this is but a map symbol. A huge problem with this segment is that Wolter never discusses the myth of Norumbega, clearly referenced on the map, making it seem unclear to viewers why Mercator would have a settlement in Rhode Island at such an early date.

Wolter next asserts that his special training in geology gives him an advantage because "I know rocks." But he uses none of that knowledge of geology, instead saying that the *shape* of the rocks was *symbolically* important, a question of *history*, not *geology*.

Egan and Wolter both claim that the Tower has significant astronomical alignments because on the winter solstice, at an unspecified time during the day (which is actually about nine in the morning), the sun shines through the west "window" and illuminates a stone on the opposite wall, which Egan thinks is important because the "Mesopotamian" symbol for Easter was the "egg," the shape of the rock hit by the sun. Of course, the rock isn't really egg-shaped—it's only very roughly egg shaped, with many irregular edges—nor is the winter solstice associated with Easter or its predecessors, the spring festivals. It's also unclear to me how this "alignment" would have been visible when the Tower was a complete "church" with a presumably finished interior. The windmill would have had a floor that would have almost certainly blocked the sunlight from reaching the egg stone, and the entire building was coated in plaster, hiding any funny-shaped rocks. (Egan believes that John Dee had pictures of the rocks painted on the plaster covering them to preserve the alignment!)

Wolter also believes that the structure has an alignment to Venus. En route we get a callback to last week's episode where Wolter gawked, seemingly without purpose, at a rare magnetic rock called cumberlandite at Paul Roberti's house. But now we know why! This rock is found only in Rhode Island, and Wolter finds that this local magnetic rock was incorporated into the Tower! Big deal: The Tower was built out of local rocks—

what a shock! An irrelevant search for more cumberlandite in the wild follows. Wolter asserts that cumberlandite is known as the "Stone of Venus," but I can find no evidence that anyone other than Wolter uses that term to describe it. In Greek and Roman times the emerald was the Stone of Venus, and in Kabala it is the amethyst. The only other reference I could find was to old claims that the magnetic iron stone at the corner of the Kaaba in Mecca, believed to be meteorite, used to be called the Stone of Venus in pagan times. But for Wolter, his assertion that the cumberlandite was known as the Stone of Venus is proof that it is tied to Cistercian and Templar symbolism of the divine female in the heavens, symbolized by the planet Venus. This claim appears only with Alan Bulter (remember him?), who recently asserted that the Templars and Cistercians worshiped the "sacred feminine" by secretly perpetuating an ancient goddess-based religion. There is no earlier connection to Venus in the literature, so far as I am able to tell, outside of ancient astronaut, diffusionist, and Holy Bloodline writers. In fact, my conversations with Rhode Islanders failed to find any *locals* who call cumberlandite the "Stone of Venus." Given its restricted geography, they'd have to be the only people who could do so.

Wolter next confuses the Templars and the Cathars by claiming the Templars promoted a feminist agenda in service of the sacred feminine. The Templars were never accused of believing in the equality of men and women; that was the Cathars, a completely different group of medieval heretics, persecuted from 1208 to 1325. The all-male Templars were actually accused of being homosexuals who worshiped a demon named Baphomet. Alternative writers have drawn connections between the two groups, but the only proof is an alleged document claiming that the Templars gave safe haven to Cathar refugees. This paper is conveniently gone, supposedly lost in World War II before anyone other than an alternative writer had ever seen it. Historians recognize no connection between the two groups.

There is no evidence that the Templars recognized anything special about Venus, nor is the presence of Venus alignments in the Tower proof of Templar influence. (Why not, say, Venus-worshiping Romans?) There is no reference to Venus in any reference book on the Templars I consulted, and it only appears in the alternative history literature very recently, in conjunction with goddess conspiracies. There is no evidence of such Venus alignments in any Templar or Cistercian buildings of the era in Europe. Nevertheless, Wolter believes that the light of Venus could be focused through the Newport Tower's second story window and "captured" by a niche on the opposite wall to bring "the goddess"—the Templars are pagans now?—into the Tower. In Episode Eleven the Templars were "pure" Christians with the "truth" about Christ; this time they're pre-Christian goddess-worshipers. Consistency is not Wolter's strong suit.

Wolter tries to explain that the light from Venus was captured by the niches in the tower, but I have problems with this. If the windows at the very top of the tower (the third story in American usage, or second story in British usage) were meant, as Wolter says, for "observations," then Venus would need to be visible *from ground level*, but it is not. The "alignment" could only be seen from halfway up the Tower, at the "niche," and no light would ever actually shine from the planet into the Tower itself. (Starlight or planet light isn't bright enough to create a focused beam through an aperture as big as a window; if that were the case, then your home telescope would be shooting lasers into your eyes.) Wolter also fails to state what time during the night this alignment should occur, nor what the azimuth of Venus would be; Venus "appearing" at 22° is not enough information. The angle needs to be measured from a given point, and Wolter won't say whether that point is at ground level, up in the sky, or what. He thinks that two such alignments together create an X like the fictitious Templar "hooked X."

Wolter next states that the engineering of the Tower was "very precise," but again I must point to the fact that (a) the Tower not perfectly round, (b) its pillars are unevenly spaced, and (c) two of its arches are of different widths from the other six. Engineers who were supposedly so precise that they encoded Venus alignments to an incredibly small angle were also incapable of building a regular structure? "Nobody but the Templars would have designed this into a structure like this!" Wolter screams as he views a laser reconstruction of the Venus X. Never mind, of course, that the X would *never* have been visible (since Venus cannot be in two places simultaneously), that the Templars have no connection to Venus, and that when Scott Wolter came to the Newport Tower in 2007 to look for Venus, he found that there "was *not* a visible opening to allow Venus to be seen" as an evening star.[14] At the time, he blamed the failure to see Venus on (a) clouds and (b) reconstruction work on the Tower after 1780 that may have altered the position of the windows. Given that the Tower's uppermost three feet have been rebuilt, there is no way to know what the original "alignment" would have been. (Other alternative believers have, on just as little evidence, proposed that the true "alignment" was to Sirius and/or the North Star on various days.)

Wolter tries to test his idea by looking for Venus atop a ladder placed inside the Tower. Neither Wolter nor Egan seems aware that it is possible to calculate the position of Venus at any given time; it is not a miracle that requires speculation. Are we to assume that the Templars stood on stilts to see Venus? Fortunately for Wolter, the weather prevented him from "proving" where Venus was in the sky, despite, again, the fact that astronomers are able to determine such positioning with great accuracy. Wolter is disappointed that Venus fails to hit the niche, and he rationalizes that "maybe in the past" the niche aligned with Venus, when the earth's axis was in a different position (!) and before earthquakes (!!) had misaligned the Tower! This is post-hoc rationalization at its worst. Again, as a geologist he should be able to find evidence if these alleged monument-moving earthquakes had occurred—is the Tower's foundation damaged? And astronomers can tell you *exactly* where Venus was on any given night, except that they are "academics" and so in on the conspiracy.

But only seconds later, Wolter then trumpets a *solar* alignment that hits a keystone at an unspecified point during the morning around the solstice. But I thought he just said *earthquakes moved the Tower out of alignment*. Which is it? The sun is seen quite high in the sky, so the "fertilization" of the keystone "egg" isn't happening at dawn, the sacred moment in ancient religion, but rather by chance sometime later in the day.

"The academic community has dropped the ball," Wolter says. "Not just with the Newport Tower but with *many* of these ancient sites and arti-facts that indicate that people have been coming to what is now America for thousands of years." Wolter fails to tell viewers that the "academic community" has been studying the Newport Tower since the 1840s, and the results of architectural, archaeological, radiocarbon, and other studies are always the same: All signs point to the mid-1600s (see above). He is being highly dishonest in ignoring actual archaeological and academic work on the site in order to claim that none exists.

"I truly believe that the society that the Templars envisioned was eventually laid out by modern Freemasons over a period of centuries, and those symbols, the signs, they're all around us, hidden in plain sight." Thus, America is actually the culmination of sacred goddess worship, the joint inheritance of the Templars and Masons: "These two orders were re-sponsible for founding our United States itself."

Wolter sees that one of the Newport Tower's keystones is very roughly shaped like a notched Masonic keystone (like the one used in Pennsylva-nia road signs—it's the keystone state), but it is so roughly shaped like one that it's hard to attribute intentional symbolic design to the rock rather than the necessity to support the circular stone placed by design directly above with a flat support that juts up above the rest of the arch. So much for precision engineering. Wolter sees this stone as a "Mark Master Ma-son's Keystone," associated with a level of Freemasonry; but such a stone is a modern invention. As recently as the nineteenth century, the mark master mason's keystone was smooth (un-notched), with a circle inscribed within. It may be possible, I suppose, that the circle above the Tower key-stone was meant to represent this, but Wolter isn't aware of the fact. It looks instead like the rock was irregular and shaped as best as possible to fit into the available space in the arch. Of course, any connection is de-pendent on accepting Wolter's contention that the Knights Templar gave rise to the Freemasons through the good offices of the Sinclair family—none of which finds any historical backing.

Instead, Wolter takes a helicopter to look at the Statue of Liberty, a statue created in France rather than America, who holds in her left hand a tablet that has two notches at the top. Although the tablet is rectangular (with parallel sides) and therefore could not possibly serve as a keystone—which by definition must taper in a wedge shape to fit into and support an arch—Wolter screams and hoots that he found a hidden Mason's symbol. In fact, the sculptor, Frédéric Bartholdi, intended the tablet to be a *tabula ansata*, an imperial Roman tablet with dovetailed (notched) ends used for votive inscriptions. Such tablets also appear in Renaissance European art from the same ancient sources. They have nothing to do with Mason's keystones, and indeed the Masons never hid the fact that they publicly laid the cornerstone for the foundation of the statue's base and that a Mason spoke at its dedication.

If this is a "hidden" cult rite, they have a funny way of doing it in public, but it did not help matters that when anti-Masons raised objections to the Masons laying the cornerstone, Grand Master William A. Brodie chose to tell the assembled crowd at the dedication ceremony that

> ...our ancient brethren erected grand old works of architecture that adorn the cities of the world, and which have come down to us covered with the mold and moss of centuries, or lie in ruin's silent data, so ancient that history fails to reach back to the distant point—so in a speculative sense, the Masonic fraternity of the present age are called upon to erect the magnificent works of modern architecture, by laying the cornerstones thereof."[15]

Despite his deputy's assurance that same day that Masons take no part in government affairs and Brodie's own (if confusing) words that the Masons only *symbolically* carried on ancient traditions, Brodie's ill-considered statement sparked more than a century of speculation about the secret Egyptian rites that the Masons must have hidden within the symbol of Liberty.

Such extreme claims about the Statue of Liberty are not uncommon in the most hysterical anti-Masonic literature. Pseudo-archaeologists Graham Hancock and Robert Bauval made such claims, fretting that the Masons, as "secret rulers of the world," had used the statue to sneak an image of the goddess Isis and a secret Egyptian cult into America.[16] This same worry permeates works of Christian prophecy, which see the Masons as Satan's minions undermining America as God's chosen land. For example, John J. Quiles wrote angrily that Freemasons used the Statue of Liberty to symbolize the New World Order and to introduce pagan Ishtar or Isis worship into America's ruling class.[17] None of these authors or their peers, however, seriously thought that the statue's plaque was a keystone; instead, they thought that the torch in her other hand was a secret Masonic lamp of reason—symbolizing the star Sirius (which, as Robert Temple explained in 1976, is where the alien overlords of the earth live).

The show concludes with Wolter expressing his certainty that the Templars gave rise to the United States and its "religious freedom" and "determined the very destiny of our nation." The final minutes serve to sum up the series' clear aim of providing an ancient (or at least medieval) rationalization for American values, continuing the project started with the mound builder myth several centuries ago of giving non-Native Americans—immigrants all—deeper connections to the land and a fictive, mythic history sufficient to assuage any doubts about who *really* belongs in America, and also who does *not* belong in America as a true member of our society.

Hunt for the Holy Grail

March 15, 2013

Episode Summary

Scott Wolter travels to Nova Scotia to investigate whether Henry Sinclair, Earl of Orkney, hid the Holy Grail among the ruins of an alleged Templar Castle. With help from treasure hunters and a sophisticated dowsing rod, Wolter digs for the Grail but finds nothing. This only deepens his belief that he is on the right track.

Historical Background

In the historical background to Episode Twelve, I mentioned the story of "Prince Henry," as Scott Wolter calls him, more properly Henry Sinclair, Earl of Orkney and Baron of Roslin. His princely style rests on the fact that Henry's Norwegian-held title of *jarl,* or earl, of Orkney was once translated as "prince" because of its higher rank in Norway, above a duke. It is this shadowy, half-formed figure whose life serves as the only slender thread connecting the Jesus Bloodline and the Knights Templar to wild claims about non-Viking Europeans in the pre-Columbian United States.

As you will recall, in 1784, a German with romantic dreams of his lost Scottish noble ancestors suggested that Henry Sinclair of Orkney could be identified with "Prince Zichmni," a fictional character in a Renaissance-era hoax called the Zeno Narrative (see Appendix Two) about two Venetian brothers' alleged trip to the North Atlantic. In the most generous reading of that hoax, the story takes Zichmni only to Greenland in the years after

1394, where he supposedly founded a colony. Only significant special pleading can extend that to America. It is the *only* evidence of a voyage by Henry Sinclair. Later, Richard Henry Major took up the claim, placing blame for any mistakes to the incorrigible hyperbole of Italians (supplemented a century later by Frederick J. Pohl's argument that Zichmni was a corruption of "d'Orkney" as transcribed by someone with bad handwriting). Major admits that taken at face value, the Zeno Narrative fails to match the life of Henry, "a dilemma from which it would be next to impossible to escape"[1] without simply asserting that the whole narrative was "rewritten" to change all the details!

> But is there no possibility that that language itself may not be perfectly correct? [...] the narrative [...] exhibits beyond all contradiction a quality excessively misleading to the critic who takes each word *au pied de la lettre,* and that quality is hyperbole: yet no one it may be hoped, who is acquainted with the genius of the southern mind, would condemn a tendency to a certain amount of hyperbole, especially in the record of the deeds of an ancestor, as involving any conscious want of integrity. [...] we must accept the exaggerations as merely the husk which surrounds a real and genuine kernel. All deviation from right is wrong, though from habit it may not be so reputed.[2]

His influential preface to his translation of the Zeno Narrative (the basis for all later Sinclair claims) later inspired in 1992 a descendant of Henry Sinclair named Andrew Sinclair to declare his ancestor a Knight Templar and a discoverer of America. Not only was Henry born too late to be a Templar (by fifty years at least), his ancestors actually testified *against* the Templars in 1309. Now, to add some details specific to the claim that Henry was active in Nova Scotia in 1398.

Henry Sinclair was made Jarl (Earl or Prince) of Orkney in 1379 by King Hakron of Norway and was in Norway that year and the one after, meaning that the Zeno narrative cannot be chronologically correct, as the Zeno brothers met Zichmni on his magic island in 1380. Zichmni engaged in various battles in the 1380s and went to live in Greenland after 1394.

Henry Sinclair, by contrast, disappears from the historical record after attending the coronation of the King of Pomerania in Norway in 1389 (meaning he could not have been in America then), and his grandson reported that Henry died in a battle to defend Orkney, probably the 1401 English invasion of Orkney that he was required by feudal obligation to Norway to repel. In fact, a copy of Henry's feudal obligations survives, and it makes plain that Henry could not have waged war against the King of Norway, as Zichmni was said to have done:

> Also, we promise in good faith that we must assume in no direction to us the lands of our lord the king, or any other rights of his which his progenitors and the king our lord are known to have reserved to themselves; and concerning those lands or jurisdictions not to intromit in any manner whatsoever. They have reserved those laws, indeed, and those pleas within the Orcadian earldom, as is before said, and the lands and pleas of that kind will remain in all cases safe for them; but if, upon this, we shall have his special letters, then we ought to be specially bound thereafter to our same lord the king.
>
> Besides, but may it be absent, if all those abovesaid things shall not have been brought to conclusion, and totally fulfilled to the same my lord the king as it has been expressed above, or if we should have attempted anything in the contrary of any of the premises, then the promotion and favour which we have experienced from the king our lord, and of his grace, ought to be of no strength; yea, the promotion and favour of that kind done to us must be broken down altogether, and in their forces be totally empty and inane, so that we and our heirs for the rest shall have no right of speaking for the beforesaid county or for the lands or beforesaid islands, or we of acting about those lands and islands in any way whatsoever, that it may be manifest to all that the promotion and grace of this kind was given by no force of law or justice.[3]

Richard Henry Major, a true believer, recognized that this presented an insoluble dilemma, and his answer was to simply assert that all the parts of the Zeno Narrative that did not agree with his conclusion were the product of the fancy of soft-minded Italians, while those scraps that could be mustered in his favor were the real, Northern European truth hidden amidst Southern fantasy.

The Icelandic historian Thormodus Torfæus, writing in his massive Latin history of the Orkneys, the *Orcades,* in 1697, claimed that Norwegian records (now lost) stated that in the late 1380s Henry was virtually running Norway and had no time to sail to America. "In the year 1388, Henry Sinclair, Jarl of Orkney (being declared the next in rank to the king, by Archbishop Vinold of Nidar and the rest of the bishops and senators, with the other councillors of the Norwegian kingdom), proclaimed, by a long document, that Eric was the true heir and successor to the kingdom of Norway."[4] Eric III took the throne in 1389, but most modern historians believe Henry Sinclair's role was entirely ceremonial, not an expression of real power. It's possible that such a gentleman as Henry *could* have decided to take a few years off to sail to America, first to build the Newport Tower, and then again to dump the Templar treasure, but I would imagine his Norwegian overlords would be particularly pissed at him since the Norwegian king had declared as a condition of making him Earl that he should always be available to aid the king with one hundred men on but three months' notice and should attend the National Council on demand. Any extended absence, like a several years' long voyage to America, would have required Royal consent, and neither Torfæus nor any extant record indicates any such thing.

The Sinclair (a.k.a. St. Clair) family has been pushing the Henry Sinclair narrative since the nineteenth century when Thomas Sinclair, Mrs. May St. Clair Whitney-Emerson, and others wrote books and delivered lectures to steal back the honor of discovering America for the Northern European race from that upstart and rogue referred to as "the Italian," Columbus, who was not of the "blood royal" of the Viking-Norman Duke Rollo, whose noble descendants the family of the time believed traveled six times to America, with Henry being the last and greatest. It is perhaps interesting to note, though, that Thomas Sinclair held that the real voyager to America was actually Henry II Sinclair, the successor to our Henry— even true believers have their differences of opinion.[5] It is perhaps to

Thomas Sinclair that we owe the unfortunate claim that Sinclair blood lived on in New England, and that the civilization of the Native Americans of New England was no indigenous development but "Norwegian and Scottish training grafted on mere savagery." In fact, he was certain that the Norse and Scots, whom he called true heroes, "ruled the Red Indians to some extent, and amalgamated with them."[6] (See Appendix Four.) This racial claim follows us down the centuries, straight into the heart of *America Unearthed*. Thomas Sinclair had racist views against both Native Americans *and* Englishmen, whom he accused of trying to cover up the Sinclair legacy.

Today, there is a group of American descendants of the Sinclair family, calling themselves the Clan Sinclair U.S.A., who organize Sinclair-themed events in America. Among the American Sinclairs is a Steve St. Clair, who claims to be a very distant cousin of Prince Henry. (Some, though, have challenged his claim.) He runs the Sinclair/St. Clair DNA Project, and part of his project involves investigating whether the Sinclairs came to America in the Middle Ages and bequeathed their very special Scottish DNA to Native Americans, whom he tests to determine whether they have Scottish ancestry. Although Steve St. Clair says he has found no evidence to support such claims, he feels the question remains open:

> Since beginning this DNA study, I've had no choice but to focus on the study of Native populations, on finding better ways to analyze the Jarl Henry St. Clair story, on the mystery of the Newport Tower, on the crusades, on ancient navigation, on population statistics, on heraldry, and more. One result of this focus was the Atlantic Conference of August 2008, described as 'the definitive gathering of world experts on early trans-Atlantic voyaging.' Clearly this is an area that affects the history of our family, but I wanted to approach it from a more scientific perspective, examining the actual proofs and reasonable likelihoods that such voyaging was possible. This was not a 'Prince Henry' conference but, rather, a scientific gathering sponsored by a family that has a great interest in the subject as a whole.[7]

Now, guess whom Steve St. Clair invited to the Atlantic Conference of

2008, and whose research he helped to support? Yes, Scott Wolter. Wolter presented a paper at the 2008 conference on the "hooked X" and its alleged connections to the Templars—and thus to Henry Sinclair. The two became close: The next year they appeared together on speculative radio shows like *Coast to Coast A.M.*[8] to promote the Committee Films production *Holy Grail in America*, airing on the History Channel that year, and to lay out the "evidence" that Henry Sinclair sailed to America, built the Newport Tower, and returned to Scotland to bequeath the secret to his grandson, who built Rosslyn Chapel to encode the truth about Jesus' DNA lineage.

Of course the Sinclair true believers (which do not include Steve St. Clair but do include many Holy Bloodline authors) feel the family members are the very special descendants of Jesus and therefore the legitimate protectors of the Holy Grail and Grail Kings. As members of the "royal blood," they are therefore in line to fulfill the medieval legend of the Last World Emperor, much loved by that Mason-Templar conspirator Christopher Columbus, who discussed it in his *Book of Prophecies*, a relatively unknown collection of his mystical writings about the apocalypse. This story, which draws on biblical and medieval mysticism, holds that a final universal monarch shall confront the Muslims, retake Jerusalem, and surrender his crown at the Second Coming of Jesus. Indeed, more than a few extremely fringe speculators have connected the Sinclairs and the Holy Bloodline to the Second Coming of Christ.

The radio appearances happened at the same time that Wolter began to claim that the Newport Tower was "aligned" to the Kensington Rune Stone! Wolter appeared in *Holy Grail in America* with Niven Sinclair, another organizer of the Atlantic Conference, and a Scottish adherent of the alternative theories of Henry Sinclair, as well as David Sinclair-Bouschor, a former grand master of Minnesota's Freemasons. Both were brought into the program because of their connection via the Atlantic Conference to Wolter, whom Committee Films credited in 2008 production documents with proposing the concept for the film. You will remember that Wolter was described as the "key expert" whose views guided the direction and claims of the film, which became the template for *America Unearthed.*

The Atlantic Conference was designed to explore, and I'll be blunt, the theory that European people have lived in America since 9000 BCE and interbred with Native Americans. That's not me accusing them of racism. That's what they say on their website, where they write that "Native traditions states [...] that the populations of Europe and North America are mixed."[9] To their credit, they also explore the idea that Native people returned the favor and "mixed" with European people in Scandinavia, part of a larger claim that trans-Atlantic contact occurred continuously since deepest prehistory.

Interestingly, the cosponsor of the 2008 Atlantic Conference was *Ancient American* magazine, the alternative history publication put out by Wayne May, the Mormon extremist, and (before his 2007 retirement) Frank Joseph, the ex-neo-Nazi convicted child predator. Both work to support Mormon narratives that white Europeans were the original inhabitants of America before God cursed some of them with dark skin.[10] This same publication has also published Scott Wolter's papers on the Bat Creek Stone, the Newport Tower Venus "alignments," and other related subjects that, of course, all serve as "evidence" for pre-Columbian European colonization of America. The magazine is one of Wolter's primary outlets for his written work.

The Episode

"Hunt for the Holy Grail," opens with a reenactment of a cloth-bound bundle being lowered by rope into what resembles a mine shaft in the presence of Knights Templar, as marked by their red crosses on white cassocks above chain mail. Then we cut to the opening credits for the final time this season. The next scene shows Scott Wolter's laboratory in winter. He is reading an email from Dennis "Den" Parada, a treasure hunter with an outfit called Finders Keepers who believes he knows the location of buried Templar treasure at Hobson Island in Nova Scotia, brought to the island by Prince Henry Sinclair. Wolter immediately calls Steve St. Clair, who is game for investigating his "family treasure."

Wolter travels to Nova Scotia to meet with the Parada, and we have long scenes of Wolter driving across Canadian highways. As he does so, Wolter asserts that "legend says that a Scottish prince named Henry Sinclair with strong ties to the Templars brought it [the treasure] here in 1398." Nothing in that sentence is true. The "legend" was created by Andrew Sinclair (yes, another Sinclair) in 1992, in *The Sword and the Grail*, based on a pseudo-scholarly argument about the Zeno Map made in 1784 and again in the mid-1800s. From 1784 to 1992, the actual family claim was that Henry came as the last of a series of *Viking* (Norse) expeditions. Only after 1992 did these transform into "Templar" expeditions. Henry had no ties to the Templars, disbanded fifty years before his birth and against whom his ancestors gave testimony at their 1309 trial.

Additionally, the Zeno Narrative states that Zichmni, whom believers equate with Henry Sinclair, actually colonized "Engronelanda," a place typically identified as Greenland. Frederick J. Pohl originated the idea that it was Nova Scotia on the strength of the idea that the Zeno Narrative describes "a great fire in the bottom of the hill, and that there was a spring from which issued a certain matter like pitch." This, Pohl felt, could only be "the Pictou region of Nova Scotia, at Stellarton, [where] an open coal seam burned at the bottom of a hill, from the top of which pitch flowed down in what is now called 'Coal Brook' and crossed the burning seam."[11] While the coal seam at Stellarton, called the Foord Seam, was reported to have caught fire more than once in historic times, including a stretch from 1870 to 1901, but I can find no evidence that the seam was actively burning prior to the start of coal mining in the area in the 1830s, when mining activity sparked several fires. In fact, according to a contemporary report made to the Geologic Survey of Canada, the fires actually occurred *within* the mines, not in the open air, and were driven by natural gas released from mining activities.[12]

But this is irrelevant because there is a much better reason that Zeno included these particular details in his narrative: He was copying from Olaus Magnus. Olaus Magnus' description of Iceland from his 1555 *History of the Northern Peoples*, published in Italy just three years before the Zeno

Narrative. There, in Book Two, chapters one and two, he describes volcanoes and burning waters. An accompanying illustration shows three burning hills, the volcanoes, *with fire at the bottom of the hills,* and rivers of hot substances (presumably lava, but someone with no knowledge of volcanoes might mistake it for pitch) flowing into large cauldrons and then onward, presumably to the sea. Another woodcut shows a lake of burning pitch and sulfur beside a smoking mountain and a village. It seems that Zeno, adapting Olaus' text, simply accepted Olaus' false but popular idea that volcanoes burned from the bottom.

Sadly, *America Unearthed* will have none of this and simply accepts that Nova Scotia was a logical destination for the disbanded Knights Templar without ever explaining why. The Holy Grail is back to being a cup again this week, though with shout outs to the "holy bloodline of Jesus and Mary," and Wolter claims that Henry was the last person to have held it—of which, of course, no documentary evidence whatsoever exists, being based entirely on the 1992 claim that Henry was a Templar. Especially interesting is Wolter's cockamamie assertion that the Templars may have found "scrolls" and "technology" under the Temple Mount in Jerusalem— shades of Laurence Gardner's monatomic gold-producing Ark of the Covenant, Graham Hancock's electric-generator Ark of the Covenant, and the ancient astronaut writers' extraterrestrial communications device Ark of the Covenant. What does Wolter really think happened in the ancient past? Aliens? Atlantis?

Parada shows Wolter a map of Oak Island, the often-discussed "mystery" island of Nova Scotia that Joe Nickell persuasively identified as a nineteenth-century Freemasons' initiation site. Parada thinks that Oak Island was actually Templar, but that Prince Henry moved the treasure to Oak Island from Hobson Island nearby. Nickell, on the other hand, explained that the very first phenomenon to spark interest in Oak Island— the discovery of a "treasure shaft" in 1795—was actually a naturally-occurring sinkhole. Afterward, the island was apparently used by local Freemasons for enacting the Secret Vault allegory (which involves a symbolic descent into a vault to touch a stand-in for the Ark of the Covenant in an allegory of death and rebirth), and many of the odd artifacts found on the island can be identified as eighteenth- and nineteenth-century Masonic ritual apparatus. Masonry had been practiced on Nova Scotia since 1738, so this is not evidence of a Templar conspiracy. But most interesting for our purposes is the ritual developed by the local Masonic Grand Master Reginald Harris in the 1930s and preserved in fragmentary form in his papers. According to Nickell, this involves an allegorical play that evokes the (fictitious) story that the prime minister of England attempted to seize the Freemasons' treasure, *including the Holy Grail*, at Glastonbury in 1535, but the Masons spirit the Grail away. Harris was also an investigator of the Oak Island mystery, and it is only *after* him that alternative writers began to locate the Holy Grail on Oak Island and its environs.[13]

Parada, treasure hunter Patrick Whelan, and Wolter travel to Hobson Island in ridiculously overproduced overhead shots of them speeding across the waters beneath waves and cresting musical accompaniment. They stroll through some rocks on which one displays a very rough, wide-angled **V**. Wolter immediately relates it to the "upper part of the hooked X" despite it, of course, not being an **X**. All involved declare it a **V** even though the image clearly shows a horizontal line connecting to the left-hand leg of the **V** at its top, something like a flattened **N**. All see the horizontal line and declare it "just like" the one on the hooked X, even though the Kensington Rune Stone's hooked X is on the *right* stave of the **X**, partway down the stave, and perpendicular to the stave (X)—all different from this figure.

Next, Parada claims to have found a treasure map made of stone. So the three men trudge across more rocks and boulders. Parada claims that the rocks and boulders have been laid out carefully in the shape of the three hundred islands off Nova Scotia, with several of the prominent rocks representing different islands the Templars visited. A computer-generated map tries to make the correlation, but I am not able to see a connection— there is no similarity of shape between rock and represented island, and the relative proportions between the rocks are not scientific in the least. For example, the rock representing Gooseberry Island is so large (proportionally twice the size of the alleged island it represents) that it covers a great deal of the ground meant to symbolize the water between it and Frog Island, another rock disproportionately large for representing its intended island. Consequently, I can see nothing here other than self-deluded individuals who are seeing what they want in the random shapes of nature.

Nevertheless, this "map" supposedly points to the "Castle at the Cross" at New Ross, an archaeological site that Sinclair researchers have been promoting as a "mini-castle" built by Henry Sinclair since the 1980s, particularly by Michael Bradley, the author of *Holy Grail across the Atlantic* (1988). So far as I know, Joan Hope's two self-published books, *The Secret City* (1987) and *A Castle in Nova Scotia* (1997) are the primary source for the claim. To my knowledge, no archaeological reports about the site have been published, but all that remains are an earthen mound, some large stones, and a well—surely not the remains of a full castle, or even a "mini-castle." The photographs of the site show some loose stones in the shape of some squares, whereas an actual castle would have had *many* more stones to build walls and battlements. Hope herself confirmed that the above-ground stones were the remains of a seventeenth-century mansion, though she also found some very scanty evidence that the site *might* have been visited by the Norse of Vinland, though an ancient Native occupation at the site complicates that claim. But Hope was a romantic, and she believed the site to be haunted, often seeing phantasmagorical scenes of ghostly visitors, ranging from whole families of the dead to a disembodied ginger-haired head. All told, she encountered several dozen ghosts and was plagued by what she felt was a poltergeist attacking her possessions. One ghost even drew elaborate artwork on her frost-covered windows. Then, of course, she started to be visited by aliens in UFOs.

She imaginatively interpreted older layers of stone on the site as the walls of a vanished castle, and she spun for herself a fanciful history where her backyard was the site of a glorious pageant of history. An ambiguous mason's mark on a stone was "linked to Stonehenge," and her yard was once a Neolithic European stone circle from the depths of time!

And it was used for penis worship! Leif Erikson built a summer home atop its ruins. A medieval castle stood there next, followed by a colonial-era mansion so wonderful that Massachusetts bought it and carried it off to become the statehouse in Boston. And of course the ghosts of all watched over the site, in their UFOs. "Phoenicians, Celts, Micmacs, Norsemen and other Europeans: all had used our property through the ages, if not to build their homes there, then as a place of worship. When all this began is lost in time; but we can say that the site has been in use, often as an important centre, for at least about 3,500 years."[14] How lucky for her.

Hope was a credulous woman, and she believed everything a local Native American told her because she believed Native people were inherently possessed of superior wisdom. One told her that her house had once been a castle completely covered in gold, and he drew her a picture of it. Right after receiving this picture she suddenly "found" evidence confirming exactly this imaginary image of a long-vanished castle. After reading Frederick J. Pohl's book *Prince Henry Sinclair: His Expedition to the New World in 1398* (1974)—itself based on Richard Henry Major's imaginary version of the Zeno Narrative—Hope adopted the most extreme claims for the Zeno text and concluded that Henry Sinclair built her castle, and she decided her castle was *also* the famous Norumbega, which Wolter elsewhere names as Newport.

Sadly, Hope was too credulous for her own good, and playing about in the ruins of a colonial mansion built atop a Native American village, she imagined a glorious Eurocentric world that never was, a romantic fantasy that fit her ghost-haunted, alien-guarded world. There is obviously no reason to privilege the medieval castle above any of her other evidence-free fantasies. Scott Wolter and Steve St. Clair refuse to tell viewers any of this and instead pretend that hers was a serious, scholarly effort to prove the reality of a medieval Sinclair settlement. Hardly: She got it from other alternative authors and applied it to her own house because it felt right to her! Wolter and St. Clair speculate that New Ross was named for Rosslyn (Roslin), the Sinclair family seat in Scotland and the home of Rosslyn Chapel, built by Henry's grandson William. How Rosslyn Chapel would encode information about Henry's activities in Nova Scotia is beyond me since the theory seems to be that he built a castle and died in Nova Scotia, never having returned to Scotland and Orkney. (Actual fact: He was succeeded no later than 1404 by Henry II Sinclair, and William Sinclair wrote that Henry I had died defending Orkney.)

The team learns that material beneath one of the rocks was carbon dated to the 1300s (though no report is cited—and Joan Hope actually said the radiocarbon dates were to around 1000 CE), but no one on the program thinks for even a minute about the actual people known to have lived in the area in the past—the First Nations (Native Americans). The Maritime tradition among native groups includes burial mounds, not unlike the earthen mound at the New Ross site, and of course Native peoples and their villages existed in the area right up to the contact period. The area was also not unreasonably far south of the known Viking settlement at L'anse-aux-Meadows (likely Vinland) located to the north in Newfoundland, and Hope had found a very few clues that might point in that direction. Further, the first colonists in the area, dating back to the 1600s built buildings in stone. Any of these possibilities, including the Viking one (which would be a significant and major find, if true), is much more probable than anything Templar.

The current owner of the land asserts that the First Nations people have a legend of men who came wearing a red cross on a white cassock, which the team interprets as representing Knights Templar. However, I am unable to find any evidence of this legend. If it did exist, I would imagine it referred to the Catholic and Anglican missionaries who came in the 1600s, with their robes and crosses—no one mentions chain mail, for example. Europeans have been settled in Nova Scotia since 1605, making this the more likely source for any legend, especially since there are very few genuine historical traditions from the 1300s retained in oral folklore. After all, Jessé Fléché, a French priest, accompanied the French explorer Poutrincourt to French Acadia, which became British Nova Scotia. There, he caused a scandal by converting the natives en masse to Catholicism without permission from the Jesuits, who were supposed to do such

things. So successful was he that the local Mi'kmaq (Micmac) took his title, "Le Patriarch," and corrupted it into Patiliasse, still their word for
"priest." They also adopted the red cross on a white background as their
flag. Fléché's activities around Port Royal are described by Marc Lescarbot
in *The Conversion of the Savages*, written in 1610. There, we can see that
the cross was not an uncommon symbol and quickly adopted by the natives:

> Now this Membertou to-day, by the grace of God, is a Christian, together
> with all his family, having been baptized, and twenty others with him, on
> last saint John's day, the 24th of June. [...] Chkoudun, a man of great in-
> fluence, of whom I have made honorable mention in my History of New
> France, because I saw that he, more than all the others, loved the French,
> and that he admired our civilization more than their ignorance: to such
> an extent, that being present sometimes at the Christian admonitions,
> which were given every Sunday to our French people, he listened atten-
> tively, although he did not understand a word; and moreover wore the
> sign of the Cross upon his bosom, which he also had his servants wear;
> and he had in imitation of us, a great Cross erected in the public place of
> his village, called Oigoudi, at the port of the river saint John, ten leagues
> from Port Royal.[15]

Surely, this type of conversion scene is what any local legend refers to.

Based on Joan Hope's fanciful blueprint of the "castle," the team plans
to dig for the Templar treasure, though I note that instead of using
ground-penetrating radar, which could seek out the foundations of the
alleged castle—and which Wolter used in Episode Two—the team instead
turns to a "long range locator," better known as a dowsing rod hooked up
to an electric beeper. The dowsing rod has its own fascinating history,
originating in the worship of Thor and the idea that certain sticks were
imbued with the power of lightning. It does not, however, have even a
shred of scientific accuracy, running entirely on the ideomotor effect
whereby the operator's hands subconsciously move the locator wand. This
is why robots and dogs can't use dowsing rods or long range locators. Anyway, the magic stick is used to find where to dig for "gold"—major

amounts of gold, they say, at least fifty ounces.

Anyone with a moment's scientific training can see that the investigation will turn up nothing related to Templar treasure. Didn't Wolter learn anything from his Minnesota "giant" investigation, when the dowsing rods returned one false hit after another? Finders Keepers' Dennis Parada later contacted me to explain that what was seen on the show was a staged event, that the actual work was done with other equipment not seen, and that some gold nuggets—not artifacts—were recovered. Parada vaguely insinuated that he was "not allowed" to report the nuggets on air. Since Nova Scotia is known to have had significant gold deposits, and had indeed been a gold mining center in the nineteenth century, this is not terribly surprising. What was surprising is that Parada informed me that he and his team had a license to drill for minerals but understood that they were forbidden by law (the 2010 Special Places Protection Act of Nova Scotia) from excavating artifacts. As a result, all of what follows was simply a sham put on for television since all involved knew they could not excavate. Parada repeated these claims in an interview with The Progress, and his son Kem added that America Unearthed, while not scripting events, did organize who would speak, in what order, and what words they were to use. Dennis Parada told the newspaper that the show's writers took his claims, turned them into an outline of what he was to do, and told him to follow it.[16]

The program describes the team—now comprised of several Finders Keepers—as using a metal detector next, but somehow the metal detector returns radar results about the shape of an underground chamber hidden near the bottom of the well. The device is apparently actually an electromagnetic conductivity meter which uses magnetic fields to map conductive material below ground, much of which would by definition be metal. This is doubly confusing when later in the episode, Parada claims that his machines found "no void" to excavate, leading to the conclusion that the chamber is filled with water. Then how did the metal detector find it? (In a later conversation with me, Parada again claimed that additional equipment was used but cut from the show.) Parada claims that an "energy force" is disturbing the readings—and Steve St. Clair suggests (probably in jest, but the show treats it seriously) that the Ark of the Covenant (recovered, of course, by the Templars) is sending out special beams to disrupt their work. Seriously, what do these people really believe about the ancient past? It is obvious that they have been seeped in alternative history to the point where any claim, no matter how outrageous, is for them a serious hypothesis so long as it appeared in someone's book.

The team sends a diver down the well, which is a superfluous action since they were planning to pump it dry anyway, and he finds the opening, a portion of the wall that has been "bricked off," probably to close off a natural opening to keep the well from collapsing. There is no arch or other support (though Parada says one exists but was not seen on camera), so the well wall must have always been there, at least since this apparently colonial-era well was sunk. Everyone is excited, and Wolter practically shouts at Steve St. Clair that they are close to finding "your family treasure." Surely the Holy Grail doesn't actually belong to Steve St. Clair—in fact legally, under Nova Scotia's recently revised Special Places Protection Act, any treasure would belong to the provincial government. They pump the well, and Wolter feels that the opening behind the well wall is the "treasure room" of the Holy Grail. Therefore, they bring in a drill to look for the chamber that is somehow both there and not there, and Wolter refers again to "strange energy" when the drilling equipment experiences brief battery problems. I can't help but think that this strange energy is a legacy of Joan Hope's ghost-soaked, UFO-cloaked tenure, and Wolter internalized her book too much.

Consider that for a moment: They told audiences they were using a *giant drill* to smash their way to priceless, fragile artifacts. Science! Parada later explained to me that the drill was brought in by the TV crew, that it was used only to create "test" holes for the camera (i.e., it was a sham), and that both Finders Keepers and the crew understood that they were forbidden by law to excavate artifacts. This is the same reason that the team never tries to prove that the "castle" is really there—which, of course, would have been strong proof of Wolter's pet theory: Doing so would require excavation, and that means submitting to actual regulation and oversight—and doing real archaeology, not staged TV stunts.

Drilling down finds boulders beneath ground, which Wolter suggests is a wall but is more likely actually rocks since this is, after all, a rocky island. There is no void, and the dowsing rod is wrong. They move the drill over a bit and try again. They bring up backfill that Wolter claims means that someone in the past has dug out the site, certainly a possibility given that the area has been used for various purposes for at least four hundred years—no Holy Grail required. In a third location, guaranteed by the "metal detector" to be the right location this time, they drill and find absolutely nothing—no hole, no void, no treasure. "We're not going to find shit," Wolter says, complaining bitterly about "all these things we've been talking ourselves into." He concludes—correctly!—that the backfill of soil created a density difference that showed up as a void on their machine— which I suppose means that it is a resistivity detector.

Wolter also asks where the gold the dowsing rod found really is. Parada makes excuses: "Something in the ground"—magic energy—is "throwing everything off." It's a classic excuse used by dowsers everywhere: When we're right, credit the rod; when we're wrong, blame unseen forces and mysterious, undetectable "energy." Parada explains that he had been "warned" that the "ghost of Prince Henry," in Wolter's words, is preventing them from finding the treasure. This appears to be another reference to Joan Hope, who saw the "ghosts" of men in medieval dress riding spirit horses and brandishing spirit swords. Parada, it would appear, is taking Hope's book as his source and thus his "warning."

Wolter concludes that the Templars or another group had moved the treasure, and Steve St. Clair appeals to the show's own Bible, *The Da Vinci Code* (weirdly, the movie and not the book), as precedent, for in the movie Robert Langdon also finds that the Holy Bloodline conspiracy had removed the evidence before he could find it. Wolter says that the Templars keep moving the treasure so it can never be found—and can keep generating new episodes! "The signs are everywhere. The clues are everywhere. It's here somewhere in North America, and I'm going to find it." Somehow, however, the complete failure of this entire investigation—finding no treasure, no chamber, no Templar artifacts (not even a lead cross!), no actual castle—leaves Wolter "more convinced than ever" that he is on the right track.

The series ends with Wolter reasserting that history is wrong and that the true history of "this country" (Canada?—or did he forget he's not in the United States this time?) needs to be unearthed. He promises that he has "thousands" of leads, "and I'm just getting started." He concludes by saying that "There's a pattern woven into the fabric of this country, something that connects the people of the past to each other, and to us in ways I'm only starting to understand."

The season concludes with Wolter drawing a line to connect selected ancient sites he chose to investigate this season. He connects them in a way that forms a Fibonacci curve emerging from the Kensington Rune Stone, which is cute, except that it connects only seven of the thirteen sites from this season (six, actually, since the Dare Stones have two locations on the map). It was Wolter—not science—that selected those sites to investigate, possibly to conform to the pattern, and there is no logical reason to select those from among the "thousands" of sites Wolter claims to know about; he didn't even choose just his alleged Templar sites, including as he did the non-Templar Dare Stones and the non-Templar Mystery Hill. The Fibonacci curve does not fit very well (some sites are off by what seems to be tens or hundreds of miles), and no accounting is made for spherical geometry, so the curve that looks good on a flat map may not actually be in the Fibonacci ratio on a spherical surface. In fact, I'm not certain Wolter's hand-drawn spiral is an actual Fibonacci spiral if one were to work out the exact proportions.

So we end with a threat for more of the same next season, continuing on the quest to find Europeans in America and more Jesus/Holy Bloodline material. I had hoped that after this season Wolter would expand to non-European, non-Caucasian claims, but after this episode he seemed dedicated to establishing a European presence in medieval America. In spring 2013 Wolter began filming the second season of the show, with trips to investigate a supposed prehistoric rock wall in Texas and Viking voyages to Martha's Vineyard, indicating a similar though possibly wider scope for the second season. I think, though, that the most fitting description summing up all of *America Unearthed* over the thirteen episodes of the first season is one Wolter delivered himself in this episode: The show is about "all these things we've been talking ourselves into."

The Meaning of AMERICA UNEARTHED

Summing Up

At the end of its first season, *America Unearthed* reigned as the highest rated program on H2. The channel issued a press release trumpeting the record ratings, which crossed the one million viewer mark in January 2013 and continued to rise. As a result, the program sparked some of the most passionate response I have ever received for anything I've written. Steve St. Clair, Dennis Parada, Jeff Lutgen, and several more show guests all stopped by my website to complain about the reviews you have just read, and Scott Wolter himself wrote to me several times to criticize my handling of his claims: "I've concluded this [is] a site driven by something closer to religious zealotry rather than truly scientific thinking. Paying lip service to 'science' doesn't mean you practice it," Wolter wrote to me a few weeks into the show's run. "In the past, the strong negative reaction I've received was based on fear and I sense that is part of what is going on here."[1] Accusations of deep-seated fear were among the milder responses.

I've received messages that ranged from positive to horrifying. I've been called a douche, an arrogant know-it-all, an elitist, a betrayer of the white race, a jealous hater, a profiteer, and part of an academic anti-Wolter conspiracy. By far, though, the most frequent complaint is that I am not "open minded," which astounds me since the very definition of being open minded is that I am willing to entertain Wolter's ideas and look for evidence rather than simply dismiss them as the impossible delusions of an ideologue. But by "open minded" most don't mean the desire for inquiry; they use it as a synonym for anti-elitism and an opposition to what they see as academic and intellectual elites who monopolize knowledge. Being "open minded" means, in essence, agreeing with their world view. Interestingly, none of these angry readers had checked my previous work before complaining. Many were surprised to discover that I have been equally critical of *Ancient Aliens* (in identical weekly reviews, collected as *A Critical Companion to Ancient Aliens* in 2012) as well as detailed reviews of specific books by Erich von Däniken, Gavin Menzies, David Childress, Frank Joseph, Alan Butler and Christopher Knight, and more—and that I've been doing this since 2001.

But after having the chance to review all thirteen episodes of the first season, I'd like to talk for a minute about the meta-narrative the show presented. This meta-narrative isn't intentional, but it is the message that the show is communicating through the editorial choices it made over thirteen investigations. Consider this:

- Number of Native Americans interviewed in 13 episodes of the show: 0
- Number of non-white people interviewed in 13 episodes of the show: 1
- Number of non-Western cultures alleged to have come to America out of 13 investigations: 1
- Number of Native American sites attributed to Native Americans in 13 episodes: 0

For the record, the non-white person was the American-trained archaeologist Alfonso Morales, and the only non-white culture was the Maya. Both were in the same episode, and that episode was designed to tie in to the December 21, 2012 "Maya Apocalypse" programming on the H2 network. Even in that episode, the Native American (Creek) mound site at Ocmulgee (Track Rock) was attributed to the Maya, a culture that alternative writers have frequently claimed was "really" from Atlantis, Phoenicia, or other non-native origins.

The discussions of Native Americans that occurred on the show are as follows:

- The Creek were slaves of or descendants of the Maya
- The Old Copper culture mined copper under the rule of the Minoans
- The native peoples of the southwest learned architecture from a medieval Englishman
- The Mound Builders were Norse Vikings
- The Mandan people were really Welsh

Additionally, Native Americans appear as background noise in several other episodes. They are referenced as hostile forces threatening the Roanoke colonists and as awed observers of the Templars' activities. Even in the season finale, when we hear of a current legend of the First Peoples (Canadian Native Americans) about cross-bedecked visitors, we don't hear it from an actual Native American but rather secondhand. Even when the Native peoples under discussion still exist and could be consulted, as in the case of the Mandan, they are ignored. It simply fails to cross anyone's mind on this show that Native Americans are and have been real people with their own intentions and actions, not just blank slates or Rousseau-style noble savages waiting for a higher civilization to give them their orders.

I'm not sure that anyone involved with *America Unearthed* is aware of the racist and nationalist background of the stories they investigate. Certainly the show betrayed no awareness of the history of the ideas under discussion. Witness, for example, the attribution of knowledge of Henry Sinclair's voyage to "legends" despite the fact that the story originated in a known publication in 1784. Similarly, you would never know from *America Unearthed* that the Episode Three "copper heist" at Lake Superior originates in the work of Ignatius Donnelly, who concluded that Native Americans were too ignorant and inferior to have mined copper, and therefore Atlantis must have done so and carried it off to start the Bronze Age in Europe. In the same way, the much earlier imagining of Native burial mounds to be the work of Vikings, Phoenicians, or a lost white race— recalled in Wolter's investigation of Minnesota giants—was intimately tied to early American efforts to colonize Native lands by delegitimizing Native land claims and was tied also to efforts to forge a new national identity.

But it's not just anti-Native American racism that drove early ideas. There's also the ethnic pride angle. The Newport Tower "mystery" was concocted in 1839 by a Scandinavian man, Carl Rafn, who wanted to attribute the discovery of America to the Vikings out of ethnic pride. (The Vikings, of course, did land in Canada, but there is no evidence they made it as far south as Rhode Island.) The Swedish-language Kensington Rune Stone just happened to show up amidst a Swedish immigrant community working hard to sink roots into newly-settled farmland. The Henry Sinclair narrative was used by one of his descendants, Thomas Sinclair, during the Chicago World's Fair in 1893 as a point of white pride, a counterpoint to the Italian narrative of Columbus, and a way to rewrite American history to exclude "Latin" peoples—Italians and Spaniards—who were not considered to be true whites at the time:

> The glorification of Columbus in the discovery centenary of 1892 was an aid towards the threatened Spanish or Latin domination; and Scandinavian energy has been in movement, especially at the Chicago Exhibition of 1893, to counteract the southern tide, by ascribing the discovery of America to Norsemen of the Teuton stock, including, as principal factors, the English and the Dutch. Caithnessmen [i.e. the Sinclair bloodline], especially of Canada and the United States, have the strongest personal interest in such a gigantic Armageddon contest of blood and belief, if it is to be early fact.[2]

None of this, of course, precludes the possibility that any one of these diffusionist claims is true; however, if the show would do the minimum to acknowledge the origins and pedigree of their claims, and the disturbing uses to which they had historically been put, it would go a long way toward mitigating the meta-narrative the show is putting out, namely, that Native Americans are primitive and ignorant wild men whom Europeans and Euro-Americans can either safely ignore or control.

So What Does It Mean?

But why is this meta-narrative returning now? The scholar of Indo-European myth Bruce Lincoln wrote an informative book in 1989 called

Discourse and the Structure of Society in which he argued that myths "can be, and have been, employed as effective instruments not only for the replication of established social forms ... but more broadly for the construction, deconstruction, and reconstruction of society itself."[3] For Lincoln, myth can serve as the vehicle whereby societies experiencing crisis can justify the practical changes needed to overcome crisis or to provide the sanction of history and the divine to maintain existing social hierarchies in the face of crisis. In *The Demon-Haunted World*, Carl Sagan offered a similar thought, though in less academic language: "Whenever our ethnic or national prejudices are aroused, in times of scarcity, during challenges to national self-esteem or nerve, when we agonize about our diminished cosmic place and purpose, or when fanaticism is bubbling up around us— then habits of thought familiar from ages past reach for the controls. The candle flames gutters. It's little pool of light trembles. Darkness gathers. The demons begin to stir."[4]

I bring this up because I am disturbed by the way *America Unearthed* host Scott Wolter has dedicated himself to a quest for the Holy Grail, which he believes is the secret set of descendants of Jesus and Mary Magdalene. In looking for a physical dimension to the Christian mysteries, this "Holy Bloodline" myth (which is not unique to Wolter, of course) seems to represent a modern yearning to make material the immaterial, to make gods into men, to give religion a physical foundation. In turn, such a yearning seems closely related to the idea that in a world where science represents the commonly accepted language of truth, the spiritual must be cast in the guise (if not the methods) of science—the same impulse behind Intelligent Design. It does, however, seem to be a bit of a step down for religion and the old faith in the transcendent.

This has nothing to do with the search for archaeological evidence for or against one particular alternative claim but rather how a multitude of claims, for which there is at very best ambiguous evidence, are sown together into an alternative worldview, one that rivals the mainstream and seems to serve a purpose beyond mere archaeological inquiry.

This also has clear parallels with what anthropology calls "revitalization movements," conscious efforts on the part of a culture under stress to restructure society. One of the best known examples is that of the Seneca prophet Handsome Lake, who in the years around 1800 preached a new religion in the guise of resurrecting traditional Iroquois (Haudenosaunee) values. His faith was particularly appealing because in a time when the Iroquois were under pressure from white Americans to adopt Euro-American culture and had lost their traditional lands to white settlers, Handsome Lake emphasized a strong, indigenous identity—but he did so by adopting and adapting the values of Christianity. He eventually descended into literal witch-hunting, accusing his followers right and left of being witches. A similar movement in those years among white Americans in search of a new national identity after the break from Britain gave rise to the lost white race theorists, culminating in Mormonism, with its recreated past of forgotten white mound builders who were the Lost Tribes of Israel come to America—a new, non-English but still "white" past. In both cases, the revivalist groups recreated the past to help negotiate the tricky politics and sociology of Euro-American settlement in lands once occupied by non-Euro-American people.

I'm certain that it is no coincidence that "alternative archaeology" tends to achieve its greatest success in periods of social upheaval. In America, it correlates well with the early Republic, Reconstruction, the Depression, the 1960s/70s, and the post-9/11 eras. (There are exceptions: American interest in Graham Hancock's lost civilization claims of the 1990s was possibly one, though its presumed web of hidden communications networks and priesthood of secret dispensers of high-tech information did parallel the technological upheavals of the Web 1.0 era.) True, it's possible to become convinced by one particular archaeological "alternative" claim, like a particular Norse expedition to Minnesota, or a stray Englishman in Anasazi territory, without becoming part of the revitalization movement. (Indeed, any one claim by itself is a scientific question.) But those who string together dozens of such claims across time and space, almost indiscriminately and largely without care about the quality of evidence, do so *because* they reject mainstream "ways of knowing," and are involved in a project designed (consciously or not) to *replace* an unsatisfying mainstream view with one that is more satisfying on an emotional level, or more useful in advocating particular cultural values that the advocate wishes society to adopt.

Making up Weird Claims

One of the problems I've often encountered in discussing speculative claims is that many readers aren't familiar with the concept of the burden of proof and therefore feel that the skeptic has an equal obligation to disprove a claim that the advocate has in proving it. But "prove me wrong" just doesn't work as science or history; otherwise, we'd spend all our days trying to disprove the existence of every wild claim ever made and have to provisionally accept anything anyone ever said as true until proved otherwise to the satisfaction of the most diehard believer. And as we've seen, no evidence will ever convince the most zealous advocates that they are wrong. That's why science deals in probabilities, not absolutes, and makes provisional claims based on evidence, not absolute truth claims from dogma.

In fact, I've had more than one person take exception to my suggestion that the evidence Scott Wolter used to spin his stories was no better than that used for other speculative claims, including patently absurd ones like unicorns. Why should Wolter have all the fun? I thought it might be entertaining and a fitting conclusion to this exploration of *America Unearthed* to use the *America Unearthed* system of speculation to see if we can "prove" that unicorns exist. So, here is my outline for how to develop a new episode of *America Unearthed* entirely from hot air. Read and enjoy, but note that nothing here is as it seems....

Unicorns in America?

T he show should start with a sepia-toned recreation of an old-timey person walking through some woods. His jaw will drop as he sees... a CGI unicorn! Then we'll need some splashy graphics and a good intro: *HISTORY AS WE KNOW IT IS WRONG! Academic elites are keeping the truth from you! Facts can lie, but TV never does.* Then we'll start the show proper. To do so, we'll need some wild stories that someone, somewhere once encountered a unicorn. This should preferably have occurred in the backwoods of rural America and have taken place sometime between 1500 and 1925 to ensure no living person survives to confirm the story. Can we do this? Yes, we can. In exploring the land of Spanish Florida in his second voyage of 1565, Sir John Hawkins recorded in his journal that he encountered evidence of unicorns:

> The Floridians have pieces of unicorns' horns, which they wear about their necks, whereof the Frenchmen obtained many pieces. Of those unicorns they have many; for that they do affirm it to be a beast with one horn, which, coming to the river to drink, putteth the same into the water before he drinketh. Of this unicorn's horn there are of our company that, having gotten the same of the Frenchmen, brought home thereof to show.[1]

An expedition led by John Davis, the arctic explorer fooled by the Zeno Map hoax, reported that that it found unicorn horns as far up as 67° 40′ north latitude in 1588, in the hands of an Inuit. This report comes from John Janes, a merchant who accompanied Davis on the expedition:

Of them I had a darte with a bone in it, or a piece of Unicornes horne, as I did judge. This dart he made store of, but when he saw a knife, he let it go, being more desirous of the knife than of his dart.[2]

Further, Dr. Olfert Dapper in *Die Unbekannte Nue Welt* (1673) writes that there were unicorns in Maine. In Odell Shepard's translation:

On the Canadian border there are sometimes seen animals resembling horses, but with cloven roofs, rough manes, a long straight horn upon the forehead, a curled tail like that of the wild boar, black eyes, and a neck like that of the stag. They live in the loneliest wildernesses and are so shy that the males do not even pasture with the females except in the season of rut, when they are not so wild. As soon as this season is past, however, they fight not only with other beasts but even with those of their own kind.[3]

So, now we have historic sightings up and down America's east coast—the very coast where the European voyagers must have landed after leaving Europe. According to Hawkins, we also have "horns" as artifacts, which means that we can then do some fake geological tests to "prove" that these horns are in fact more than five hundred years old and therefore genuine. Fossilized bone can't easily be tested for DNA, so as long as it's fossilized no one can prove it's *not* a unicorn horn. How did unicorns get here, and what don't academics want you to know?

We should also see if a famous historical figure, preferably a major European with occult connections, had anything to say about unicorns. Oh, here we go. Leonardo da Vinci talked about unicorns in his notebooks: "The unicorn, through its intemperance and not knowing how to control itself, for the love it bears to fair maidens forgets its ferocity and wildness; and laying aside all fear it will go up to a seated damsel and go to sleep in her lap, and thus the hunters take it."[4] The traveler Marco Polo also claimed to have seen one in Asia: "Here are wild elephants, and unicorns not much smaller, being double the size of buffalo. They have a large black horn in the middle of the forehead..."[5] According to Polo, unicorn leather was a leading export from India to Arabia. Obviously, there is a deep conspiracy connection that the academic elite are covering up. What could it be, and what is the connection to America?

We should fly to Britain to find out because that's what our travel budget already expensed for other episodes. Experts in medieval lore will explain that the unicorn's association with virginity and purity meant that it was a symbol of Christ. We will also be amazed to discover that the unicorn is prominently featured on the coat of arms of the United Kingdom. Could this be a coincidence? Of course not. The unicorn, we will learn, was added as a supporter to the heraldic arms of England in 1603, when England, symbolized by a lion, joined with... wait for it... *Scotland*, in personal union under King James. The unicorn was meant to symbolize Scotland because the unicorn was associated with purity and freedom, but those of us in the know understand that Scotland has an occult connection to the Knights Templar, who fled to Scotland after the suppression of their order, hid the Holy Grail in Rosslyn Chapel, and became the Scottish Rite Freemasons.

We're getting in deep now.

At Rosslyn Chapel, we learn that the Holy Grail (*San greal*) was in fact a symbol of the womb of Mary Magdalene, who is believed by occult speculators to have been the wife of Jesus and the mother of his child. Spirited away to France, the bloodline (*sang real*) spawned by this union gave rise to Merovingian kings on the Continent. Kicked out of power by the Carolingians, they lay hidden, protected by various orders including the Knights Templar until the Catholic Church disbanded the Templars, who moved to Scotland and became Freemasons. We know this because Scott Wolter tells us so, on the strength of his hooked X. In Scotland, the Christ bloodline eventually became, according to ancient astronaut theorist Laurence Gardner, the Stuarts in Scotland, whose most famous scion was James I of England (James VI of Scotland)!

But what did King James know about unicorns?

To find out, we turn to the King James Bible, commissioned by that monarch, where shockingly we find the mysterious unicorn mentioned throughout, in Job 39:9–12; Psalms 22:21, 29:6; Numbers 23:22, 24:8; and Deuteronomy 33:17.

In fact, the King James Bible seems to encode in its unicorn references a clear description of Templar-Freemason-Holy Grail activities. Job 39 seems to tell us about the Templars' historic role preserving the lineage (or "seed") of Christ, hiding it safe in their towers and temples:

> Will the unicorn be willing to serve thee, or abide by thy crib?
>
> Canst thou bind the unicorn with his band in the furrow? or will he harrow the valleys after thee?
>
> Wilt thou trust him, because his strength is great? or wilt thou leave thy labour to him?
>
> Wilt thou believe him, that he will bring home thy seed, and gather it into thy barn?

Psalm 22:21 appears to tell us that the Templars saved the Scottish bloodline of Christ from English corruption: "Save me from the lion's mouth: for thou hast heard me from the horns of the unicorns." This secretly-encoded message in the King James Bible seems to be a clear instruction to seek out the true divine bloodline in Scotland, not England. But there's more: Psalm 29:6 says that God "maketh them also to skip like a calf; Lebanon and Sirion like a young unicorn." But Sirion is an historical name for Mount Hermon, where the Book of Enoch states that the Fallen Angels descended to mate with human women. Is this a reference to the fact that the unicorn represents the bloodline of divine Christ and mortal Mary Magdalene? Numbers 23:22 tells us what happened next: "God brought them out of Egypt; he hath as it were the strength of an unicorn." Clearly, the King James Bible is telling us that the bloodline escaped the Old World (the evil, corrupt "Egypt") for the New! This is confirmed in Deuteronomy 33:17, where we read that the Templars decided to take the Bloodline of Christ from Scotland to America: "His glory is like the firstling of his bullock, and his horns are like the horns of unicorns: with them he shall push the people together to the ends of the earth." What was the farthest point on the sixteenth century earth? The New World. Obviously, this passage means that God's chosen people will gather in America.

But the Knights Templar connection doesn't end there. The unicorn was also said to be the special possession of Prester John, a shadowy medieval figure who ruled in either Ethiopia, where the Templars are said to have spirited the Ark of the Covenant and introduced Christianity (as Graham Hancock informed us in *The Sign and the Seal*), or in India, where the Greek writer Ctesias recorded the presence of the unicorn in his *History of India* 2,500 years ago: "In India there are wild asses as large as horses, or even larger. Their body is white, their head dark red, their eyes bluish, and they have a horn in their forehead about a cubit in length."[6] (Ethiopia is also the only land where the Book of Enoch was preserved... coincidence?)

This same unicorn appears in the art of the Indus Valley civilization thousands of years earlier still. The Indus Valley civilization, one of the oldest on earth, lost its place to the Aryan invasion, according to nineteenth century scholars, who of course must be correct because they are old and therefore smarter than twenty-first century scholars. These Aryans spread from India to England, and they must have adopted the unicorn as their symbol when they became civilized after conquering India. As a result, the warrior caste of these Aryans (confirmed to exist by the preeminent scholar of Indo-European society, Georges Dumézil) must have been the precursors to the Knights Templar. Consider: Both groups rode horses, used weapons and armor, recited epic poetry, and took orders from a high-ranking spiritual elite. Clearly they are the same people.

Now, *America Unearthed* already established that medieval and ancient peoples did not make up fanciful depictions of, say, *dinosaurs*, and rock drawings of boats are accurate enough to identify the specific type of ship, so any depiction must be a real creature. Given the wide range of unicorns depicted in art from the Indus Valley to the Middle Ages, we must conclude that there is good evidence for unicorns, especially since medieval apothecaries stocked "unicorn horn" among their medical offerings and we all know that if there is an artifact attached, it must be a real animal. In 1663, an entire unicorn skeleton was uncovered in Germany, buried in limestone—like the famous Tucson *caliche*—and was reconstructed by Gottfried Wilhelm von Leibniz, becoming the toast of Europe. This unicorn was, like that of Polo and Ctesias, "the size of a horse" or greater,[7] and its horn still exists today and can be geologically tested to "prove" it is ancient... no, wait, let's "prove" it's medieval instead. Caliche only takes a few hundred years to form, right?

So what does this tell us? *America Unearthed* established that the Knights Templar came to America and explored the East Coast (where they built the Newport Tower). Certainly a branch of them came prior to Columbus, but why? Could they have been looking for their predecessors, the "precursors" who buried the Tucson Artifacts in the 800s CE? And would they have used unicorns to find them? Clearly, when the precursors left Europe for Arizona because "some Muslim group," as Scott Wolter has established, had forced them from Europe, they took with them their most precious cargo: A member of the Bloodline of Christ and his guardian unicorns. Every divine figure had his or her guardian animals. Just as Zeus had his bulls and Marduk his dragon, so too did Christ have his unicorn. His descendant would, of course, have needed an escort of unicorns to serve at his court.

We also know that when the conquistador Hernando de Soto arrived in the New World to explore the southern United States, he brought pigs with him. Some of these pigs escaped and went feral, becoming the razorbacks of the South. Some of the unicorn herd the Templar precursors brought with them must have escaped as they made their way down the East Coast, producing the herds of wild unicorns found in Maine and in Florida. From the distribution of unicorns, we know that the Templar precursors must have sailed the northerly route, from Scotland to Iceland to Greenland to Canada and then down the East Coast.

Or perhaps the more recent Templars of the 1300s brought their unicorns with them when they built the Newport Tower. We know from John of Hesse that unicorns roamed the Holy Land in 1389, when he saw one,[8] so obviously the Templars had access to unicorns during the two centuries when they were headquartered atop Jerusalem's Temple Mount. Unicorns were still active in the Sinai region in 1483 when Felix Fabri saw one,[9] but by then they were by then on the brink of extinction. The last unicorn supposedly died at Mecca around 1600. Did the Templars bring these unicorns to America to save them from Muslim and Catholic hostility and extinction? We'll never know until we perform some spurious geological testing on the unicorn horns in the possession of Native American groups to see if any date back before 1300 CE. This will let us establish which Templar or pre-Templar group brought unicorns and a descendant of Christ to America.

But what happened to the last descendant of Christ? Tune in next season to find out which digital-tier cable host is the lineal descendant of Jesus and a candidate to be the Last World Emperor!

And Now, the Truth

The above speculation is based on actual facts, though the interpretations given above are of course complete lies. The actual truth is this:

- The unicorns of the King James Bible are a translation of the Greek *monoceros*, translating the Hebrew *re'em* in light of a stylized form of Assyrian art where bulls were depicted in profile, so only one horn was visible.
- There is no bloodline of Christ; this myth was fabricated in the twentieth century.
- The Knights Templar had no connection to the Freemasons, nor were they descended from an Aryan warrior priesthood.
- Medieval apothecaries ground up narwhal horns, mammoth tusks, and other bones they believed belonged to unicorns; some just committed fraud and called *anything* unicorn horn.
- Marco Polo reported on a rhinoceros, as Ctesias was also likely doing in a confused way.
- The unicorn horns seen by John Hawkins were probably various animal teeth and bones.
- The unicorn horns seen by John Janes actually belonged to narwhals.
- Leibniz's unicorn skeleton was actually a fossil elephant from the Pleistocene. He creatively "reconstructed" the skeleton into a two-legged, one-horned unicorn.
- There are no unicorn herds in the United States.

Final Thoughts

Since the first season of *America Unearthed* is the story of Scott Wolter and his quest to find Jesus' descendants in America, it only seems fair to let Wolter finish out our story. Each week Wolter asserts to an audience of a million people that scientists are conspirators and that history is a lie. That is a tremendously audacious claim, and when I tried to evaluate it, Wolter told me that he suspected I was secretly terrified he was right and that all of American history is a fraud. This is what I told him:

It's up to you to prove that case, and since no one else is willing to discuss the shortcoming of your claims, I will do that job to the best of my ability. But if you want to sit here and tell me that only you are qualified to evaluate evidence and draw conclusions to share with others, let me share this with you: You have a bachelor's in geology and no special training in archaeology and deign to tell the world that every other scientist is wrong. I have a bachelor's in archaeology and in broadcast journalism, so when I tell you that your program is bad television and bad archaeology, that isn't just me blowing smoke. That's my "expert" opinion. By your own logic, that means something.

And this is how Scott Wolter responded:

Your points are well taken and I respect your opinion. I still find your criticism a little extreme given the context of our show. It is not intended to [be] the final word (well, maybe in a couple cases), it is intended to incite reasoned debate and follow-up. As I stated before, we simply cannot go into the level of detail these matters require. However, the opinions I express are based on the facts I have in front of me and if you listen carefully, I try to make it clear when I am speculating and what I consider to be fact. I'm sure we miss the mark sometimes, but I try to be careful.[10]

I hope that this book serves as the "debate and follow-up" Scott Wolter said he hoped to incite. I doubt, though, that my reviews can be considered any more extreme than Wolter's own claim at the beginning of every episode that history is a lie and that historians and archaeologists are purposely deceiving the public to cover up a hidden history, a claim that is breathtaking in its audacity. As we have seen, the only people who have manipulated reality to craft a fictitious story are Scott Wolter, Committee Films, and H2. Through deceptive editing, selective omission, and staged material, they falsified and fabricated sections of *America Unearthed*, presented extreme speculation as solid research, and declared those who disagreed "close-minded."

Documents on Meriwether Lewis and Welsh Indians

Although America Unearthed *asserts that Thomas Jefferson provided Meriwether Lewis with secret instructions to find Welsh Indians, no such instructions survive. The following documents demonstrate the actual order of events. The first is Morgan John Rhys's letter discussing his interest in Welsh Indians. The second is Jefferson's secret message to Congress, and the third his official instructions to Lewis, which make no mention of Welsh Indians. The fourth is Jefferson's letter of 1804—after the expedition was underway—indicating that Morgan John Rhys, a Welsh expatriate and supporter of the Welsh Indian theory, would write with information about the same. This letter clearly indicates that such an investigation was not part of the original plan, as Jefferson references the Welsh Indians only in passing, without interest, and apparently uninformed about them. He is more concerned about the utility of the regional map an earlier searcher for Welsh Indians had made. Nor was this secret: The journals of expedition members Joseph Whitehouse and John Ordway, our final documents, make mention of the group's encounter with a tribe they thought might be Welsh—quite possibly due to the arrival of Rhys's letter.*

A. Letter of Morgan John Rhys[1]

Philadelphia Nov. 24th 1795

Dr. Sir,

No, you shall not say 'The Editor of the Welsh Magazine is gone! We shall hear no more from him!' I acknowledge I should have wrote sooner; but I wanted to give you some information concerning this country. I have now finish'd my tour, through the greater Part of the United States, the south & north western territories—In the course of last year I travell'd, at least, on this continent between 4 & 5000 miles—It would but spoil the story to begin a relation of it here should you at any future period wish to obtain any particular acct of this part of the world I shall be ready to relate, according to the dictates of truth.

You have heard I expect before this time that John Evans is at length gone up the Missouri. I was the beg[inn]ing of last May within about 300 miles of him—I had a full account of his peregrinations to that time from G. Turner one of the supreme Judges for the North Western territory—wh[o] saw him at St. Louis N. West of the Mississipi 12 miles below the mouth of the Missouri. Poor John Evans had been imprisoned by the order of the Commandant of St. Louis—and had it not been for the interference of Judge Turner, his enterprising spirit must have died in that place. Turner pleaded for him to some purpose. He has obtained from the Commandant passports in Spanish french & English to go on his journey. He has likewise gone up the Missouri with the Indian traders with proper articles to introduce himself to the different tribes—According to his present directions he is to trace the Missouri to its source—to approach the burning mountain as near as he can—to follow the Western Waters to the passific—and whether he meets with the Welsh Madogians or not—he will receive on his return 2 or 3000 dollars from the Spanish government—I have heard many additional tales concerning what they call the Welsh Indians but as yet I have my doubts about them. I have conversed with the acting partner in the Missouri Co. He has been among more Indians than any other white man on this continent. He knows nothing of the Welsh language but by my conversing in Welsh—he could not recognize the words nor the idiom altogether among the Indians North of the Missouri—he thinks the *Padoucas* are out of the question. however I deliver'd him a Welsh Vocabulary & begg'd of him to give all the assistance he could to John Evans should he meet him. This man is to remain on the Missouri for 3 or 4 years to trade with the Indians. He has promised to write to me from time to time, and I do assure you it afforded me much pleasure to meet with a man of his disposition & information engaged in the Indian trade.

It is a confirmed fact that there are white Indians on the Missouri and in many places far west of the Mississippi. I have seen deer and buffaloe skins with various other articles dressed by them in a most capital manner. A frenchman has lately been up the Missouri for fifteen hundred miles and by what he could judge of the stream & country, that river must be about 2,400 miles in length. I have seen a map likewise of the Mississipi by actual survey to its source. It is no more like the present Mississipi on paper, than a cow is to a snake. It forms an elbow and runs westward long before it meets the line appointed for the limits of the United States. Every part of this continent affords sufficient proofs of a more civilised people having existed here than the present Indians—At the last treaty, North West of the Ohio, I had an opportunity of conversing with & seeing somthing of the manners of a great No of the tribes. There was between 6 and 700 of them together, among whom were a greater number of Chiefs than ever was seen together on this continent—I began a vocabulary of their different languages, the finishing part of which I was oblig'd to leave to the chaplain of the Army and one of the surgeons. I have heard from a freind in the north of England that another attempt is to be made to enlighten the Welsh people thro ye medium of a Welsh register—Should it be carried into execution, perhaps I may give some assistance by telling some Indian tales, or at some future time, I may transmit to you a description of the ancient fortifications, mounds, barrows, graves, & the curiosities found in them on the Ohio etc. etc.

[*The rest of the letter is missing.*]

B. Thomas Jefferson's Secret Message to Congress
January 18, 1803.

Gentlemen of the Senate, and of the House of Representatives:

As the continuance of the act for establishing trading houses with the Indian tribes will be under the consideration of the Legislature at its present session, I think it my duty to communicate the views which have guided me in the execution of that act, in order that you may decide on the policy of continuing it, in the present or any other form, or discontinue it altogether, if that shall, on the whole, seem most for the public good.

The Indian tribes residing within the limits of the United States, have, for a considerable time, been growing more and more uneasy at the constant diminution of the territory they occupy, although effected by their own voluntary sales: and the policy has long been gaining strength with them, of refusing absolutely all further sale, on any conditions; insomuch that, at this time, it hazards their friendship, and excites dangerous jealousies and perturbations in their minds to make any overture for the purchase of the smallest portions of their land. A very few tribes only are not yet obstinately in these dispositions. In order peaceably to counteract this policy of theirs, and to provide an extension of territory which the rapid increase of our numbers will call for, two measures are deemed expedient. First: to encourage them to abandon hunting, to apply to the raising stock, to agriculture and domestic manufacture, and thereby prove to themselves that less land and labor will maintain them in this, better than in their former mode of living. The extensive forests necessary in the hunting life, will then become useless, and they will see advantage in exchanging them for the means of improving their farms, and of increasing their domestic comforts. Secondly: to multiply trading houses among them, and place within their reach those things which will contribute more to their domestic comfort, than the possession of extensive, but uncultivated wilds. Experience and reflection will develop to them the wisdom of exchanging what they can spare and we want, for what we can spare and they want. In leading them to agriculture, to manufactures, and civilization; in bringing together their and our settlements, and in preparing them ultimately to participate in the benefits of our governments, I trust and believe we are acting for their greatest good. At these trading houses we have pursued the principles of the act of Congress, which directs that the commerce shall be carried on liberally, and requires only that the capital stock shall not be diminished. We consequently undersell private traders, foreign and domestic, drive them from the competition; and thus, with the good will of the Indians, rid ourselves of a description of men who are constantly endeavoring to excite in the Indian mind suspicions, fears, and irritations towards us. A letter now enclosed, shows the effect of our competition on the operations of the traders, while the Indians, perceiving the advantage of purchasing from us, are soliciting generally, our establishment of trading houses among them. In one quarter this is particularly interesting. The Legislature, reflecting on the late occurrences on the Mississippi, must be sensible how desirable it is to possess a respectable breadth of country on that river, from our Southern limit to the Illinois at least; so that we may present as firm a front on that as on our Eastern border. We possess what is below the Yazoo, and can probably acquire a certain breadth from the Illinois and Wabash to the Ohio; but between the Ohio and Yazoo, the country all belongs to the Chickasaws, the most friendly tribe within our limits, but the most decided against the alienation of lands. The portion of their country most important for us is exactly that which they do not inhabit. Their settlements are not on the Mississippi, but in the interior country. They have lately shown a desire to become agricultural; and this leads to the desire of buying implements and comforts. In the strengthening and gratifying of these wants, I see the only prospect of planting on the Mississippi itself, the means of its own safety. Duty has required me to submit these views to the judgment of the Legislature; but as their disclosure might embarrass and defeat their effect, they are committed to the special confidence of the two Houses.

While the extension of the public commerce among the Indian tribes, may deprive of that source of profit such of our citizens as are engaged in it, it might be worthy the attention of Congress, in their care of individual as well as of the general interest, to point, in another direction, the enterprise of these citizens, as profitably for themselves, and more usefully for the public. The river Missouri, and the Indians inhabiting it, are not as well known as is rendered desirable by their connexion with the Mississippi, and consequently with us. It is, however, understood, that the country on that river is inhabited by numerous tribes, who furnish great supplies of furs and peltry to the trade of another nation, carried on in a high latitude, through an infinite number of portages and lakes, shut up by ice through a long season. The commerce on that line could bear no competition with that of the Missouri, traversing a moderate climate, offering according to the best accounts, a continued navigation from its source, and possibly with a single portage, from the Western Ocean, and finding to the Atlantic a choice of channels through the Illinois or Wabash, the lakes and Hudson, through the Ohio and Susquehanna, or Potomac or James rivers, and through the Tennessee and Savannah, rivers. An intelligent officer, with ten or twelve chosen men, fit for the enterprise, and willing to undertake it, taken from our posts, where they may be spared without inconvenience, might explore the whole line, even to the Western Ocean, have conferences with the natives on the subject of commercial intercourse, get admission among them for our traders, as others are admitted, agree on convenient deposits for an interchange of articles, and return with the information acquired, in the course of two summers. Their arms and accoutrements, some instruments of observation, and light and cheap presents for the Indians, would be all the apparatus they could carry, and with an expectation of a soldier's portion of land on their return, would constitute the whole expense. Their pay would be going on, whether here or there. While other civilized nations have encountered great expense to enlarge the boundaries of knowledge by undertaking voyages of discovery, and for other literary purposes, in various parts and directions, our nation seems to owe to the same object, as well as to its own interests, to explore this, the only line of easy communication across the continent, and so directly traversing our own part of it. The interests of commerce place the principal object within the constitutional powers and care of Congress, and that it should incidentally advance the geographical knowledge of our own continent, cannot be but an additional gratification. The nation claiming the territory, regarding this as a literary pursuit, which is in the habit of permitting within its dominions, would not be disposed to view it with jealousy, even if the expiring state of its interests there did not render it a matter of indifference. The appropriation of two thousand five hundred dollars, "for the purpose of extending the external commerce of the United States," while understood and considered by the Executive as giving the legislative sanction, would cover the undertaking from notice, and prevent the obstructions which interested individuals might otherwise previously prepare in its way.

C. Thomas Jefferson's Instructions to Capt. Meriwether Lewis
June 20, 1803

To Meriwether Lewis esq. Capt. of the 1st regimt. of infantry of the U. S. of A.

Your situation as Secretary of the President of the U. S. has made you acquainted with the objects of my confidential message of Jan. 18, 1803 to the legislature; you have seen the act they passed, which, tho' expressed in general terms, was meant to sanction those objects, and you are appointed to carry them into execution.

Instruments for ascertaining, by celestial observations, the geography of the country through which you will pass, have been already provided. Light articles for barter and presents among the Indians, arms for your attendants, say for from 10. to 12. men, boats, tents, & other travelling apparatus, with ammunition, medecine, surgical instruments and provisions you will have prepared with such aids as the Secretary at War can yield in his department; & from him also you will recieve authority to engage among our troops, by voluntary agreement, the number of attendants above mentioned, over whom you, as their commanding officer, are invested with all the powers the laws give in such a case.

As your movements while within the limits of the U.S. will be better directed by occasional communications, adapted to circumstances as they arise, they will not be noticed here. What follows will respect your proceedings after your departure from the United states.

Your mission has been communicated to the ministers here from France, Spain & Great Britain, and through them to their governments; & such assurances given them as to its objects, as we trust will satisfy them. The country [of Louisiana] having been ceded by Spain to France, the passport you have from the minister of France, the representative of the present sovereign of the country, will be a protection with all its subjects; & that from the minister of England will entitle you to the friendly aid of any traders of that allegiance with whom you may happen to meet.

The object of your mission is to explore the Missouri river, & such principal stream of it, as, by it's course & communication with the waters of the Pacific Ocean, whether the Columbia, Oregan, Colorado or and other river may offer the most direct & practicable water communication across this continent, for the purposes of commerce.

Beginning at the mouth of the Missouri, you will take *careful* observations of latitude & longitude, at all remarkeable points on the river, & especially at the mouths of rivers, at rapids, at islands, & other places & objects distinguished by such natural marks & characters of a durable kind, as that they may with certainty be recognised hereafter. The courses of the river between these points of observation may be supplied by the compass the log-line & by time, corrected by the observations themselves. The variations of the compass too, in different places, should be noticed.

The interesting points of the portage between the heads of the Missouri, & of the water offering the best communication with the Pacific ocean, should also be fixed by observation, & the course of that water to the ocean, in the same manner as that of the Missouri.

Your observations are to be taken with great pains & accuracy, to be entered distinctly & intelligibly for others as well as yourself, to comprehend all the elements necessary, with the aid of the usual tables, to fix the latitude and longitude of the places at which they were taken, and are to be rendered to the war-office, for the purpose of having the calculations made concurrently by proper persons within the U.S. Several copies of these as well as of your other notes should be made at leisure times, & put into the care of the most trustworthy of your attendants, to guard, by multiplying them, against the accidental losses to which they will be exposed. A further guard would be that one of these copies be on the paper of the birch, as less liable to injury from damp than common paper.

The commerce which may be carried on with the people inhabiting the line you will pursue, renders a knolege of those people important. You will therefore endeavor to make yourself acquainted, as far as a diligent pursuit of your journey shall admit, with the names of the nations & their numbers;

the extent & limits of their possessions; their relations with other tribes of nations; their language, traditions, monuments;

their ordinary occupations in agriculture, fishing, hunting, war, arts, & the implements for these;

their food, clothing, & domestic accommodations;

the diseases prevalent among them, & the remedies they use;

moral & physical circumstances which distinguish them from the tribes we know; peculiarities in their laws, customs & dispositions;

and articles of commerce they may need or furnish, & to what extent.

And, considering the interest which every nation has in extending & strengthening the authority of reason & justice among the people around them, it will be useful to acquire what knolege you can of the state of morality, religion, & information among them; as it may better enable those who endeavor to civilize & instruct them, to adapt their measure to the existing notions & practices of those on whom they are to operate.

Other objects worthy of notice will be

the soil & face of the country, it's growth & vegetable productions, especially those not of the U.S.

the animals of the country generally, & especially those not known in the U.S. the remains or accounts of any which may be deemed rare or extinct;

the mineral productions of every kind; but more particularly metals, limestone, pit coal, & salt-petre; salines & mineral waters, noting the temperature of the last, & such circumstances as may indicate their character;

volcanic appearances;

climate, as characterized by the thermometer, by the proportion of rainy, cloudy, & clear days, by lightening, hail, snow, ice, by the access & recess of frost, by the winds prevailing at different seasons, the dates at which particular plants put forth or lose their flower, or leaf, times of appearance of particular birds, reptiles or insects.

Altho' your route will be along the channel of the Missouri, yet you will endeavor to inform yourself, by enquiry, of the character & extent of the country watered by it's branches, & especially on it's Southern side. The North river or Rio Bravo which runs into the gulph of Mexico, and the North river, or Rio colorado which runs into the gulph of California, are understood to be the principal streams heading opposite to the waters of the Missouri, and running Southwardly. Whether the dividing grounds between the Missouri & them are mountains or flatlands, what are their distance from the Missouri, the character of the intermediate country, & the people inhabiting it, are worthy of particular enquiry. The Northern waters of the Missouri are less to be enquired after, becaue they have been ascertained to a considerable degree, & are still in a course of ascertainment by English traders, and travellers. But if you can learn any thing certain of the most Northern source of the Missisipi, & of its position relatively to the lake of the woods, it will be interesting to us.

Some account too of the path of the Canadian traders from the Missisipi, at the mouth of the Ouisconsin to where it strikes the Missouri, & of the soil and rivers in it's course, is desireable.

In all your intercourse with the natives, treat them in the most friendly & conciliatory manner which their own conduct will admit; allay all jealousies as to the object of your journey, satisfy them of its innocence, make them acquainted with the position, extent, character, peaceable & commercial dispositions of the U.S. of our wish to be neighborly, friendly & useful to them, & of our dispositions to a commercial intercourse with them; confer with them on the points most convenient as mutual emporiums, and the articles of most desireable interchange for them & us. If a few of their influential chiefs, within practicable distance, wish to visit us, arrange such a visit with them, and furnish them with authority to call on our officers, on their entering the U.S to have them conveyed to this place at the public expense. If any of them should wish to have some of their young people brought up with us, & taught such arts as may be useful to them, we will receive, instruct & take care of them. Such a mission, whether of influential chiefs or of young people, would give some security to your own party. Carry with you some matter of the kinepox; inform those of them with whom you may be, of it'[s] efficacy as a preservative from the small-pox; & instruct & incourage them in the use of it. This may be especially done wherever you winter.

As it is impossible for us to foresee in what manner you will be recieved by those people, whether with hospitality or hostility, so is it impossible to prescribe the exact degree of perseverance with which you are to pursue your journey. We value too much the lives of citizens to offer them to probable destruction. Your numbers will be sufficient to secure you against the unauthorised opposition of individuals or of small parties: but if a superior force, authorised, or not authorised, by a nation, should be arrayed against your further passage, and inflexibly determined to arrest it, you must decline its further pursuit, and return. In the loss of yourselves, we should lose also the information you will have acquired. By returning safely with that, you may enable us to renew the essay with better calculated means. To your own discretion therefore must be left the degree of danger you may risk, and the point at which you should decline, only saying we wish you to err on the side of your safety, and to bring back your party safe even it if be with less information.

As far up the Missouri as the white settlements extend, an intercourse will probably be found to exist between them & the Spanish post of St. Louis opposite Cahokia, or Ste. Genevieve opposite Kaskaskia. From still further up the river, the traders may furnish a conveyance for letters. Beyond that, you may perhaps be able to engage Indian to bring letters for the government to Cahokia or Kaskaskia, on promising that they shall there receive such special compensation as you shall have stipulated with them. Avail yourself of these means to communicate to us, at seasonable intervals, a copy of your journal, notes & observations, of every kind, putting into cypher whatever might do injury if betrayed.

Should you reach the Pacific ocean inform yourself of the circumstances which may decide whether the furs of those parts may not be collected as advantageously at the head of the Missouri (convenient as it supposed to the waters of the Colorado & Oregan or Columbia) as at

Nootka sound, or any other point of that coast; and that trade be consequently conducted through the Missouri & U.S. more beneficially than by
the circumnavigation now practised.

On your arrival on that coast endeavor to learn if there be any port
within your reach frequented by the sea-vessels of any nation, & to send
two of your trusty people back by sea, in such way as shall appear practicable, with a copy of your notes: and should you be of opinion that the
return of your party by the way they went will be eminently dangerous,
then ship the whole, & return by sea, by way either of cape Horn, or the
cape of good Hope, as you shall be able. As you will be without money,
clothes or provisions, you must endeavor to use the credit of the U.S. to
obtain them, for which purpose open letters of credit shall be furnished
you, authorising you to draw upon the Executive of the U.S. or any of its
officers, in any part of the world, on which draughts can be disposed of, &
to apply with our recommendations to the Consuls, agents, merchants, or
citizens of any nation with which we have intercourse, assuring them, in
our name, that any aids they may furnish you, shall be honorably repaid,
and on demand. Our consuls Thomas Hewes at Batavia in Java, Win. Bu-
chanan in the Isles of France & Bourbon, & John Elmslie at the Cape of
good Hope will be able to supply your necessities by draughts on us.

Should you find it safe to return by the way you go, after sending two
of your party around by sea, or with your whole party, if no conveyance
by sea can be found, do so; making such observations on your return, as
may serve to supply, correct or confirm those made on your outward journey.

On re-entering the U.S. and reaching a place of safety, discharge any
of your attendants who may desire & deserve it, procuring for them immediate paiment of all arrears of pay & cloathing which may have in-
curred since their departure, and assure them that they shall be recom-
mended to the liberality of the legislature for the grant of a souldier's portion of land each, as proposed in my message to Congress: & repair yourself with papers to the seat of government.

To provide, on the accident of your death, against anarchy, dispersion,

& the consequent danger to your party, and total failure of the enterprize, you are hereby authorised, by any instrument signed & written in your own hand, to name the person among them who shall succeed to the command on your decease, and by like instruments to change the nomination from time to time as further experience of the characters accompanying you shall point out superior fitness: and all the powers and authorities given to yourself are, in the event of your death, transferred to, & vested in the successor so named, with further power to him, and his successors in like manner to name each his successor, who, on the death of his predecessor, shall be invested with all the powers & authorities given to yourself.

Given under my hand at the city of Washington this 20th day of June 1803.

Th. Jefferson

Pr. U.S. of America

D. Thomas Jefferson to Meriwether Lewis
January 22, 1804

Washington Jan. 22. 1804.

Dear Sir

My letters since your departure have been of July 11 & 15. Nov. 16 and Jan. 13. Yours recieved are of July 8, 15, 22, 25, Sep. 25, 30 & Oct. 3. Since the date of the last we have no certain information of your movements. With mine of Nov. 16. I sent you some extracts made by myself from the journal of an agent of the trading company of St. Louis up the Missouri. I now inclose a translation of that journal in full for your information. In that of the 13th inst. I inclosed you the map of a Mr. Evans, a Welshman, employed by the Spanish government for that purpose, but whose original object I believe had been to go in search of the Welsh Indians, said to be up the Missouri. On this subject a Mr. Rees[2] of the same nation, established in the Western parts of Pennsylvania, will write to you. N. Orleans was delivered to us on the 20th of Dec. and our garrisons &

government established there. the order for the delivery of the Upper posts were to leave N. Orleans on the 28th and we presume all those posts will be occupied by our troops by the last day of the present month. When your instructions were penned, this new position was not so authentically known as to effect the complection of your instructions. Being now become sovereigns of the country, without however any diminution of the Indian rights of occupancy we are authorised to propose to them in direct terms the institution of commerce with them. It will now be proper you should inform those through whose country you will pass, or whom you may meet, that their late fathers the Spaniards have agreed to withdraw all their troops from all the waters & country of the Missisipi, that they have surrendered to us all their subjects Spanish & French settled there, and all their posts & lands: that henceforward we become their fathers and friends, and that we shall endeavor that they shall have no cause to lament the change: that we have sent you to enquire into the nature of the country & the nations inhabiting it, to know at what places and times we must establish goods among them, to exchange for their peltries: that as soon as you return with the necessary information we shall prepare supplies of goods and persons to carry them and make the proper establishments: that in the mean time, the same traders who reside among or visit them, and who now are a part of us, will continue to supply them as usual: that we shall endeavor to become acquainted with them as soon as possible, and that they will find in us faithful friends and protectors. Although you will pass through no settlements of the Sioux (except seceders) yet you will probably meet with parties of them. On that nation we wish most particularly to make a friendly impression, because of their immense power, and because we learn they are very desirous of being on the most friendly terms with us.

I inclose you a letter which I believe is from some one on the part of the Philosophical society. They have made you a member, and your diploma is lodged with me; but I suppose it safest to keep it here & not to send it after you. Mr. Harvie departs tomorrow for France as the bearer of the Louisiana stock to Paris. Capt. William Brent takes his place with me.

Congress will probably continue in session through the month of March. your friends here & in Albemarle, as far as I recollect are well. Trist will be the Collector of N. Orleans, & his family will go to him in the spring. Dr. Bache is now in Philadelphia & probably will not return to N. Orleans.

Accept my friendly salutations & assurances of affectionate esteem & respect.

Th: Jefferson

E. Journal of Joseph Whitehouse
September 5-6, 1805

Thursday 5th Sep^t. 1805.

a clear cold morning, the Standing water froze a little last night. we hoisted our large flag this morning. Several men went out a hunting, about 10 oClock our officers held a Council with the flat head nation and told them nearly the Same as they told other nations, only told them that we wanted a flew horses from them, and we would give them Some marchandize in return. Gave 4 of their principal men meddles made them chiefs gave each of them a Shirt and a nomber of other articles also 2 flags &c. then told them that we could not Stop long with them and that we were ready to purchase their horses, and that we could not talk with them as much as we wish, for all that we Say has to go through 6 languages before it gits to them and it is hard to make them understand all what we Say. these Savages has the Strangest language of any we have ever Seen, they appear to us to have an Empeddiment in their Speech or a brogue or bur on their tongue but they are the likelyest and honestst Savages we have ever yet Seen, our officers lay out Some marchandize in different piles to trade with the natives for horses, our officers bought twelve horses and gave a Small quantity of marchandize for each horse, we swapped 7 horses which were lame &c. Gave Some Small articles to boot. we bought 10 or a Dozen pack Saddles from the natives, our hunters all came to Camp towards evening, one of them had killed 2 young Deer and one brarow.

Friday 6ᵗʰ Sepᵗ. 1805.

a clear cold morning, we began to pack up our baggage and look up our horses &c. bought a nomber of lash chords and other Small articles from the natives at 10 oClock A. M. the natives all got up their horses and Struck their lodges in order to move over on the head of the Missourie after the buffalow. they make a large Show as they are numerous and have abundance of horses, we take these Savages to be the Welch Indians if their be any Such from the Language. So Capᵗ. Lewis took down the names of everry thing in their Language, in order that it may be found out whether they are or whether they Sprang or origenated first from the welch or not. about noon we got ready to Set out. we have now 40 good pack horses, and three Colts, we loaded the horses Several men had to take 2 horses &c. 4 hunters were furnished horses without loads to hunt constant. about 1 oClock P. M. we Set out. the natives Set out at the Same time to go over on the Missourie. we proceeded on our journey, crossed a large creek went over a mountain about 7 miles came down on the Same creek and Camped nothing to eat but a little pearched corn. on[e] hunter Stayed out all night. light Sprinklings of rain through the course of the day.

F. Journal of John Ordway
September 5–6, 1805

Wednesday 4ᵗʰ Sepᵗ 1805. the morning clear, but very cold. the ground covred with frost our mockasons froze the mountains covred with snow. 2 mountain Sheep Seen by one of the men who was a hunting the horses. we delayed untill about 8 oClock A. M. then thoughed our Sailes by the fire to cover the loads and set out. ascended the mountain on to the dividing ridge and followed it some time. the Snow over our mockasons in places. we had nothing but a little pearched corn to eat the air on the mountains verry chilley and cold. our fingers aked with the cold proceeded on de-scended the mountain down a rough way passed through a large thicket of pine and balsom fer timber. in which we killed a dozen partridges or fessents. went down in to a valley on a branch running about a north course and halted. our hunter killed a deer on which we dined. our guide and the young Indian who accompanied him eat the verry guts of of the deer. Saw fresh sign of Indians. proceeded on down this valley towards evening we arived at a large encampment of the flat head nation of Indians about 40 lodges and I Suppose about 30 persons, and they have between 4 or 5 hundred horses now feeding in the plains at our view and they look like tollarable good horses the most of them. they received us in a friendly manner, when our officers went to their lodges they gave them each a white robe of dressed skins, and spread them over their Shoulders and put their arms around our necks instead of Shakeing hands as that is their way they appeared glad to see us. they smoaked with us, then gave us a pleanty Such as they had to eat, which was only Servis berrys and cherries pounded and dryed in Small cakes. Some roots of different kinds. our officers told them that we would speak to them tomorrow and told them who we were and what our business is and where we are going &. C. these natives are well dressed, descent looking Indians. light complectioned. they are dressed in mo. Sheep leather Deer & buffalow robes &C. they have the most curious language of any we have seen before. they talk as though they lisped or have a bur on their tongue. we suppose that they are the welch Indians if their is any Such from the language. they have feather lodges to live in Some other Skins among them, they tell us that they or Some of them have Seen bearded men towards the ocean, but they cannot give us any accurate *accoun* of the ocean, but we have 4 mountains to cross to go where they saw white men which was on a river as we suppose the Columbian River. came [blank in Ms.] miles to day and pitched our Camp near the creek on the right of the Indian lodges.1 considerable of large pitch pine timber in this valley our hunter killed another deer this evening.

Thursday 5ᵗʰ Sepᵗ 1805. a clear cool morning. the Standing water froze a little. the Indian dogs are so ravinous that they eat several pair of the mens Moccasons. a hard white frost this morning. Several men went out to hunt our officers purchased Several horses of the natives after Counsiling with them. they are a band of the Flat head natives. our officers made four chiefs gave them meddles 2 flags Some other Small presents and told them our business and that we were friends to all the red people &. C. which they appeared verry friendly to us. they have a great stock of horses but have no provision only roots and berrys, at this time but are on their way to the Meddison River or Missourie whire they can kill pleanty of buffalow. our officers bought 12 horses from them and gave a Small quantity of Marchandize for each horse. our officers took down Some of their language found it verry troublesome Speaking to them as all they Say to them has to go through Six languages, and hard to make them understand. these natives have the Stranges language of any we have ever yet seen. they appear to us as though they had an Impedement in their Speech or brogue on their tongue. we think perhaps that they are the welch Indians, &. C. they are verry friendly to us. they Swaped to us some of their good horses and took our worn out horses, and appeared to wish to help us as much as lay in their power.1 accommodated us with pack Saddles and chords by our giving them any small article in return towards evening our hunters came in had kild 1 deer.

Carl Rafn on the Newport Tower

1839

Wild claims about the Newport Tower derive ultimately from the work of Carl Christian Rafn (1795-1864), a Danish antiquarian who was convinced that the Norse had colonized America based upon his readings of the Norse literature. Rafn's 1839 publication about the Tower were the length of a small book. Here I present lengthy excerpts from that book to demonstrate the types of arguments Rafn used to "prove" the Tower's Norse origin, the exact same arguments Scott Wolter repurposed to "prove" a Templar connection. The complete, unabridged text is available on JasonColavito.com.

SUPPLEMENT TO THE ANTIQUITATES AMERICANÆ
ACCOUNT OF AN ANCIENT STRUCTURE IN NEWPORT, RHODE-ISLAND,
THE VINLAND OF THE SCANDINAVIANS,

communicated by Thomas H. Webb, M. D., in letters to Professor Charles C. Rafn; with remarks annexed by the latter.

Boston May 22, 1839.

In the town of Newport, near the Southern extremity of the island of Rhode-Island, stand the ruins of a structure, bearing an antique appearance, known to the inhabitants and to the numerous visitors, who flock there in the summer season, from various quarters of the Union to enjoy the pure air and the luxury of seabathing, by the homely appellation of the OLD STONE MILL.

It is situated on the west side, (near the summit), of the hill, upon which the upper part, or rear of the town is built, and is so placed as to command a view of the noble harbor, that lies to the West. This has, for a long time, been an object of wonder to beholders, exciting the curiosity of all who visit it, and giving rise to many speculations and conjectures, among both the learned and the unlearned. But nothing entirely satisfactory has ever been decided about it; it still remains shrouded with mystery; and the only reply that can be obtained to any interrogatory, addressed even to the oldest inhabitants, is that "from the time that the memory of man runneth not to the contrary it has been styled the Old Stone Mill."

Every thing about it, as many think, throws discredit upon the supposition that it was erected for a Mill, although from what we can gather we doubt not but that it may have been at some period used as such. No similar structure built in ancient or in modern times, for any purpose whatever, is to be met with in the vicinity referred to, nor indeed, so far as we have any reason to believe, in any other section of this Country. The State of Rhode-Island was first settled by the whites in *Post-Columbian* times, (using that expression, by way of distinction from the Ante-Columbian times, as, since the satisfactory evidence that has been adduced of the early visits of the Northmen, it would be manifestly incorrect to speak of the period we are now referring to, as that in which the *first* white settlers located themselves here,) we repeat, the State of Rhode-Island was first settled by the whites or Europeans, in Post-Columbian times in the year 1636. [...] The earliest manuscript record, wherein an allusion is made to the stone structure, is the Will of Governor Benedict Arnold; this was executed in 1678 being but 40 years from the settlement of the place. In this instrument it is alluded to, as his "stone built wind mill". So that it will be observed, that even then it was denominated the *mill* as though it had been built, or at least used, for one.

The question may perhaps be asked, — "If this structure were here when the English first located themselves at Newport, would they not have taken particular notice and made especial mention of it?" But on the other hand it may be said, "If it were erected subsequently, is it not reasonable to suppose that such a remarkable transaction would have been duly chronicled?" — The singularity of erecting such a unique piece of architecture, at such a time, would have been noised far and wide throughout the Colonies, and some of the writers, who were taking due note of the events of the day to transmit to the mother country, or for the information of those dwelling in the land of their adoption, would certainly, we should suppose, have penned a line or two in reference to the strange building fancies of the Rhode-Islanders. That the neighboring inhabitants were not ignorant of passing transactions in the Island Colony is abundantly evident, and that they watched with a scrutinizing eye every thing that was there going on, cannot for a moment be doubted, knowing as we do that they entertained a great jealousy towards them. But we will not extend these remarks at present.

In investigations of this description we should, where there is any rational hope of success, examine into possibilities as well as probabilities. I therefore transmit, for your inspection, drawings of the structure, thinking it at least among the possibilities that your investigations relative to the early history of America and your acquaintance with ancient structures in the North may enable you to throw some light upon the matter; at all events in so far as to decide, if this be probably the work of a period more recent than that of the Ante-Columbian settlement of this Country, which in fact I am inclined to think is the case, although my mind is not conclusively made up.

The drawings sent may be relied upon as accurate in all essential particulars, being copies from some taken expressly for me, by my friend F. Catherwood, architect, who is familiar with the relicks of bygone times, having spent years in wandering among the ruins of the East and in making researches in the Holy Land.

[Hereafter Webb describes the structure in detail and wonders why the locals made no mention of it while it was being built.]

View the subject as we may, difficulties will still meet us. It has perhaps occupied more of my time, and your attention than it really deserves. It was natural however, considering the doubts that exist, for me to direct your notice to it; as I reasonably conjectured, if there were any similarity between this structure and any in the North of Europe, supposed to have been erected about the time of the Scandinavian voyages, you would readily recognize it. The settling of the question, however it may be decided, will be advantageous, inasmuch as it will either advance us one step farther in our investigations, or by removing an obstacle aid in preparing the way for such advancement.

SUPPLEMENT TO THE ANTIQUITATES AMERICANÆ,
by Charles C. Rafn.
(Translated by John M'Caul, M.A. Oxford.)

In the Disquisitions, wherewith in the ANTIQUITATES AMERICANÆ I accompanied my edition of the Old Northern MSS relating to the Ante-Columbian history of America, I endeavoured to assign the position of those regions in that country, which were discovered by the Scandinavians in the 10th century, and of the places mentioned in the ancient accounts as having been frequented by them in the times immediately following the discovery. The situation of KIALARNES and FURDUSTRANDIR, as also of the VÍNLAND of the Northmen, is, as far as I can observe, no longer considered as doubtful. But having ventured to suggest as a probable conjecture, that the ancient Northmen not only made a settlement in those parts, but also continued to reside there during a considerable period — for several generations — it has been found difficult to reconcile this conjecture with the circumstance, that in the district in question there never has been found any building of a remote antiquity, "not a stone which appears to have been laid upon another stone, according to the principles of European Art". This has appeared inexplicable, inasmuch as the very same people erected in Greenland edifices, of which numerous ruins to this day bear Witness of the race by whom they were constructed. To this it must, however, be observed that Greenland was entirely without woods, and consequently quite destitute of timber fit for the purpose of building. The ancient MSS inform us that the inhabitants used to procure drift timber from the North of Baffin's Bay, and it would even seem from Lancaster Sound. But the quantity so obtained must have fallen very short of what they required. They were obliged, therefore, to import this material partly from

Norway, and in part also, as we find expressly stated, from Vinland. From places so remote did the European inhabitants of Greenland fetch their building timber in the 11th century. Their increased acquaintance with America would doubtless at a subsequent period render it more easy for them to procure their supplies of this material, inasmuch as they could fetch it from countries situated nearer to their own, as for example, from Markland (*Nova Scotia, New Brunswick or Lower Canada*) as is reported in the Annals of 1347. Still the supply obtained from these sources, must, from the difficulties attending its importation, have been very inadequate for the erection of the buildings themselves, and must have been nearly exclusively employed in the fitting up of the interior of their houses. Buildings, public as well as private, were therefore in Greenland erected of stone, necessity compelling the inhabitants to make use of the more accessible material, even although the working and employment of it required a greater degree of toilsome labour. Thus the church in Kakortok is built of stone obtained from the adjacent cliffs, as is still clearly perceptible in comparing those with the walls of that structure. The same inference is confirmed by the rest of the ruins in Greenland. In Iceland on the other hand, where building timber was more easy to be procured, as also in Scandinavia itself, by far the greater part of the buildings were constructed of wood, and only a very few of stone, cathedral churches and a few castles forming almost the only exceptions. The employment of wood instead of stone, even in the erection of public buildings, has been adhered to in many parts of Norway down to the latest times, and even in our own days we find in many, if not in a great majority of instances, the country churches in Norway built of wood.

The earliest settlement in Vinland occurs in the 11th century, when wooden edifices were far more general than in the subsequent centuries. The country abounded with building timber, which the Northmen exported thence to Greenland. It is natural, therefore, to conclude that also in Vinland itself they made use of this material in the construction of their dwelling houses, as is likewise confirmed by the Sagas, which expressly call the great houses (*mikil hús*) erected by Leif and Thortinn Karlsefne *búðir*, i.e. wooden houses. Wood is a substance very subject to decay. The wooden buildings which were erected in Vinland in the 11th and 12th centuries must have long ago perished. After the 13th century it seems probable that the Northmen gradually intermixed with the Aborigines of the country, as was the case in a somewhat later period in Greenland. They accordingly more and more lost their original civilization, and as the connexion with the mother country in the subsequent centuries ceased to be upheld, they gradually degenerated into a state of savagism, no longer erecting such buildings, nor feeling any interest in the maintenance of those, which they had inherited from their ancestors. It will accordingly be perceived that the circumstance of no remains of stone buildings being hitherto found in those regions affords no proof whatever against their having been in days of yore inhabited by a civilized European nation. Here, however, an opportunity presents itself of calling in question the correctness of the assertion, that in the Vinland of the Scandinavians no remains are to be found of stone buildings from the Ante-Columbian period. The ancient structure in Newport, respecting which Dr. Webb has given us the preceding account, merits a more attentive consideration.

There is no mistaking in this instance the style in which the more ancient stone edifices of the North were constructed, the style which belongs to the Roman or Ante-Gothic architecture, and which, especially after the time of Charlemagne, diffused itself from Italy over the whole of the West and North of Europe, where it continued to predominate until the close of the 12th century; that style which some authors have from one of its most striking characteristics called the round arch style, the same which in England is denominated Saxon and some times Norman architecture.

On the ancient structure in Newport there are no ornaments remaining, which might possibly have served to guide us in assigning the probable date of its erection. That no vestige whatever is found of the pointed arch, nor any approximation to it, is indicative of an earlier rather than of a later period. From such characteristics as remain, however, we can scarcely form any other inference than one, in which I am persuaded that all who are familiar with Old-Northern architecture will concur, THAT THIS

BUILDING WAS ERECTED AT A PERIOD DECIDEDLY NOT LATER THAN THE 12TH CEN-
TURY. This remark applies, of course, to the original building only, and not
to the alterations that it subsequently received; for there are several such
alterations in the upper part of the building which cannot be mistaken,
and which were most likely occasioned by its being adapted in modern
times to various uses, for example as the substructure of a windmill, and
latterly as a hay magazine. To the same times may be referred the windows, the fire place, and the apertures made above the columns. That this
building could not have been erected for a windmill, is what an architect
will easily discern.

[…] The history of art in the ancient countries of the North, more especially as regards architecture, has been as yet but very little explored.
There remain, besides, very few structures of the 11th and 12th centuries
in such a state as to enable us to trace the original style of building. But as
these structures merit by means of delineations and descriptions to be
rendered accessible to a greater number of investigators, the Royal Society
of Northern Antiquaries intend, in their Annals of next year, to commence
a series of communications on some of the more important architectural
remains of the olden time of the North, for which purpose one of our
ablest artistical historians has promised his assistance. Referring to the
more detailed descriptions to be given in the Annals, I shall at present con-
fine myself to exhibiting, for the purpose of being compared with the ancient structure in Newport, three buildings in Denmark, belonging to the
remote epoch in question.

VESTERVIG CHURCH IN JUTLAND situated near the western inlet of
Lümfiord. This church, *Ecclesia Scti Theodgari*, belonged originally to the
Augustine Monastery of this place, and was founded about the year 1110
in honor of St. Thöger, *St. Theodgarus*, who lived in the 11th century, is
said to have been born in Thüringen, went from thence first to England,
from whence he repaired to Norway and was made chaplain to St. Olave,
but came after the fall of that monarch to Denmark. The church was not
finished till towards the end of the century (1197). This church is an ob-
long building: the side walls of its nave […] are constructed of blocks of

hewn granite, and each of them is supported on five semicircular arches, the pillars of which are alternately round and square. The walls rest on the low shafted pillars alone, without being supported by buttresses. This edifice, which has so much in common with the ancient structure in Newport, and, like it, recommends itself to us by its architectural simplicity, has for its model the early style of the Christian Roman Basilica.

What is also characteristical in the ancient structure at Newport, is the low shafted columns which support the superstructure; they are of unusual thickness both in proportion to their distance from one another and to their height. The intervals between the pillars are equal to about 1½ of their diameter, and the columns, including the base and capital, are little more than three diameters of the column in height.

THE CRYPT AT VIBORG in Jutland under the Cathedral Church of that place, formerly called *Ecclesia Cathedralis beatœ Mariœ Virginis*. This church is said to have been originally built in the 11th century during the reign of Canute the Great, or of his immediate successors; but, being found too small, it was during the reign of King Nicolas, about the year 1128, rebuilt from the foundation on a much larger scale. It was not, however, finished till about the year 1169. Meanwhile the Crypt may be referred to the commencement of the 12th century, like that under the Cathedral Church of Lund in Scania to which it bears so great a resemblance.

BIERNEDE CHURCH NEAR SORÖ in Seeland, first erected about the middle of the 12th century by Ebbe, a son of Skialm White and brother of Archbishop Absalon's father Asker Ryg; and it was rebuilt of stone by Ebbe's son Sune, the hero celebrated in the Knytlinga Saga, who during the expedition against Rügen in 1168 was sent by King Waldemar the I to the castle of Arcona to break down the idol of Swantevit. [...] Here in Denmark there are still other round buildings to be met with from that early period. Of these I may mention Thorsager Church in Jutland, which from its description appears to resemble that at Biernede; and four in Bornholm, viz. St. Laurence's, St. Nicolas's, St. Olave's, and All Saints' or New Church. Of these St. Laurence's or, as it is now called, Öster Lars Church may perhaps be the most deserving of our attention here, on account of an inner round building in the same; but respecting the construction of which I am for the present unable to give a detailed account for want of correct drawings.

"For what use was this Ante-Columbian building originally intended?" is a question naturally suggested by the first view of it, That the primary and principal object of its being erected was to serve as a watch tower, is what I cannot admit, although very possibly it may have been occasionally used as a station from whence to keep a look out over the adjacent sea. On the contrary I am more inclined to believe that it had a sacred destination, and that it belonged to some monastery or Christian place of worship of one of the chief parishes in Vinland. In GREENLAND there are still to be found ruins of several *round buildings* in the vicinity of the churches. One of this description, the diameter of which is about 26 feet, is situate at the distance of 300 feet to the eastward of the great church in Igalikko; another of 44 feet in diameter at the distance of 440 feet to the eastward of the church in Kakortok; this is constructed of rough stones of from 2 to 5 feet in height; a third of 32 feet in diameter among the ruins of 111 buildings at Kanikitsok or Iglorsoït in the firth of Sermelik. These lie on an area of about 600 feet in length, which is, as it were, sown with prostrate ruins, now so completely over grown that their original plan cannot with any certainty be discerned. The most discernible is the circular building in the southeastern corner of the area. Very close to it is a ruin about 20 feet long and 16 feet broad, respecting which it is difficult to say whether it was formerly connected with the other or not. These round buildings have been most likely *Baptisteries*; for it was the practice in elder times to erect separate buildings as Baptisteries, distinct from the churches near them, it being the received opinion that no one could enter the sacred edifice of the church, until he had first been initiated by the rite of baptism. As a separate Baptistery we may mention the Constantine Baptistery near the Lateran Basilica in Roule; and similar ones are also found in other of the considerable towns of Italy, for example, in Florence, Ravenna, Parma, Pisa.

Among the ruins of MELLIFONT ABBEY in the county of Louth in Ireland, there is found, close to the Chapel of St. Bernard, an octagonal structure in the Roman style of the 12th century, probably coeval with the foundation of the Monastery A. D. 1141. [...] Each side is perforated by an arched doorway, and the exterior angles are formed by pilasters, on which the whole structure rests. The inhabitants of the neighbourhood call it a bath; but it seems more probable, and this is also the conjecture of the Irish Antiquarians, that it was a *Baptistery*. The ornaments were all of blue marble, both within and without, and when perfect it must have been master piece of its kind. A structure, on which so much pains had been bestowed, may doubtless seem to have been intended for a nobler destination than to serve as a bath.

The Ante-Columbian structure in Newport bears so much resemblance to this octagonal building that it must appear probable, that it was intended for a similar Christian use, and has possibly belonged to a church, or a monastery founded in Vinland by the ancient Northmen.

The idea which I have formed from the scanty information of the 12th century respecting the relations with America the epoch in question, I shall now proceed to lay before my readers, leaving to a more fortunate futurity, which will doubtless he possessed of much additional light, to clear up, correct, or confirm the views, which, guided merely by the feeble glimpses of the present moment I have been able to discern.

At the commencement of the century in question the population of Greenland had considerably increased, churches had been built in many of the firths both in the eastern and western settlement, or *Bygð*. Colonies had been settled in Vinland, to which country many were allured by the superior mildness of the climate and more abundant supply of the means of subsistence. [...] In different expressions, so that we cannot suppose the one to have copied from the other, the best annal codices make mention of Bishop Eric's voyage to Vinland. But about his proceedings in Vinland such ancient records as we have in our possession make no mention. We must therefore leave to future investigations and researches, whether a more clear light may be discerned in this obscure part of the Ante-Columbian history of America. Haply they may lead to a more certain decision as to whether the ancient Tholus in Newport, of which the erection appears to be coeval with the time of Bishop Eric, did really belong to a Scandinavian church or monastery, where in alternation with Latin masses the old Danish tongue was heard seven hundred years ago.

The Voyage of the Zeno Brothers

Nicolò Zeno
1558

Translated by Richard Henry Major

In the year of our Lord 1200, there was in the city of Venice a very famous gentleman named Messire Marino Zeno, who, for his great virtue and wisdom, was elected president over some of the republics of Italy; in the government of which he bore himself so discreetly, that his name was beloved and held in great respect, even by those who had never known him personally. Among other honourable actions of his, it is specially recorded that he set at rest some very serious civil disturbances which had arisen among the citizens of Verona, and from which were to be apprehended great provocations to war, had it not been for the interposition of his extreme activity and good advice.

This gentleman had a son named Messire Pietro, who was the father of the Doge Rinieri, who, dying without issue, left his property to Messire Andrea, the son of his brother Messire Marco. This Messire Andrea was Captain-General and Procurator, and held in the highest reputation for his many rare qualities. His son, Messire Rinieri, was an illustrious Senator, and several times Member of the Council. His son was Messire Pietro, Captain-General of the Christian Confederation against the Turks, and bore the name of Dragone because, on his shield, he bore a Dragon in lieu of a Manfrone, which he had borne previously. He was father of the great Messire Carlo, the famous Procurator and Captain-General against the Genoese in those perilous wars which were organised amongst nearly all the leading princes of Europe against our liberty and empire, and in which, by his great prowess, as Furius Camillus delivered Rome, so he delivered his country from an imminent risk which it ran of falling into the hands of the enemy. On this account he obtained the name of the Lion, which he bore painted on his shield as an enduring memorial of his deeds of prowess. Messire Carlo had two brothers, Messire Nicolò the Chevalier and Messire Antonio, the father of Messire Dragone. This latter was the father of Messire Caterino, father of Messire Pietro, whose son was another Messire Caterino, who died last year, being the father of Nicolò, now living.

Now M. Nicolo, the Chevalier, being a man of great courage, after the aforesaid Genoese war of Chioggia, which gave our ancestors so much to do, conceived a very great desire to see the world and to travel and make himself acquainted with the different customs and languages of mankind, so that when occasion offered, he might be the better able to do service to his country and gain for himself reputation and honour. Wherefore having made and equipped a vessel from his own resources, of which he possessed an abundance, he set forth out of our seas, and passing the Strait of Gibraltar, sailed some days on the ocean, steering always to the north, with the object of seeing England and Flanders. Being, however, attacked in those seas by a terrible storm, he was so tossed about for the space of many days with the sea and wind that he knew not where he was j and at length when he discovered land, being quite unable to bear up against the violence of the storm, he was cast on the Island of Frislanda. The crew, however, were saved, and most of the goods that were in the ship. This was in the year 1380. The inhabitants of the island came running in great numbers with weapons to set upon Messire Nicolo and his men, who being sorely fatigued with their struggles against the storm, and not knowing in what part of the world they were, were not able to make any resistance at all, much less to defend themselves with the vigour necessary under such dangerous circumstances; and they would doubtless have been very badly dealt with, had it not fortunately happened that a certain chieftain was near the spot with an armed retinue. When he heard that a large vessel had just been wrecked upon the island, he hastened his steps in the direction of the noise and outcries that were being made against our poor sailors, and driving away the natives, addressed our people in Latin, and asked them who they were and whence they came; and when he learned that they came from Italy, and that they were men of the same country, he was exceedingly rejoiced. Wherefore promising them all that they should receive no discourtesy, and assuring them that they were come into a place where they should be well used and very welcome, he took them under his protection, and pledged his honour for their safety. He was a great lord, and possessed certain islands called Porlanda, lying not far from Frislanda to the south, being the richest and most populous of all those parts. His name was Zichmni, and besides the said small islands, he was Duke of Sorano, lying over against Scotland.

Of these north parts I have thought good to draw a copy of the sailing chart which I find that I have still amongst our family antiquities, and, although it is rotten with age, I have succeeded with it tolerably well; and to those who take pleasure in such things, it will serve to throw light on the comprehension of that which, without it, could not be so easily understood. Zichmni then, being such as I have described him, was a warlike, valiant man, and specially famous in naval exploits. Having the year before gained a victory over the King of Norway, who was lord of the island, he, being anxious to win renown by deeds of arms, had come with his men to attempt the conquest of Frislanda, which is an island somewhat larger than Ireland. Whereupon, seeing that Messire Nicolò was a man of judgment, and very experienced in matters both naval and military, he gave him permission to go on board his fleet with all his men, and charged the captain to pay him all respect, and in all things to take advantage of his advice and experience.

This fleet of Zichmni consisted of thirteen vessels, whereof two only were rowed with oars; the rest were small barks and one ship. With these they sailed to the westwards, and with little trouble gained possession of Ledovo and Ilofe and other small islands in a gulf called Sudero, where in the harbour of the country called Sanestol they captured some small barks laden with salt fish. Here they found Zichmni, who came by land with his army, conquering all the country as he went. They stayed here but a little while, and making their course still westwards, they came to the other cape of the gulf, and then turning again they fell in: with certain islands and lands which they brought into possession of Zichmni. This sea through which they sailed, was in a manner full of shoals and rocks; so that had Messire Nicolò and the Venetian mariners not been their pilots, the whole fleet, in the opinion of all that were in it, would have been lost, so inexperienced were Zichmni's men in comparison with ours, who had been, one might say, born, trained np, and grown old in the art of navigation. Now the fleet having done as described, the captain, by the advice of Messire Nicolò, determined to go ashore at a place called Bondendon, to learn what success Zichmni had had in his wars, and there to their great satisfaction they heard that he had fought a great battle and put to flight the army of the enemy; in consequence of which victory, ambassadors were sent from all parts of the island to yield the country up into his hands, taking down their ensigns in every town and village. They decided therefore to stay in that place to await his coming, taking it for granted that he would be there very shortly. On his arrival there were great demonstrations of joy, as well for the victory by land as for that by sea; on account of which the Venetians received from all such great honour and praise that there was no talk but of them, and of the great valour of Messire Nicolo. Whereupon the chieftain, who was a great lover of valiant men, and especially of those that were skilled in nautical matters, caused Messire Nicolò to be brought before him, and after having honoured him with many words of commendation, and complimented his great zeal and skill, by which two things he acknowledged himself to have received a very great and inestimable benefit, viz. the preservation of his fleet and the winning of so many places without any trouble to himself, he conferred on him the honour of knighthood, and rewarded his men with very handsome presents. Departing thence they went in triumphant manner towards Frislanda, the chief city of that island, on the south-east of it, lying inside a bay in which there is such great abundance of fish that many ships are laden therewith to supply Flanders, Brittany, England, Scotland, Norway and Denmark, and by this trade they gather great wealth.

The description thus far is taken from a letter sent by Messire Nicolò to Messire Antonio, his brother, requesting that he would find some vessel to bring him out to him. Whereupon, he having as great a desire as his brother to see the world and make acquaintance with various nations, and thereby make himself a great name, bought a ship, and, directing his course that way, after a long voyage in which he encountered many dangers, at length joined Messire Nicolò in safety, and was received by him with great' gladness, not only as being his brother by blood, but also in courage.

Messire Antonio remained in Frislanda and dwelt there fourteen years, four years with Messire Nicolò, and ten years alone. Here they won such grace and favour with the prince that, to gratify M. Nicolò, and still more because he knew full well his value, he made him captain of his navy, and with much warlike preparation they went out to attack Estlanda [Shetland], which lies off the coast between Frislanda and Norway; here they did much damage, but hearing that the King of Norway was coming against them with a great fleet to draw them off from this attack, they departed under such a terrible gale of wind, that they were driven upon certain shoals and a good many of their ships were wrecked. The remainder took shelter in Grislanda, a large island but uninhabited. The king of Norway's fleet being caught in the same storm, was utterly wrecked and lost in those seas. When Zichmni received tidings of this from one of the enemy's ships that was driven by chance upon Grislanda, he repaired his fleet, and perceiving that the Shetlands lay not far off to the northward, determined to make an attack upon Islanda [or Shetland], which together with the rest was subject to the king of Norway. Here, however, he found the country so well fortified and defended, that his fleet being but small and very ill-appointed both with weapons and men, he was fain to give up that enterprise without effecting anything, but removed his attack to the other islands in those channels which are called Islande, [or the Shetlands] which are seven in number, viz., Talas, Broas, Iscant, Trans, Mimant, Dambere, and Bres; and having taken them all he built a fort in Bres, where he left Messire Nicolò, with some small vessels and men and stores. For his

own part, thinking that he had done enough for the present, he returned
with those few ships that remained to him, in all safety to Frislanda.
Messire Nicolò being left behind in Bres, determined the next season to
make an excursion with the view of discovering land. Accordingly he fit-
ted out three small barks in the month of July, and sailing towards the
North arrived in Engroneland. Here he found a monastery of the order of
Friars Preachers, and a church dedicated to St. Thomas, hard by a hill
which vomited fire like Vesuvius and Etna. There is a spring of hot water
there with which they heat both the church of the monastery and the
chambers of the Friars, and the water comes up into the kitchen so boiling
hot, that they use no other fire to dress their victuals. They also put their
bread into brass pots without any water, and it is baked the same as if it
were in a hot oven. They have also small gardens covered over in the winter time, which being watered with this water, are protected against the
effect of the snow and cold, which in those parts, being situate far under
the pole, are very severe, and by this means they produce flowers and
fruits and herbs of different kinds, just as in other temperate countries in
their seasons, so that the rude and savage people of those parts, seeing
these supernatural effects, take those friars for Gods, and bring them many
presents, such as chickens, meat, and other things, holding them as Lords
in the greatest reverence and respect. When the frost and snow are very
great, these friars heat their houses in the manner described, and by letting in the water or opening the windows, they can in an instant temper
the heat and cold of an apartment at their pleasure. In the buildings of the
monastery they use no other material than that which is supplied to them
by the fire; for they take the burning stones that are cast out like cinders
from the fiery mouth of the hill, and when they are at their hottest they
throw water on them and dissolve them, so that they become an excellent
white lime which is extremely tenacious, and when used in building never
decays. These clinkers when cold are very serviceable in place of stones
for making walls and arches; for when once chilled they will never yield
or break unless they be cut with some iron tool, and the arches built of
them are so light that they need no strong support, and are everlasting in

their beauty and consistency. By means of these great advantages these good friars have constructed so many buildings and walls that it is a curiosity to witness. The roofs of their houses are for the most part made in the following manner: first, they raise up the wall to its full height; they then make it incline inwards, by little and little, in form of an arch, so that in the middle it forms an excellent passage for the rain. But in those parts they are not much threatened with rain, because the pole, as I have said, is extremely cold, and when the first snow is fallen, it does not thaw again for nine months, which is the duration of their winter. They live on wild fowl and fish; for, where the warm water falls into the sea, there is a large and wide harbour, which, from the heat of the boiling water, never freezes all the winter, and the consequence is, that there is such an attraction for sea-fowl and fish that they are caught in unlimited quantity, and prove the support of a large population in the neighbourhood, which thus finds abundant occupation in building and in catching birds and fish, and in a thousand other necessary occupations about the monastery.

Their houses are built about the hill on every side, round in form, and twenty-five feet broad, and narrower and narrower towards the top, having at the summit a little hole, through which the air and light come into the house; and the ground below is so warm, that those within feel no cold at all. Hither, in summer time, come many vessels from the islands thereabout, and from the Cape above Norway, and from Trondheim, and bring the Friars all sorts of comforts, taking in exchange fish, which they dry in the sun or by freezing, and skins of different kinds of animals. By this means they obtain wood for burning, and admirably carved timber, and corn, and cloth for clothes. For all the countries round about them are only too glad to traffic with them for the two articles just mentioned; and thus, without any trouble or expense, they have all that they want. To this monastery resort Friars from Norway, Sweden, and other countries, but the greater part come from the Shetland Islands. There are continually in the harbour a number of vessels detained by the sea being frozen, and waiting for the next season to melt the ice. The fishermen's boats are made like a weaver's shuttle. They take the skins of fish, and fashion them with the bones of the self-same fish, and, sewing them together and doubling them over, they make them so sound and substantial that it is wonderful to see how, in bad weather, they will shut themselves close inside and expose themselves to the sea and the wind without the slightest fear of coming to mischief. If they happen to be driven on any rocks, they can stand a good many bumps without receiving any injury. In the bottom of the boats they have a kind of sleeve, which is tied fast in the middle, and when any water comes into the boat, they put it into one half of the sleeve, then closing it above with two pieces of wood and opening the band underneath, they drive the water out; and this they do as often as they have occasion, without any trouble or danger whatever.

Moreover, the water of the monastery being sulphureous, is conveyed into the apartments of the principal friars in vessels of brass, or tin, or stone, so hot that it heats the place like a stove, and without carrying with it any stench or offensive odour whatever.

Besides this they have another means of conveying hot water by a conduit under the ground, so that it should not freeze. It is thus conducted into the middle of the court, where it falls into a large vessel of brass that stands in the middle of a boiling fountain. This is to heat their water for drinking and for watering their gardens. In this manner they derive from the hill every comfort that can be desired. These good friars devote the greatest attention to the cultivation of their gardens, and to the erection of handsome, but, above all, commodious buildings, nor are they wanting in ingenious and painstaking workmen for this purpose; for they are very liberal in their payments, and in their gifts to those who bring them fruits and seeds they are unlimited in their generosity. The consequence is that workmen and masters in different handicrafts resort there in plenty, attracted by the handsome pay and good living.

Most of them speak the Latin language, and specially the superiors and principals of the monastery. This is all that is known of Greenland as described by Messire Nicolò, who gives also a special description of a river that he discovered, as may be seen in the map that I have drawn. At length Messire Nicolò, not being accustomed to such severe cold, fell ill, and a little while after returned to Frislanda, where he died.

Messire Antonio succeeded him in his wealth and honours; but although he strove hard in various ways, and begged and prayed most earnestly, he could never obtain permission to return to his own country. For Zichmni, being a man of great enterprise and daring, had determined to make himself master of the sea. Accordingly, he proposed to avail himself of the services of Messire Antonio by sending him out with a few small vessels to the westwards, because in that direction some of his fishermen had discovered certain very rich and populous islands. This discovery Messire Antonio, in a letter to his brother Messire Carlo, relates in detail in the following manner, saving that we have changed somo old words and the antiquated style, but have left the substance entire as it was.

Six and twenty years ago four fishing boats put out to sea, and, encountering a heavy storm, were driven over the sea in utter helplessness for many days; when at length, the tempest abating, they discovered an island called Estotiland, lying to the westwards above one thousand miles from Frislanda. One of the boats was wrecked, and six men that were in it were taken by the inhabitants, and brought into a fair and populous city, where the king of the place sent for many interpreters, but there were none could be found that understood the language of the fishermen, except one that spoke Latin, and who had also been cast by chance upon the same island. On behalf of the king he asked them who they were and where they came from; and when he reported their answer, the king desired that they should remain in the country. Accordingly, as they could do no otherwise, they obeyed his commandment, and remained five years on the island, and learned the language. One of them in particular visited different parts of the island, and reports that it is a very rich country, abounding in all good things. It is a little smaller than Iceland, but more fertile; in the middle of it is a very high mountain, in which rise four rivers which water the whole country.

The inhabitants are very intelligent people, and possess all the arts like ourselves; and it is believed that in time past they have had intercourse with our people, for he said that he saw Latin books in the king's library, which they at this present time do not understand. They have their own language and letters. They have all kinds of metals, but especially they abound with gold. Their foreign intercourse is with Greenland, whence they import furs, brimstone and pitch. He says that towards the south there is a great and populous country, very rich in gold. They sow corn and make beer, which is a kind of drink that northern people take as we do wine. They have woods of immense extent. They make their buildings with walls, and there are many towns and villages. They make small boats and sail them, but they have not the loadstone, nor do they know the north by the compass. For this reason these fishermen were held in great estimation, insomuch that the king sent them with twelve boats to the southwards to a country which they call Drogio; but in their voyage they had such contrary weather that they were in fear for their lives. Although, however, they escaped the one cruel death, they fell into another of the cruellest; for they were taken into the country and the greater number of them were eaten by the savages, who are cannibals and consider human flesh very savoury meat.

But as that fisherman and his remaining companions were able to shew them the way of taking fish with nets, their lives were saved. Every day he would go fishing in the sea and in the fresh waters, and take great abundance of fish, which he gave to the chiefs, and thereby grew into such favour that he was very much liked and held in great consideration by everybody.

As this man's fame spread through the surrounding tribes, there was a neighbouring chief who was very anxious to have him with him, and to see how he practised his wonderful art of catching fish. With this object in view, he made war on the other chief with whom the fisherman then was, and being more powerful and a better warrior, he at length overcame him, and so the fisherman was sent over to him with the rest of his company. During the space of thirteen years that he dwelt in those parts, he says that he was sent in this manner to more than five-and-twenty chiefs, for they were continually fighting amongst themselves, this chief with that, and solely with the purpose of having the fisherman to dwell with them;

so that wandering up and down the country without any fixed abode in one place, he became acquainted with almost all those parts. He says that it is a very great country, and, as it, were, a new world; the people are very rude and uncultivated, for they all go naked, and suffer cruelly from the cold, nor have they the sense to clothe themselves with the skins of the animals which they take in hunting. They have no kind of metal. They live by hunting, and carry lances of wood, sharpened at the point. They have bows, the strings of which are made of beasts' skins. They are very fierce, and have deadly fights amongst each other, and eat one another's flesh. They have chieftains and certain laws among themselves, but differing in the different tribes. The farther you go south-westwards, however, the more refinement you meet with, because the climate is more temperate, and accordingly there they have cities and temples dedicated to their idols, in which they sacrifice men and afterwards eat them. In those parts they have some knowledge and use of gold and silver.

Now this fisherman, after having dwelt so many years in these parts, made up his mind, if possible, to return home to his own country; but his companions despairing of ever seeing it again, gave him God's speed, and remained themselves where they were. Accordingly he bade them farewell, and made his escape through the woods in the direction of Drogio, where he was welcomed and very kindly received by the chief of the place, who knew him and was a great enemy of the neighbouring chieftain; and so passing from one chief to another, being the same with whom he had been before, after a long time and with much toil he at length reached Drogio, where he spent three years. Here by good luck he heard from the natives that some boats had arrived off the coast; and full of hope of being able to carry out his intention, he went down to the seaside, and to his great delight found that they had come from Estotiland. He forthwith requested that they would take him with them, which they did very willingly, and as he knew the language of the country, which none of them could speak, they employed him as their interpreter.

He afterwards traded in their company to such good purpose, that he became very rich, and fitting out a vessel of his own, returned to Frislanda, and gave an account of that most wealthy country to this nobleman [Zichmni]. The sailors, from having had much experience in strange novelties, give full credence to his statements. This nobleman is therefore resolved to send me forth with a fleet towards those parts, and there are so many that desire to join in the expedition on account of the novelty and strangeness of the thing, that I think we shall be very strongly appointed, without any public expense at all. Such is the tenor of the letter I referred to, which I [i.e. Nicolò Zeno, Junior] have here detailed in order to throw light upon another voyage which was made by Messire Antonio. He set sail with a considerable number of vessels and men, but had not the chief command, as he had expected to have, for Zichmni went in his own person; and I have a letter describing that enterprise, which is to the following effect:— Our great preparations for the voyage to Estotiland were begun in an unlucky hour, for exactly three days before our departure the fisherman died who was to have been our guide; nevertheless Zichmni would not give up the enterprise, but in lieu of the deceased fisherman, took some sailors that had come out with him from the island. Steering westwards, we discovered some islands subject to Frislanda, and passing certain shoals, came to Ledovo, where we stayed seven days to refresh ourselves and to furnish the fleet with necessaries. Departing thence we arrived on the first of July at the Island of Ilofe; and as the wind was full in our favour, we pushed on; but not long after, when we were on the open sea, there arose so great a storm that for eight days we were continuously kept in toil, and driven we knew not where, and a considerable number of the boats were lost. At length, when the storm abated, we gathered together the scattered boats, and sailing with a prosperous wind, we discovered land on the west. Steering straight for it, we reached a quiet and safe harbour, in which we saw an infinite number of armed people, who came running furiously down to the water side, prepared to defend the island. Zichmni now caused his men to make signs of peace to them, and they sent ten men to us who could speak ten languages, but we could understand none of them, except one that was from Shetland. He, being brought before our prince, and asked what was the name of the island,

and what people inhabited it, and who was the governor, answered that the island was called Icaria, and that all the kings that reigned there were called Icari, after the first king, who as they said, was the son of Daedalus, King of Scotland, who conquered that island, left his son there for king, and gave them those laws that they retain to the present time; that after this, when going to sail further, he was drowned in a great tempest; and in memory of his death that sea was called to this day the Icarian Sea, and the kings of the island were called Icari; that they were contented with the state which God hath given them, and would neither alter their laws nor admit any stranger. They therefore requested our prince not to attempt to interfere with their laws, which they had received from that king of worthy memory, and observed up to the present time: that the attempt would lead to his own destruction, for they were all prepared to die rather than relax in any way the use of those laws. Nevertheless, that we might not think that they altogether refused intercourse with other men, they ended by saying that they would willingly receive one of our people, and give him an honourable position amongst them, if only for the sake of learning my language and gaining information as to our customs, in the same way as they had already received those other ten persons from ten different countries, who had come into their island. To all this our prince made no reply, beyond enquiring where there was a good harbour, and making signs that he intended to depart. Accordingly, sailing round about the island, he put in with all his fleet in full sail, into a harbour which he found on the eastern side. The sailors went on shore to take in wood and water, which they did as quickly as they could, for fear they might be attacked by the islanders; and not without reason, for the inhabitants made signals to their neighbours with fire and smoke, and taking to their arms, the others coming to their aid, they all came running down to the seaside upon our men with bows and arrows, so that many were slain and several wounded. Although we made signs of peace to them, it was of no use, for their rage increased more and more, as though they were fighting for their own very existence. Being thus compelled to depart, we sailed along in a great circuit about the island, being always followed on the hill tops and along the sea coasts by an infinite number of armed men. At length, doubling the northern cape of the island, we came upon many shoals, amongst which we were for ten days in continual danger of losing our whole fleet; but fortunately all that while the weather was very fine. All the way till we came to the east cape, we saw the inhabitants still on the hill tops and by the sea coast, keeping with us, howling and shooting at us from a distance to show their animosity towards us. We therefore resolved to put into some safe harbour, and see if we might once again speak with the Shetlander, but we failed in our object; for the people, more like beasts than men, stood constantly prepared to beat us back if we should attempt to come on land. Wherefore Zichmni, seeing that he could do nothing, and that if he were to persevere in his attempt, the fleet would fall short of provisions, took his departure with a fair wind and sailed six days to the westwards: but the wind afterwards shifting to the south-west, and the sea becoming rough, we sailed four days with the wind aft, and at length discovering land, as the sea ran high and we did not know what country it was, were afraid at first to approach it; but by God's blessing, the wind lulled, and then there came on a great calm. Some of the crew then pulled ashore, and soon returned to our great joy with news that they had found an excellent country and a still better harbour. Upon this we brought our barks and our boats to land, and on entering an excellent harbour, we saw in the distance a great mountain that poured forth smoke, which gave us good hope that we should find some inhabitants in the island; neither would Zichmni rest, although it was a great way off, without sending a hundred soldiers to explore the country, and bring an account of what sort of people the inhabitants were. Meanwhile, they took in a store of wood and water, and caught a considerable quantity of fish and sea fowl. They also found such an abundance of birds' eggs, that our men, who were half famished, ate of them to repletion. Whilst we were at anchor here, the month of June came in, and the air in the island was mild and pleasant beyond description; but, as we saw nobody, we began to suspect that this pleasant place was uninhabited. To the harbour we gave the name of Trin, and the headland which stretched out into the sea we called Capo de Trin.

After eight days the hundred soldiers returned, and brought word that they had been through the island and up to the mountain, and that the smoke was a natural thing proceeding from a great fire in the bottom of the hill, and that there was a spring from which issued a certain matter like pitch, which ran into the sea, and that thereabouts dwelt great multitudes of people half wild, and living in caves.

They were of small stature, and very timid; for as soon as they saw our people they fled into their holes. They reported also that there was a large river, and a very good and safe harbour. When Zichmni heard this, and noticed that the place had a wholesome and pure atmosphere, a fertile soil, good rivers, and so many other conveniences, he conceived the idea of fixing his abode there, and founding a city. But his people, having passed through a voyage so full of fatigues, began to murmur, and to say that they wished to return to their own homes, for that the winter was not far off, and if they allowed it once to set in, they would not be able to get away before the following summer. He therefore retained only the row boats and such of the people as were willing to stay with him, and sent all the rest away in the ships, appointing me, against my will, to be their captain. Having no choice, therefore, I departed, and sailed twenty days to the eastwards without sight of any land; then, turning my course towards the south-east, in five days I lighted on land, and found myself on the island of Neome, and, knowing the country, I perceived I was past Iceland; and as the inhabitants were subject to Zichnini, I took in fresh stores, and sailed with a fair wind in three days to Frislanda, where the people, who thought they had lost their prince, in consequence of his long absence on the voyage we had made, received us with a hearty welcome.

What happened subsequently to the contents of this letter, I know not beyond what I gather from conjecture from a piece of another letter, which is to the effect: That Zichmni settled down in the harbour of his newly-discovered island, and explored the whole of the country with great diligence, as well as the coasts on both sides of Greenland, because I find this particularly described in the sea charts; but the description is lost. The beginning of the letter runs thus:—

Concerning those things that you desire to know of me, as to the people and their habits, the animals, and the countries adjoining, I have written about it all in a separate book, which, please God, I shall bring with me. In it I have described the country, the monstrous fishes, the customs and laws of Frislanda, of Iceland, of Shetland, the kingdom of Norway, Estotiland, and Drogio; and, lastly, I have written the life of my brother, the Chevalier, Messire Nicolò, with the discovery which he made, and all about Greenland. I have also written the life and exploits of Zichmni, a prince as worthy of immortal memory as any that ever lived for his great bravery and remarkable goodness. In it I have described the discovery of Greenland on both sides, and the city that he founded. But of this I will say no more in this letter, and hope to be with you very shortly, and to satisfy your curiosity on other subjects by word of mouth.

All these letters were written by Messire Antonio to Messire Carlo his brother; and I [Nicolò the younger] am grieved that the book and many other writings on these subjects have, I don't know how, come sadly to ruin; for, being but a child when they fell into my hands, I, not knowing what they were, tore them in pieces, as children will do, and sent them all to ruin: a circumstance which I cannot now recall without the greatest sorrow. Nevertheless, in order that such an important memorial should not be lost, I have put the whole in order, as well as I could, in the above narrative; so that the present age may, more than its predecessors have done, in some measure derive pleasure from the great discoveries made in those parts where they were least expected; for it is an age that takes a great interest in new narratives and in the discoveries which have been made in countries hitherto unknown, by the high courage and great energy of our ancestors.

Excerpt of a Speech to the De Sancto Claro Society

Thomas Sinclair
1893

*Thomas Sinclair was deeply disturbed by the glorification of Christopher Co-
lumbus on the four hundredth anniversary of his first voyage across the Atlantic. Worried that it represented a rising tide of Italian and Spanish Catholic
domination of the United States, he proposed that America should recognize
Henry Sinclair (the Second, as he thought) as the true discoverer of America.
In so doing, he explained that Sinclair had raised up the primitive Natives
through sexual contact with superior Europeans, who reigned over them as
kings. The following excerpts of his extremely lengthy speech detail his views
on the Sinclair myth and race.*

Norse and Scotch were hardly the kind of people to neglect the possession
of lands, not to say kingdoms; and there is no proof that they did not,
again and again, plant colonists whose descendants are now in New England and on other parts of the Atlantic shore. White men would have thus
been continuous in America from the ninth century till now, a most interesting problem to authenticate. It is true that Prince Henry, according to
the Zeno biography, gave up at one time a colony there; but the book does
not come to the close of his life; and he and his great-hearted son, Prince
William of Orkney, Lord Nithsdale, Baron of Roslin, and the first recorded
Earl of Caithness of his surname, were not the men to be baulked of their
high objects. A land without limit like America, would appeal to their heroic persistency; and it is almost assured that they repeated again and
again their occupation of the continent. Everyone knows of the traditional
rumours that Christian bishops were among the Red Indians, some ascribing their advent to Ireland, some to Wales, whose Celtic books are full of a

western land beyond the seas in much earlier centuries than those of Prince Henry and Prince William. It is most akin to historical fact that the clerical and laic white men of Indian legend, were colonists and conquerors from Scandinavia and Scotland; the annexing of savage kingdoms to the church of the pope being, especially in the 14th and 15th centuries, a positive madness of the brain. The Spaniards led by Columbus thought more of the conversion of the Indians to Christianity than they did of gold, though of this they are credited to have been supreme lovers. Later, Mexico and Peru had to be saved, and such salvation! The former, it is true, was by priest-sanctioned cannibalism a pandemonium of blood; and Christian fire may have purified that cookery horror off the face of the earth, as moral sanitation. The New England districts have yet a tale to tell, of Europeans, a century earlier than the Spaniards, carrying the religious and material civilisation of Europe and Asia there; and it may be provable that the remnant never died out, though the puritans of the "May Flower" claim to have been the pioneers of Yankeeland or Englishland. Englishmen, at all periods, have had the useful trick of assuming too much in their own favour; and the nonconformists who left old Plymouth of England to found the new Plymouth of America, had enough of this valuable quality of Emerson's self-reliance about 1620, when they fled from Archbishop Laud's ecclesiastical tyranny, to forget that there were whites there long before them. Indeed, the marvellously developed social condition of the Red Indians, with their communal long houses, suggests Norwegian and Scottish training grafted on mere savagery. Fiske exhibits the Delawares and the rest of the native tribes, or six nations or more, in lights absolutely novel to those with the preconceived ideas obtained from Fenimore Cooper's romantic novels. But enough, in so untrodden but not unpromising field. The De Sancto Claro Society has, however, inquiries and successes in this direction also, as nothing has been more striking than recent American advance in knowledge of the primitive races; scientific precision by and bye perhaps to be able to distinguish external influences over their highly-articulated popular life. Celtic and Norse literature is full of shadowings of ancient intercourse from Europe to America; and such dreamings nearly always, in research, prove to be founded on facts of some extent. The want of historians and the accidents of time have blotted out many a chapter of human experience, now beyond our imagination to fathom; but the acuteness of learning recovers wonderful gold-dust from the river of the past, which becomes in due time coin and currency. It is already pretty certain that the Norse and Scotch heroes left a sprinkling of population, who ruled the Red Indians to some extent, and amalgamated with them. The French half-breeds of Canada show how it could have been done; for before the "brave" was taught the use of gunpowder, he was not the cruel intractable creature with whom the modern mind is familiar. Who is not aware of the freedom with which missionaries went from tribe to tribe in the earlier European periods of America? One lay stranger was so beloved by them that he was called universally their "father." He, Dr. Patrick Sinclair, was only one of many, from others, too, than the English and Scotch, who experienced ease in guiding these so-called savages; the French at all times most insinuating and charming visitors, whom they never tired of welcoming, with whatever excess or want of wisdom.

[...] But to some of the brightest minds of America the burning question has of late been whether the Latin or Saxon race is to have the supremacy of their country; the intense activity of Roman Catholicism contrasted with the apathy of Protestantism giving philosophers and statesmen pause as to the near results, notwithstanding the power of science and reason. The glorification of Columbus in the discovery centenary of 1892 was an aid towards the threatened Spanish or Latin domination; and Scandinavian energy has been in movement, especially at the Chicago Exhibition of 1893, to counteract the southern tide, by ascribing the discovery of America to Norsemen of the Teuton stock, including, as principal factors, the English and the Dutch. Caithnessmen [i.e. the Sinclair bloodline], especially of Canada and the United States, have the strongest personal interest in such a gigantic Armageddon contest of blood and belief, if it is to be early fact. That the ancestor of many of them, and one in affinity with more, such as Mowats, Bremners [...], Cormacks, Millers, Sutherlands, Bruces, Keiths, and others, is the principal figure to oppose to the renowned Italian Christopher, makes Prince Henry Sinclair II. of as much present as past relation, not only to district, but to the widest of the world's movements; parochialism not the note of the northern vikings, roving now for property, knowledge, and rule as of yore.

NOTES

Introduction

[1] Adapted from George T. Flom, *The Kensington Rune-stone: An Address by George T. Flom Delivered before the Illinois State Historical Society at Its Annual Meeting, May 5-6, 1910, at Springfield, Illinois* (Springfield: Author, 1910), 28, to reflect Henrik Williams's 2012 version.

[2] Arthur's Icelandic adventure is recorded in Geoffrey of Monmouth, *History of the Kings of Britain* 9.10: "After an entire conquest of Ireland, he made a voyage with his fleet to Iceland, which he also subdued" (trans. J. A. Giles). Interestingly, Geoffrey also said Arthur ruled the Orkneys and defeated the King of Norway, paralleling the tale told of Henry Sinclair when myth-makers tried to make that medieval noble into the discoverer of America.

[3] E. G. R. Taylor, "A Letter Dated 1577 from Mercator to John Dee," *Imago Mundi* 13 (1956): 58.

[4] Scott Wolter, comment posted on JasonColavito.com, January 22, 2013.

[5] Cheryl Reitan, "Romance of the Stones," *Bridge* 18, no. 2 (Summer 2001).

[6] Jeanine Poggi, "H2 Network Is a Hit with Men, Advertisers," *Ad Age*, February 18, 2013, [online].

[7] Poggi, "H2 Network."

[8] Pre-production 1-sheet, *America Unearthed*.

[9] Ibid.

[10] "H2 Renews 'America Unearthed' for a Second Season," press release, History, January 29, 2013.

Episode One

[1] Recorded in the *Notes on the State of Virginia*.

[2] Alex W. Barker, Craig E. Skinner, M. Steven Shackley, Michael D. Glascock, and J. Daniel Rogers, "Mesoamerican Origin for an Obsidian Scraper from the Precolumbian Southeastern United States," *American Antiquity* 67, no. 1 (2002): 103-108

[3] John A. Walthall, *Prehistoric Indians of the Southeast* (Tuscaloosa: University of Alabama, 1990), 194-196.

[4] Stuart J. Fiedel, *Prehistory of the Americas,* 2nd ed. (Cambridge: Cambridge University Press, 1992), 252.

[5] Scott Wolter, "Tennessee's Ancient Hebrew Inscription," in *Lost Worlds of Ancient America*, ed. Frank Joseph (Pompton Plains, New Jersey: New Page, 2012), 37-43.

[6] See discussion in Mark Duell, "Did the Mayans Get to Georgia," *Daily Mail*, January 5, 2012.

[7] Ibid.

[8] Richard Thornton, "Scandal at Wikipedia," *Examiner.com*, March 26, 2013 [online].

[9] *Letter of Hernando de Soto and Memoir of Hernando de Escalante Fontaneda*, trans. Buckingham Smith (Washington: 1854), 19.

Episode Two

[1] M. W. Greenslade and J. G. Jenkins, *A History of the County of Stafford,* vol. 2 (A. Constable, 1967), 344ff.

[2] Personal communication, Staffordshire Record Office, March 15, 2013.

[3] "The Cave-Dwellers of England," *Country Life,* April 8, 1905, 479.

Episode Three

[1] Mrs. Clyda Reid Johnson, "Copper Mining in the Lake Superior District," *Locomotive Firemen's Magazine,* October 1906, 565.

[2] Angus Murdoch, *Boom Copper: The Story of the First U.S. Mining Boom* (New York: Macmillan, 1943), 8-13.

[3] S. G. W. Benjamin, *The Atlantic Islands as Resorts of Health and Pleasure* (New York: Harper & Brothers, 1878), 130.

[4] Ignatius Donnelly, *Atlantis: The Antediluvian World* (New York: Harper & Brothers, 1882), 238, 246-247.

[5] Ibid., 385.

[6] Murdoch, *Boom Copper,* 14.

[7] Susan R. Martin, "The State of Our Knowledge about Ancient Copper Mining in Michigan," *The Michigan Archaeologist* 41, no. 2-3 (1995), 119-138; accessed via *Doug's Archaeology Site* [online].

[8] Ibid.

[9] Michael L. Wyman, "Neutron Activation of Metals: A Case Study," *MASCA Research Papers in Science and Archaeology,* vol. 6: History of Technology: The Role of Metals (University of Pennsylvania Museum of Archaeology, 1989), 68.

[10] A. Mark Pollard and Carl Heron, *Archaeological Chemistry* (Cambridge: Royal Society of Chemistry, 2008), 226-227.

[11] John A. Vucetich and Rolf O. Peterson, *Wolves: Ecological Studies of Wolves on Isle Royale 2011-2012* (Wolves and Moose of Isle Royale, 2012), 4-7.

[12] David Hatcher Childress, *Lost Cities of Atlantis, Ancient Europe & the Mediterranean* (Stele, Illinois: Adventures Unlimited Press, 1996), 64.

Episode Four

[1] Giovanni Boccaccio, *Genealogia deorum gentilium* 4.68 (my translation).

[2] G. Cuvier, "Memoir upon Living and Fossil Elephants," *The Philosophical Magazine* 27 (1806).

[3] Joseph Dudley to Cotton Mather, July 10, 1706, in *Collections of the Massachusetts Historical Society,* second series, vol. 1 (Boston, 1838), 264.

[4] Walter Keating Kelly, *Curiosities of Indo-European Tradition and Folk-lore* (London: Chapman & Hall, 1864), 169.

[5] Snorri Struluson, *King Harald's Saga*, ch. 104. A Norse ell was defined as the distance from the elbow to the tip of the third finger, averaging between 18 and 19.5 inches.

[6] "Another island ... is called Vinland because vines grow there naturally, producing the best of wines. That unsown fruits grow there in abundance we have ascertained not from fabulous reports but from the trustworthy relations of the Danes. After this island, habitable land is not to be found in the ocean, but all the regions beyond are filled with impenetrable ice and immense darkness. Of this, Martianus [*Marriage of Mercury and Philology* 6.666] makes reference as follows: 'Beyond Thule,' he says, 'the sea is congealed after one day's voyage.' The most enterprising prince of the Norsemen, Harald, recently tried this sea. After he searched the breadth of the northern ocean in ships, at last before their eyes lay the darkening limits of a fading world, and by retracing his steps he only just escaped in safety the vast pit of the abyss." (Adam of Bremen, *Gesta Hammaburgensis ecclesiae pontificum* 4.38 or 39 in some editions [my translation]).This is the first record of Vinland in world literature.

[7] Samuel Robinson's "Notes on the Coast of Labrador," *Transactions of the Literary and Historical Society of Quebec* 4, no. 1 (1843), 28.

[8] Private Cemeteries Act (MN 307.08).

Episode Five

[1] "Mithra," *Encyclopædia Iranica,* 2006 [online].

[2] Plutarch, *On Isis and Osiris* 46, translated by Charles William King.

[3] The Persian origin of the Mithras cult was proposed by Franz Cumont in 1900, but this theory was rejected in 1971 at an international conference of Mithraic studies after the publication of new evidence.

[4] Justin Martyr, *Dialogue with Trypho* 70.

[5] Porphyry, *De antro Nympharum* 6.24; Tertullian, *De corona* 15.

[6] Tertullian, *De baptismo* 5.1; Jerome, *Letters* 107.2.

[7] Sir James Frazer, *The Golden Bough*, third ed., part IV, Adonis, Attis, Osiris, vol. I (London: Macmillan, 1919), 302.

[8] Tertullian, *Prescription against Heretics* 40, translated by Peter Holmes.

[9] Justin Martyr, *Apology* 1.66, translated by Marcus Dods and George Reith.

[10] Justin Martyr, *Dialogue with Trypho* 70.

[11] James Keyser, review of *Ancient American Inscriptions: Plow Marks or History?* by William R. McGlone et al., *Plains Anthropologist* 40 (1995): 290-294.

[12] Christopher Haigh (ed.), *Cambridge Historical Encyclopedia of Great Britain and Ireland* (Cambridge: Cambridge University Press, 1985), 48.

[13] *De Baptismo* 5.1, translated by S. Thelwall.

[14] Firmicus Maternus, *De errore profanarum religionem* 22. This is the only direct ancient attestation of the resurrection of Attis; however, the god whose resurrection is described is

not explicitly named as Attis but must be inferred from chapter 3. Nearly all scholars accept that he was discussing Attis, but there are many who deny that Attis was believed to have risen from the dead; at any rate, his body was incorruptible, his little finger wiggled, and his hair continued to grow.

[15] Frazer, *The Golden Bough*, 274.

[16] Jaime Alvar, *Romanizing Oriental Gods: Myth, Salvation, and Ethics in the Cults of Cybele, Isis and Mithras* trans. and ed. Richard Gordon (Leiden: Brill, 2008), 263.

[17] See discussion in Alvar, *Romanizing Oriental Gods*, 163. The oft-quoted claim that Firmicus Maternus (*De errore profanarum religionem* 28.8) supported the bull blood rite is false; he merely claims that pagans are *morally* stained by their blood rites of animal sacrifice (and the blood that falls on them while killing animals), not that they physically bathe in the blood. The only other source for the rite, a poem called *Contra paganos*, is believed to contain material derivative of Prudentius and therefore is no independent confirmation.

[18] Edward Carpenter, *Christian and Pagan Creeds: Their Origin and Meaning* (New York: Harcourt, Brace and Company, 1920), 43ff.

[19] The post disappeared from Facebook after he posted it, but not before I archived a copy. Another page on which he posted, an *America Unearthed* fan site, was closed at the request of H2 and/or Committee Films for alleged copyright violations, according to the owner, shortly after Rose voiced his displeasure at the show on the page.

Episode Six

[1] Edgar Gilbert, *The History of Salem, N.H.* (Concord, N.H.: Rumsford Press, 1907), 418.

[2] David R. Starbuck, *The Archaeology of New Hampshire: Exploring 10,000 Years in the Granite State* (Lebanon, N.H.: University of New Hampshire Press, 2006), 106-108.

[3] I told the story in an audition tape I made for the Discovery Channel family of networks last year, for a proposed series that would have investigated alternative claims about ancient American history. Sound familiar? To be titled *Ancient America*, the program never made it out of preproduction, probably due to *America Unearthed* on the competing H2 channel. The two programs would have shared eight out thirteen episode topics in common. (The Discovery program would have added some aliens in, too.)

[4] Diodorus Siculus, *Library of History* 5.19-20, trans. C. H. Oldfather; the quotation is from 5.20.

Episode Seven

[1] John Lawson, *A New Voyage to Carolina* (London, 1709), 48.

[2] Alexander Hume Ford, "The Finding of Raleigh's Lost Colony," *Appleton's Magazine*, July 1907, 31.

[3] Jim Miles, "Weird Georgia: The Dare Stones," parts 1 and 2, *Brown's Guide to Georgia* [online].

⁴ "Roanoke: The Lost Colony," *Digging for the Truth* (season 2, episode 5), History Channel, February 20, 2006.

⁵ "America Unearthed Taken to the Woodshed (Lost Colony)," February 25, 2013, video clip, *YouTube*, [online].

Episode Eight

¹ James Orchard Halliwell-Phillipps, *The Early History of Freemasonry in England* (London: Thomas Rodd, 1840), 43.

² Genesis 4:20-22, although he is never described as a mason. The story is told in the oldest Masonic guild documents, the Regius Poem (c. 1390-1425) and the Cooke Manuscript (c. 1450), the so-called Gothic Constitutions.

³ Franklin was not a Mason at that point, and he incorrectly noted that "several" lodges were active then, while documentary evidence suggests only a single lodge.

⁴ Andrew Michael Ramsay, "Discourse Pronounced at the Reception of Freemasons by Monsieur de Ramsay, Grand Orator of the Order," in Robert Freke Gould, *The History of Freemasonry*, vol. 5 (New York: John Beacham, 1886), 87-88.

⁵ Scott Wolter, posting on JasonColavito.com, January 27, 2013.

⁶ Jacob Grim, *The Shaman: Patterns of Religious Healing Among the Ojibway Indians* (University of Oklahoma Press, 1983), 71.

⁷ "Masonry among the Chippewa Indians," *The Builder* 8, no. 4 (April 1922).

⁸ W. J. Hoffman, "The Midē´wiwin or 'Grand Medicine Society' of the Ojibwa," in *Seventh Annual Report of the Bureau of American Ethnology* (Washington: Government Printing Office, 1885-1886), 143-300.

⁹ Ibid., 257. "The chief reason of this delay is attributed to the fact that the fee to the officiating priests alone must equal in value and quantity four times the amount paid at the first initiation, and as the success in gathering the robes, skins, blankets, etc., depends upon the candidate's own exertions it will readily appear why so few ever attain the distinction sought."

Episode Nine

¹ British Library Additional MS 59681, p. 14; cited in Robert Barone, "Madoc and John Dee: Welsh Myth and Elizabethan Imperialism," *The Elizabethan Review* (Spring 2000).

² Adapted from Richard Eden, *The First Three English Books on America (?1511-1555 A.D.)*, ed. Edward Arber (Westminster: Archibald Constable and Co., 1895), 347.

³ John Evans to Samuel Jones, July 15, 1797.

⁴ See Introduction, note 2.

⁵ Elliot Coues, *History of the Expedition under the Command of Lewis and Clark*, new edition, vol. 1 (New York: Francis P. Harper, 1893), 159.

Episode Ten

[1] *Lovecraft Annual* no. 2 (2004).

[2] Marshall Payn, "The Tucson Artifacts—Case Closed," *NEARA Journal* 30, nos. 3-4 (1996):

[3] Albert Harkness, *A Complete Latin Grammar* (New York: American Book Company, 1901), 320.

[4] Cyclone Covey, "Calalus Reopened," *Migration & Diffusion* 5, no. 19 (2004): 109.

[5] Ti Alkire and Carol Rosen, *Romance Languages: A Historical Introduction* (Cambridge: Cambridge University Press, 2010), 60-61.

[6] Payn, "The Tucson Artifacts," 80.

[7] The story is fascinating, and it's told in Stanley M. Horde's *To the End of the Earth: A History of the Crypto-Jews of New Mexico* (New York: Columbia University Press, 2008).

[8] Charles Hazelius Sternberg, *Hunting Dinosaurs in the Bad Lands of the Red Deer River, Alberta, Canada* (Lawrence, Kansas: Author, 1917), 59.

[9] "New Cretaceous Reptiles from German East Africa," *American Review of Reviews*, July 1911, 97.

[10] Don Burgess, "Romans in Tucson? The Story of an Archaeological Hoax," *Journal of the Southwest* 51, no. 1 (2009), accessed via Questia.

[11] Sir Daniel Wilson, *The Lost Atlantis and Other Ethnographic Studies* (New York: Macmillan, 1892), 37.

[12] Translated by C. Raymond Beasley in *The Dawn of Modern Geography*, vol. 1 (London: John Murray, 1897), 234.

[13] Vol. 1, dec. 1, book 1, chap. 2, translated by John Stevens in Woodbury Lowery, *The Spanish Settlements within the Present Limits of the United States, 1513-1561* (New York: G. Putnam's Sons/Knickerbocker Press, 1901), 255.

[14] Translated by Walter Frederick Walker in *The Azores: or Western Islands* (London: Trübner & Co., 1886), 11.

[15] Matthew 13:55 and Mark 6:3, with Josephus, *Antiquities* 20.9.1.

Episode Eleven

[1] See discussion in Richard Barber, *The Holy Grail: Imagination and Belief* (Cambridge: Harvard University Press, 2004).

[2] Richard Price, preface to *History of English Poetry*, vol. 1 by Thomas Wharton (London: Thomas Tegg, 1824), 55-66.

[3] Ibid., 66.

[4] Ibid., 308-309.

[5] Claude Charles Fauriel, "Romans Provençeaux," *Reveu des Deux Mondes* 8 (1832): 185; my translation.

[6] Quoted in Mrs. Cooper Oakley, *Traces of a Hidden Tradition in Masonry and Medieval Mysticism* (London: Theosophical Publishing Society, 1900), 182.

[7] Michel Roger Lafosse, who claims to be Prince Michael of Albany. The Belgian-born son of a shopkeeper, he fabricated a new birth certificate to claim noble parentage and on these false credentials received British citizenship and the proceeds from two charities formed to fund his claim to the throne of Scotland. After the Belgian government confirmed the forgery, his British citizenship was revoked and he moved back to Belgium to live with his (real) mother.

[8] Chris Church, "Missing Rune Stone off Pojac Point Was Focus of Study," *The Independent*, August 30, 2012 [online].

[9] Ibid.

[10] Full disclosure: I have spoken with Richard Nielsen, and he provided me with links to some of his material. While I disagree with him on many points, he has provided a compelling counterargument to Wolter's views.

[11] Richard Nielsen, "The Evaluation by 3D Imaging of the Purported Coded Runes on the Kensington Rune Stone," *RichardNielsen.org*, April 2011 [online].

[12] Simcha Jacobovici, "Smoking Templar Gun," *Simcha Jacobovici Television*, March 6, 2013 [online].

[13] Jaroslav Folda, *Crusader Art in the Holy Land, from the Third Crusade to the Fall of Acre, 1187-1291* (Cambridge: Cambridge University Press, 2005), 145-146.

[14] Ibid., 145.

[15] 35.5.1. "As to the Greeks, some say that it was invented at Sicyon, others at Corinth; but they all agree that it originated in tracing lines round the human shadow" (translated by John Bostock and H. T. Riley).

Episode Twelve

[1] Mary Sarah Bilder, *The Transatlantic Constitution: Colonial Legal Culture and the Empire* (Cambridge: Harvard University Press, 2004), 102.

[2] "Newport," *American Magazine of Useful and Entertaining Knowledge*, September 1834, 63.

[3] Nicolò Zeno, *The Voyage of the Venetian Brothers, Nicolò & Antonio Zeno to the Northern Seas, in the XIVth Century*, translated by Richard Henry Major (London: Hakluyt Society, 1873).

[4] Ibid., 34-35. As a result of the destruction, he "reconstructed" their content from memory, years afterward, to write his book.

[5] Ibid., 23.

[6] "...the family tree of the Zeni family was drawn up by the Venetian patrician Marco Barbaro and inserted into T. VII of his MS. work, *Discendente patrizie*, a copy of which is

owned by the eminent Venetian nobleman Lorenzo Antonio da Ponte... Barbaro worked on writing this until 1536, i.e. before Nicolò Zeno the younger compiled his History, which was in 1557, as we saw; and moreover, Barbaro is supremely renowned for his assiduous studies and his accuracy in such matters." This is my translation from *Dissertazione Intorno ai Viaggi* e *Scoperti Settentrionali di Nicolò et Antonio, Fratelli Zeni* (Venice: Dalle Stampe Zerletti, 1808), 39-30. Zurla was working from a copy of Barbaro, not the original, and may have made a mistake in the date. All later claims descend from this one.

[7] Translated by Richard Henry Major in *Voyage of the Venetian Brothers*, xlv.

[8] G. M. Asher, *Henry Hudson the Navigator* (London: Hakluyt Society, 1860), clxvi-clxvii.

[9] Ibid., clxv-clxvi.

[10] Ibid., clxvii.

[11] Ibid., clxvii-clxix.

[12] Johann Reinhold Forster, *History of the Voyages and Discoveries Made in the North* (London: 1786), 181.

[13] Translated in B.F. DeCosta, *Ancient Norumbega, or the Voyages of Simon Ferdinando and John Walker to the Penobscot River, 1579-1580* (Albany, NY: Joel Munsell's Sons, 1890), 99.

[14] Scott Wolter, "Venus Alignments in the Newport Tower of Rhode Island," in Richard V. Simpson, *Historic Tales of Colonial Rhode Island* (Charleston, SC: History Press, 2012), 98. The monograph first appeared in *Epigraphic Society Occasional Papers* 26, no. 1 (2010) and *Ancient American* 12 (February 2008).

[15] Peter Ross, *A Standard History of Freemasonry in the State of New York*, vol. 1 (New York and Chicago: Lewis Publishing Company, 1899), 576.

[16] Graham Hancock and Robert Bauval, *The Master Game: Unmasking the Secret Rulers of the World* (New York: Disinformation, 2011), 498-501. Hancock would later admit that much of his alternative history writing was fueled by paranoia brought on from chronic cannabis abuse.

[17] John J. Quiles, *America in Prophecy* (Xulon Press, 2008), 124-125.

Episode Thirteen

[1] Richard Henry Major (ed. and trans.), *The Voyages of the Venetian Brothers, Nicolò and Antonio Zeno, to the Northern Seas in the XIVth Century* (London: Hakluyt Society, 1873), xxxii.

[2] Ibid., xxvii-xxviii, xxix.

[3] Translated by Thomas Sinclair, "Prince Henry Sinclair II., the Pre-Columbian Discoverer of America, One of the Ancestors of the Caithness Family," *Caithness Events,* 2nd ed. (Wick: W. Rae, 1899), 160.

[4] *Orcades* (1697), p. 177; translation corrected from Thomas Sinclair, who gave the wrong date (*Caithness Events*, p. 141).

[5] Thomas Sinclair, "Prince Henry Sinclair II."

[6] Ibid., 166-167.

[7] "About St. Clair Research," *St. Clair Research: The Sinclair/St. Clair DNA Study* [online].

[8] *Coast to Coast A.M.*, August 9, 2009.

[9] "Our Aims," *The Atlantic Conference*, 2008 [online].

[10] 2 Nephi 2:21: "And he had caused the cursing to come upon them, yea, even a sore cursing, because of their iniquity. For behold, they had hardened their hearts against him, that they had become like unto a flint; wherefore, as they were white, and exceedingly fair and delightsome, that they might not be enticing unto my people the Lord God did cause a skin of blackness to come upon them." Although the modern Mormon church views this passage symbolically, it was historically interpreted as referring to the creation of dark-skinned Native Americans.

[11] Frederick J. Pohl, "A Nova Scotia Project," *Bulletin of the Massachusetts Archaeological Society* 20, no. 3 (1959): 40.

[12] Henry S. Poole, *Report on the Pictou Coal Field, Nova Scotia* (Ottawa: S. E. Dawson, 1904), 35.

[13] Joe Nickell, "The Secrets of Oak Island," *Investigating the Paranormal* (New York: Barnes & Noble, 2001), 219-234.

[14] Joan Hope, *A Castle in Nova Scotia* (Author, 1997), *The Library of Hope* [online].

[15] Marc Lescarbot, *Conversion of the Savages*, in Reuben Gold Thwaites (ed.), *Travels and Explorations of the Jesuit Missionaries in New France*, vol. 1: Acadia: 1610-1613 (Cleveland: Burrows Brothers, 1896), 77, 79.

[16] Josh Woods, "Paradas Filmed for 'America Unearthed,'" *The Progress*, March 25, 2013 [online].

Conclusion

[1] Scott Wolter, posting on JasonColavito.com, January 27, 2013.

[2] Thomas Sinclair, *Caithness Events*, 178.

[3] Bruce Lincoln, *Discourse and the Construction of Society: Comparative Studies of Myth, Ritual, and Classification* (Oxford: Oxford University Press, 1989), 3.

[4] Carl Sagan, *The Demon-Haunted World: Science as a Candle in the Dark* (New York: Ballantine, 2008), 26-27.

[1] "Hawkins' Second Voyage," in *Voyages of the Elizabethan Seamen to America*, ed. E. J. Payne (London: Thos. de la Rue & Co., 1880), 48.

[2] John Janes, "The Third Voyage North-Westward Made by John Davis," in *The Voyages and Works of John Davis the Navigator*, ed. Albert Hastings Markham (London: Hakluyt Society, 1880), 43.

[3] Odell Shepard, *The Lore of the Unicorn* (London: George Allen & Unwin, 1930), 98.

[4] *The Literary Works of Leonardo da Vinci*, vol. II, ed. Jean Paul Richter (London: Sampson, Low, Marston, Searle & Rivington, 1883), 320.

[5] Marco Polo, *The Travels of Marco Polo*, trans. and ed. Hugh Murray (New York: Harper & Brothers, 1855), 249.

[6] Photius, *Biblioteca*, codicil 72, trans. J. H. Freese.

[7] Claudine Cohen, *The Fate of the Mammoth: Fossils, Myth, and History*, trans. William Rodarmor (Chicago: University of Chicago, 2002), 59.

[8] Shepard, *Lore of the Unicorn*, 152.

[9] Ibid., 93.

[10] Scott Wolter, posting on JasonColavito.com, January 27, 2013.

Appendix One

[1] Reproduced in John Rothwell Slater, "Letters of Morgan John Rhys," *University of Rochester Library Bulletin* 2, no. 2 (1947) and G. J. Williams, "Original Documents," *National Library of Wales Journal* 2, no. 3-4 (1942): 137-138.

[2] Morgan John Rhys, an expatriate Welshman who founded a Welsh colony in American and supported the search for Welsh Indians as part of a Welsh revitalization movement. His letter to Lewis does not survive.

INDEX

ABOUT THE AUTHOR

Jason Colavito is an author and editor based in Albany, NY. His books include *The Cult of Alien Gods: H. P. Lovecraft and Extraterrestrial Pop Culture* (Prometheus, 2005), *Cthulhu in World Mythology* (Atomic Overmind, 2013), and others. His research has been featured on the History Channel and H2, and he has consulted on and provided research assistance for programs on the National Geographic Channel (US and UK), the History Channel, and more. Colavito is internationally recognized by scholars, literary theorists, and scientists for his pioneering work exploring the connections between science, pseudoscience, and speculative fiction. His investigations examine the way human beings create and employ the supernatural to alter and understand our reality and our world.

Visit his website at http://www.JasonColavito.com and follow him on Twitter @JasonColavito.

6968997R00180

Printed in Great Britain
by Amazon.co.uk, Ltd.,
Marston Gate.